THE NEW ENVIRONMENT IN INTERNATIONAL ACCOUNTING

THE NEW ENVIRONMENT IN INTERNATIONAL ACCOUNTING

Issues and Practices

Ahmed Belkaoui

QUORUM BOOKS
New York • Westport, Connecticut • London

Library of Congress Cataloging-in-Publication Data

Belkaoui, Ahmed, 1943-
The new environment in international accounting.

Includes bibliographies and index.
1. International business enterprises—Accounting.
2. Comparative accounting. I. Title.
HF5686.I56B45 1988 657'.95 87-7252
ISBN 0-89930-267-X (lib. bdg. : alk. paper)

British Library Cataloguing in Publication Data is available.

Library of Congress Catalog Card Number: 87-7252
ISBN: 0-89930-267-X

First published in 1988 by Quorum Books

Greenwood Press, Inc.
88 Post Road West, Westport, Connecticut 06881

Printed in the United States of America

The paper used in this book complies with the Permanent Paper Standard issued by the National Information Standards Organization (Z39.48-1984).

10 9 8 7 6 5 4 3 2 1

To Janice and Hédi
"Piano Piano Arriva Sano"

CONTENTS

EXHIBITS

PREFACE

At the same time that international standard setters strive to harmonize international accounting standards, various innovative forms of reporting, disclosure, and taxation continue to emerge from various countries in an attempt at providing a better level of reporting adequacy. These international innovations find acceptance in one or several countries before gaining more acceptance internationally, in spite of resistance from a few reluctant countries. What results is a slow but steady emergence of new accounting, reporting, disclosure, and taxation techniques of importance to the international accounting arena.

This book presents the principal developments in international accounting. Seven important issues are identified and examined in the following chapters:

1. Value-Added Reporting
2. Employee Reporting
3. Value-Added Taxation
4. Comparative Management and Accounting Research
5. Segmental Reporting
6. Cash-Flow Accounting
7. Accounting for the Developing Countries

This book has various roots. It is intended to provide a thorough examination of the new developments in international accounting, not only from an accounting perspective, but also from an economic and social perspective. It should be of interest to practicing accountants and financial

managers involved in multinational operations. It is also intended for second-year master's degree candidates in accounting and business, and for final-year students in undergraduate accounting and business programs.

Many people helped in the development of this book. The feedback of colleagues and students was very constructive and helpful. Also, I wish to express appreciation to the institutions and/or individuals for their permission to reprint very "valuable" and original material.

Finally, I would like to thank all the people at Quorum Books, and Eric Valentine in particular, for their cheerful and intelligent assistance.

THE NEW ENVIRONMENT IN INTERNATIONAL ACCOUNTING

1

VALUE-ADDED REPORTING

Conventional reporting as it exists in most countries of the world includes a measurement and disclosure of (a) the financial position of the firm through the balance sheet, (b) the financial performance of the firm through the income statement, and (c) the financial conduct of the firm through the statement of changes in the financial position. While the usefulness of the statements has been established by their sheer use over time, they fail to give important information on the total productivity of the firm and the share of the team of members involved in the management of resources, namely, shareholders, bondholders, workers, and the government. The value-added statement is assumed to fill that crucial-role. Therefore, the objective of this chapter is to introduce the reader to the notion, measurement, and evaluation of this new mode of reporting.

THE VALUE ADDED: NOTION AND RATIONALE

Value added refers to the increase in wealth generated by the productive use of the firm's resources before its allocation among shareholders, bondholders, workers, and the government. Thus while the profit is the final return earned by the shareholders, the value added refers to the total return earned by the team of workers, capital providers, and the government. Thus the value added may be obtained by adding pretax profit to payroll costs and interest charges. Another way of computing value added is to deduct bought-in costs from sales revenues where bought-in costs represent all costs and expenses incurred in buying goods and services from other firms.

As an example of value added let's assume that Manufacturer No. 1 has

determined to sell a product at $100. The $100 does not constitute the value added if the manufacturer had bought goods and services from Manufacturer No. 2 for $40. In such a case Manufacturer No. 1 should show a value added of $60 ($100 − $40) as a measure of wealth creation in his or her going concern. All things being equal, an aggregation of all the value added of the going concerns would constitute the total wealth created in a given economy.

Various rationales have been provided for the use of the value-added concept. The first rationale has been provided in the economist's use of the value-added concept in the measurement of national income. Richard Ruggles and Nancy D. Ruggles describe the rationale for the economist's model of value added as follows:

> The value added by a firm, i.e., the value created by the activities of the firm and its employees above, can be measured by the difference between the market value of the goods that have been turned out by the firm and the cost of those goods and materials purchased from other producers. This measure will exclude the contributions made by other producers of the total value of this firm's production, so that it is essentially equal to the market value created by this firm. The value added measure assesses the net contribution made by each firm to the total value of production; by adding up all of those contributions, therefore, it is possible to arrive at a total for the whole economy that will represent the market value of production.[1]

The economist's rationale is deemed applicable to financial accounting providing the beginning of an integration of financial accounting to macroeconomic accounting. Naturally this assumes that other things being equal, the value-added model is additive in the sense that individual measures for the firm may be summed to equal aggregate value added. A second rationale stems from the need to minimize the importance of the one dominant objective which is the maximization of shareholders' profit. The general atmosphere surrounding the business environment put the focus on all the partners rather than singly on the shareholders. Therefore, the value added provided a measure of the return due to all the partners, namely, the shareholders, the bondholders, the workers, and the government. The exact rationale, stemming from the change of attitudes, is that the accounting indicator of performance to be provided should be the total return to the team of workers and capital providers rather than merely to the shareholders. The firm now has an obligation to the welfare of the whole team rather than merely the shareholders. Like the shareholders, the other members of the team have a right to the total return, that is, the value added, as well as a right to information about the total return. This widens the responsibility of the economic entities to report the total return to the cooperating team of workers, investors, and government.

A final rationale stems from the phenomena of social change requiring adjustments in financial reporting. With government as representative of

society and labor taking a more powerful role in its demands for special rights, the importance of the shareholders has slightly diminished leading to a reduction in the importance of profit; the social change dictates then a production and disclosure of value added to meet the needs of government and labor. This importance of the phenomena of social change in the production of value-added information is stated as follows:

> Accountants have reported on profit for many centuries. Why do we now need to report on Value Added as well? One answer is that the Value Added Statement reflects a social change: shareholders have become less powerful and central government and organized labour have become more powerful.[2]

A question, however, arises over whether value added is a determining factor in the process of social change, a harbinger of social change, or a consequence of social change. Michael F. Morley distinguished three different views on this:

> (i) One might report Value Added in order to hurry the change along and to give impetus to the movement of power from capital owners towards labour and central government.
>
> (ii) One might report Value Added in order to alert the business community to this change, hoping that it may thereby be reversed.
>
> (iii) One might report Value Added in the hope that it would help one's new masters to make sensible decisions.
>
> These three attitudes may perhaps explain why Value Added enthusiasts are to be found at both ends of the political spectrum. One encounters both left and right wingers who support this new Statement though their expectations from it differ greatly.[3]

HISTORICAL DEVELOPMENT

The value-added statement can be traced back to the U.S. treasury in the eighteenth century.[4] It remained a debated subject with at various times attempts and/or suggestions made for having it included in financial accounting practice.[5] The emergence and introduction of value-added taxation in the European countries gave impetus to the value-added reporting although the new type of tax did not require the computation of a value-added statement.

The value-added concept was given serious attention during the late 1970s in various European countries. It has reached greater popularity in the United Kingdom with the publication of the *Corporate Report*, a discussion paper prepared by a working party drawn from the accounting bodies, which was published by the Accounting Standards Steering Committee (now the Accounting Standards Committee) in August 1975.[6] It recommended, among other things, a statement of value added, showing

how the benefits of the efforts of an enterprise are shared between employees, providers of capital, the state, and reinvestment. The rationale for the value-added statement appears to be contained in paragraphs 6.7 and 6.10:

> 6.7. The simplest and most immediate way of putting profit into proper perspective vis-à-vis the whole enterprise as a collective effort by capital, management and employees is by presentation of a statement of value added (that is, sales income less materials and services purchased). Value added (that is, sales income less materials and services purchased) is the wealth the reporting entity has been able to create by its own and its employees' efforts. This statement would show how value added has been used to pay those contributing to its creation. It usefully elaborates on the profit and loss account and in time may come to be regarded as a preferable way of describing performance.[7]
>
> 6.10. The statement of value added provides a useful measure to help in gauging performance and activity. The figure of value added can be a pointer to the net output of the firm; and by relating other key figures (for example, capital employed and employee costs) significant indicators of performance may be obtained.[8]

The recommendation was obviously accepted when one of the legislative proposals contained in the U.K. government report *The Future of Company Reports* included a legislative proposal for a statement of value added.[9] What followed was an increasing number of companies each year producing value-added statements. One survey reported even more than one-fifth of the largest U.K. companies disclosed value-added statements.[10] The growth of value-added reporting was helped by the trade union support of the concept. For example, a document produced by one of the trade unions stated the following: "The Federation therefore aims to encourage the use of the added value as a discipline, so that all managers, with or without experience of accounting practices, will appreciate the financial environment within which decisions affecting manpower are taken."[11]

To the labor movement the value-added report was deemed a good vehicle for information disclosure and a basis for determining wages and rewards, namely, what is termed value-added incentive payment scheme (VAIPS).[12] In addition to these uses, Stuart Burchell, Colin Clubb, and Anthony Hopwood[13] mention its occasional use in the context of (a) the performance of British industry,[14] (b) in reforming company-wide profit-sharing schemes,[15] and (c), in facilitating financial performance analysis.[16] Aware of these developments, the various U.K. accounting bodies produced research reports on the value-added concept, namely, the Institute of Chartered Accountants in England and Wales,[17] the Institute of Chartered Accountants of Scotland,[18] the Institute of Cost and Management Accountants,[19] and the Association of Certified Accountants.[20]

THE STRUCTURE OF THE VALUE-ADDED STATEMENT

Value-Added Equations and Format

The value-added statement may be conceived as a modified version of the income statement. Consequently, it can be derived from the income statement as follows:

Step 1. The income statement computes retained earnings as a difference between sales revenues on one hand and costs, taxes, and dividends on the other hand, thus:

$$R = S - B - DP - W - I - DD - T \tag{1}$$

where R = retained earnings
S = sales revenue
B = bought-in materials and services
DP = depreciation
W = wages
I = interest
DD = dividends
T = taxes

Step 2. The value-added equation can be obtained by rearranging the profit equation as

$$S - B = W + I + DP + DD + T + R \tag{2}$$

or

$$S - B - DP = W + I + DD + T + R \tag{3}$$

Equation 2 expresses the gross-value-added method. Equation 3 expresses the net-value-added method. Note that in either case the left part of the equation shows the value added (gross or net) and the right part the allocation of the value added among the groups involved in the managerial production team, namely, the workers, the shareholders, the bondholders, and the government. The righthand side is also known as the additive method and the lefthand side the subtractive method.

Exhibit 1.1 shows how the value-added statement can be derived from a regular income statement. It shows how the company deducted bought-in materials, services, and depreciation from sales to arrive at a value added of $1,120,000. The second part shows how the $1,120,000 was divided among the team of workers ($400,000), shareholders ($100,000), bondholders and creditors ($120,000), and the government ($300,000), leaving $200,000 for retained earnings.

Exhibit 1.1
Deriving the Value-Added Statement

A. The conventional income statement of a company for 19x8 was:

Sales		$2,000,000
Less: Materials Used	$200,000	
Wages	400,000	
Services Purchased	600,000	
Interest Paid	120,000	
Depreciation	80,000	
Profit Before Tax		600,000
Income Tax (Assume a 50% tax rate)		300,000
Profit After Tax		$ 300,000
Less Dividend Payable		100,000
Retained Earnings for the Year		200,000

B. A value added statement for the same year would be:

Sales		$2,000,000
Less: Bought-in Materials and Services and Depreciation		880,000
Value-added available for distribution or retention		$1,120,000
Applied as follows:		
To Employees		$ 400,000
To Providers of Capital		
Interest	$120,000	
Dividends	100,000	220,000
To Government		300,000
Retained Earnings		200,000
Value Added		$1,120,000

Gross Value Added versus Net Value Added

Because of the options available to present the value-added statement on either the gross or net format, the relative merits of each need to be appraised.

The gross-value-added format was the only one suggested by the *Corporate Report* which may explain its popularity. In addition, various other reasons may be advanced in its favor. Morley suggests the following reasons:

1. The value added would be more objective given the flexibility and subjectivity involved in the computation of depreciation. The objectivity may also serve as a way of reassuring the workers of the validity of the base used to determine their productivity bonuses, given that the gross value added may be interpreted by the workers to be less amenable to manipulation or normalization.
2. The gross value added statement allows it to show the total amount available in a given year for reinvestment, namely depreciation and retained earnings. The gross value added statement has features of more full disclosure.
3. The gross value added statement is congruent with the economists' views and preferences for gross measures of national income.[21]

The net-value-added format, as expressed in equation 3, has also some merits worth considering.

1. The net value added has a better connotation for wealth creation ready for distribution than the gross value method. The gross value method is overstated by depreciation as a measure of wealth creation and its total distribution may lead to asset depletion. The net value added is distributable while the gross value added is not.
2. The net-value-added method is a fairer base for the determination of productivity of bonuses for workers than the gross value method given the allowance it makes for capital changes.
3. The net value method presents the advantage of being able to conform to the accounting principles of consistency and matching.
4. The net value method eliminates some double-counting by deducting depreciation when the asset exchange between two firms is a depreciable fixed asset.[22]
5. Net value added would appear more congruent with the notion of a return to the team of workers, capital providers, and the government. This will be an improvement in "team spirit" within the company.[23]

Treatment of Some Items in the Value-Added Statement

While the treatment of some items is obviously defined by the value-added equation cited earlier, some other items have been the subject of various treatments. These include nontrading credits (defined as those

revenues not arising out of a firm's own manufacturing or trading activities) and extraordinary gains and losses.

While revenues (referring to operating revenues) and bought-in materials and services are subjected to a unique treatment, the nonoperating revenues (also labeled nontrading credits) have been treated as follows:

1. Understatement of input costs. If it is accepted that non-trading credits do not represent the organization's own value added, this treatment effectively overstates value added.
2. Presentation as a separately disclosed addition to value added calculated by subtractive method.
3. Netting against an application of value added. If it is accepted that non-trading credits do not represent the organization's own value added, this measure yields a proper measure of the organization's value added, but understates the total value added available for application by understating the application in question.
4. Presentation as a separately disclosed deduction from value added calculated by the additive method.
5. Elimination from the statement entirely. This treatment poses the problem of determining what application is to be matched with the credit as the SVA [Statement of Value Added], so that the amount of the applications included in the SVA is reduced; the solution is invariably retained profit.[24]

The extraordinary gains and losses also pose a problem because each item has a different impact on value added. Morley concludes that the best treatment of an extraordinary credit depends on the nature of the income or gain or whether value can be said to be added by it. The same applies to extraordinary losses.[25] Needless to say, this potentially leads to a diversity of treatments and lack of comparability. The *Corporate Report* did not make things easier by recognizing that "the presentation of value added statements involves overcoming many of the problems associated with the presentation of profit and loss accounts, for example, the treatment of extraordinary profits and losses."[26]

There is definitely a need for more experimentation before final accounting policy is enacted on all the issues subject to diverse treatments. However, this optimistic view for a large trial of experimental innovations is not shared by all.[27] There are also some possible misconceptions. One misconception about value added is that it could not be prepared in the service industry because of the absence of creation of tangible wealth.[28] Needless to say, services are considered as valuable today as any tangible product, and a value-added statement can be easily prepared for a company in a service industry.

Another misconception is the relationship between the value-added statement and value-added taxation. Although both are based on the concept of deducting input costs from sales, they can and do exist separately.

EVALUATION OF VALUE-ADDED REPORTING

Although the concept has not yet reached the level of expansion experienced by more conventional modes of reporting, various authors have already examined some of the benefits and limitations associated with value-added reporting.

Advantages of Value-Added Reporting

The advantages of value-added reporting stem basically from the multidimensional scope of the technique when compared to the conventional mode of reporting the financial affairs of a going concern. Among the most cited advantages are the following.

1. Value-added reporting generates a good organizational climate for the workers by highlighting their importance to the final results of the firm. What is expected from the disclosure of the value-added statement is an increased favorable and positive attitude of the employees toward their employing companies. Considering the employees as major participants in the making of the firm may act as a good motive for better work, more cooperation, and a closer identification with the company.

2. Value-added reporting may provide a more practical way of introducing productivity bonus increases and link rewards to changes in the value-added amounts.[29]

3. A claim is made that value-added-based ratios may act as good diagnostic and predictive cues. In other words, they may be more useful in detecting or predicting economic events of importance to the firm. An example of a useful ratio suggested is the VA/payroll ratio. It is assumed to draw attention to trends in labor costs and may be useful in wage bargaining as a means of informing labor representatives.[30] Another example is the taxation/VA ratio as an indicator of the government share in the activities of the firm. Another popular ratio is VA/sales used as a measure of the degree of vertical integration of a group of companies, and possibly as an index of vulnerability to disruptive action affecting supplies of materials and services.[31]

Cox mentions the potential use of (a) value added/capital employed as a measure of the productivity of the capital used in the business, (b) value added/operating assets as a measure of the productivity of operating assests, (c) value added/capital expenditure, (d) value added/cost of capital consumed (depreciation) as a noble measure of the productivity of physical assets, (e) operating profit/value added as a measure of the profit contribution to value added, (f) value added/sales as a measure of the impact of sales, (g) value added/number of employees as a measure of the value added per person, (h) value added/direct labor hour, and (i) value added/payroll costs as a measure of the labor contribution to value

added.[32] Gokul Sinha mentions the potential use of (a) net value added over total capital employed as an index of managerial efficiency, (b) net value added over sales as a measure of productive efficiency, (c) wages over net value added as a measure of how much of net value added is shared by wages, and (d) net value added over wages as an index of labor productivity.[33]

4. Value-added reporting is more congruent with the concepts used to measure national income and may create a useful link to the macroeconomic data bases and techniques used by economists. It is useful to government in measurements of national income, which involves aggregating (among other things) the value added (net output) of firms. Basically,

> The reason why value added rather than sales or the sales value of production (both measures of gross output) is used is to avoid "double counting" in the aggregation process, since the cost of materials and services which would be included in the gross output measures of one firm will probably already have been included in the gross output measures of its supplier. Hence national income, if it involved aggregating gross outputs would be a function of the degree of vertical integration in the economy. Thus, value added information from firms forms a useful function in macro-economic measurement and forecasting, from government's point of view. In line with this, therefore, it will presumably be useful to individual economists in constructing and testing explanatory models of the economy.[34]

There are, however, qualifications to the general rules equating the sum of the value added by all companies to national income. Morley lists them as follows:

1. National income includes Value Added by government and by other public bodies. For example, the Value Added by defense expenditures is assumed to be equal to its costs.
2. The VA of a company may rise partly in foreign territories. Similarly, Value may be Added in the domestic country by a foreign concern.
3. Economic measures of national income concentrate on production rather than on sales. Differences arise, therefore, in the valuation of increases/decreases in inventories.
4. National income conventions involve several major simplifying assumptions which are not used by financial accountants. For example, the output of durable consumer goods is assumed to have been consumed in the year of manufacture. In effect, the economist depreciates a car by 100 percent in the first year while the accountant would write off his company's fleet of vehicles at, say, 25 percent of cost in each year.[35]

5. Value-added reporting may act as a good measure of the size and importance of companies. It is a better measure of the net creation of wealth a company has achieved. Both sales and capital, generally used as surrogate for size, may be misleading. This case is argued as follows:

When an accountant is asked "Is BP bigger than ICI?," his first reaction is to decide which is the best measure of size for the purpose in question. For some purposes sales might be appropriate, but that figure can give a false impression if a large proportion of a company's turnover is merely representing the passing on to customers of costs incurred in buying-in from other companies. For some purposes, net capital employed may be appropriate, but this can overstate the company's importance if the industry is a very capital intensive one.[36]

6. Value-added reporting may be useful to the employee group because it could affect its aspirations and those of their negotiating representatives. Value-added reporting may be used as a measure of "relative equity," in relation to other stockholder groups. The same argument is made by K. T. Maunders:

This is because such a statement reveals (or should reveal) the comparative shares of each of the stockholder groups in the firm's net output for a given period. For this purpose compared with, say, the profit and loss account, it has the advantage that it shows explicitly what relative share each group takes. It should be noted, however, that its usefulness in this respect will be dependent on both its coverage and classification of group rewards.[37]

The rules may also be used as a measure of "ability to pay" and a measure of total productivity in the bargaining process.

7. Value-added reporting may be useful to the equity investor group. The argument would have validity in that the value-added information could be related to the prediction of either the systematic risk of a firm's securities or the expected return and total risk of those securities, dependent upon which view of the efficiency of the market is considered relevant. The link can be made by the possible indirect impact of value added in the earnings of a firm. Maunders offers the following rationale:

Value added information can affect the conduct of collective bargaining and hence the company's future labor costs. Unless such changes in labor costs are exactly cancelled by increases in the values of output (an unlikely coincidence), company earnings will also change. So, on the presumption that we are able to show . . . that value added information may affect collective bargaining, we can also deduce that it is potentially useful to investors for forecasting a company's earnings and, hence, the expected returns and total risk associated with securities.[38]

Disadvantages of Value-Added Reporting

It is naturally expected that while some see advantages to the adoption of value-added reporting, others will only see disadvantages. Among the disadvantages we may cite the following.

1. Value-added reporting relies on the erroneous assumption that a company is a team of cooperating groups. The facts may show that in general the groups implied have a basic conflict relationship as to the allocation of the firm's resources, the firm's increase in wealth, and as to the best way of managing the firm. Besides, some may question the legitimacy of including the government as a cooperating or even invited member. Another point raised is that some legitimate member of the cooperating team may be included. The case in point is the specialist supplier to a sole customer who would be excluded from the team even though the supplier had no other outlet for his production.[39]

2. The value-added statement can lead to confusion, especially in those cases where the value added is increasing while earnings are decreasing. If the shareholders understand that the value-added statement is not a report to shareholders, the problem would be resolved. Some would then argue that there is still a need to use the earnings statement as a special report to shareholders and the value-added statement as a special report on the welfare of a more broadly defined team. Needless to say, this argument would certainly lead to cries of information overload and information redundancy.

3. The inclusion of the value-added statement may lead management to wrongly seek to maximize the firm's value added. This unwise objective has already been unfortunately advocated in some publications.[40] The impact of such unsound objectives has been demonstrated as follows:

> Suppose a company is buying a component for £5 and the question is asked, "Should we make it ourselves?" An investigation reveals that the cost of a self-made component would be £4 for direct materials plus £10 for direct labour (we shall ignore overhead for simplicity). Assume that the labour costs are all variable and therefore the company's management does not need to incur losses as the price of keeping together the workforce. In these circumstances any sensible manager would be grateful for the outside supplier and forget about the idea of in-house manufacture of the component. But not so for the value-added maximizers. They would cancel the order to buy at £5 from outside and manufacture the component themselves for £14. They would make this inefficient and wasteful decision because it would raise their value added by £9. The amount to be shared out among the company team (value added) would have risen by £1 per component, but the workers would require £10 extra per component for the additional hours worked and the £9 difference represents the loss to the shareholders. Here, the attempt to maximize value added resulted in a disastrous decision.[41]

Diversity of Applications in the United Kingdom

The application of the value-added statement in the United Kingdom suffers from the lack of uniformity and standardization. Writers view this

lack of uniformity as detrimental to the potential success of value-added reporting:

> Published statements of value added have, to date, been characterized by ambiguous terminology and by the treatment of items in ways inconsistent with the model of value added, and inconsistent within and between individual statements. The impression received by lay users of SVAs must be one of confusion—though possibly, with a conviction that value added, like profit can be made to mean whatever the accountant wishes it to mean.[42]

> The advantages offered by Value Added Statement are, however, currently jeopardized by a great diversity of practice.[43]

> Most of those [value-added statements] available seem to be designed to show, often by a "sales-cake" diagram, how much of the value-added goes to the employees themselves, how much the government absorbs and how little the shareholder receives.[44]

A survey of three years' experience with the published statements of value added showed a variety of treatments used.[45]

1. The location of the statement was mainly in the main accounts although some firms included it in the employee report and supplementary report addressed to several groups.

2. The title of the statement included orthodox titles as the statement of value added, the added-value statement, the group value added, and statement of value added and its distribution. Unorthodox titles included examples as (a) where the money goes, (b) how the group spends the money it receives, (c) who benefits from our increase in sales, (d) statement of use of total income, (e) share of the operating profit cake, (f) how we created wealth and share it out, (g) our year's work in money terms—the "value added" way of looking at our profit and loss account, and (h) how sales were built up.[46]

3. The format included both subtractive and additive methods as well as various mixes of tabular, graphic, proportions, and narrative presentations.

4. Deferred taxes may be handled in several ways: (a) inclusion with taxation payable by companies describing taxation as applied to government, (b) shown separately but described as applied to government, (c) included with taxation described neutrally, (d) shown separately and described neutrally, and (e) included with retentions.

5. The treatment of minority interest included (a) the total amount shown as a separate application, (b) the minority interest dividends and retentions included with group allocation, (c) the total included with dividends, (d) the total included with retentions, and (e) minority interests included in input costs.

6. The treatments of nontrading credits like associated companies' results, interest receivable, and other investment income included (a) an understatement of input costs, (b) presentation as a separately disclosed addition to value added calculated by the subtractive method, (c) netting against an application of value added, (d) presentation as a separately disclosed deduction from value added calculated by the additive method, and (e) elimination from the statement entirely.[47]

7. Methods of treating extraordinary items included (a) inclusion in input costs, (b) exclusion from statement, (c) inclusion in NTCs (nontrading credits) added to value added, and (d) separate application of value added.

CONCLUSIONS

Value-added reporting is becoming more and more popular in Europe. Its adoption seems to reflect a greater European concern for the public interest and for what may be perceived as socioeconomic accounting. The greater concern for the rights and opportunities of individuals in the United States and Canada, for example, has not yet created a favorable climate for the introduction of value-added reporting. As accounting becomes more and more actively and explicitly recognized as an instrument of social management and change, value-added reporting will gain a higher status in financial reporting. When it happens, it will constitute a definite example of the intertwining of the accounting and the social, because valued-added reporting reveals something about the social character of production, something which is occluded by conventional reporting. With value-added reporting, the clear message would be that the wealth created in production is the result of the combined effort of a team of cooperating members.

NOTES

1. R. Ruggles and N. D. Ruggles, *National Income Accounts and Income Analysis*, 2d ed. (New York: McGraw-Hill, 1965), p. 50.

2. M. F. Morley, *The Value Added Statement* (London: Gee & Co. for the Institute of Chartered Accountants of Scotland, 1978), p. 3.

3. Ibid, pp. 5-6.

4. B. Cox, *Value Added: An Application for the Accountant Concerned with Industry* (London: Heinemann and the Institute of Cost and Management Accountants, 1978).

5. W. W. Suojanen, "Accounting Theory and the Large Corporation," *Accounting Review* (July 1954), pp. 391-98.

6. Accounting Standards Steering Committee, *The Corporate Report* (London: Accounting Standards Steering Committee, 1975), p. 48.

7. Ibid.

8. Ibid.

9. Department of Trade, *The Future of Company Reports* (London: HMSO, 1977), pp. 7-8.

10. S. J. Gray and K. T. Maunders, *Value Added Reporting: Uses and Measurement* (London: Association of Certified Accountants, 1980).

11. Engineering Employers Federation, *Business Performance and Industrial Relations* (London: Kogan Page, 1977).

12. M. Woodmansay, *Added Value: An Introduction to Productivity Schemes* (London: British Institute of Management, 1978).

13. Stuart Burchell, Colin Clubb, and Anthony G. Hopwood, "Accounting and Its Social Context: Towards a History of Value Added in the United Kingdom," *Accounting, Organizations and Society* 10, no. 4 (1985), p. 387.

14. F. C. Jones, *The Economic Ingredients of Industrial Success* (London: James Clayton Lecture, Institution of Mechanical Engineers, 1976); F. C. Jones, "Our Manufacturing Industry: The Missing $100,000 Million," *National Westminster Bank Quarterly Review* (May 1978), pp. 8-17; C. New, "Factors in Productivity That Should Not Be Overlooked," *The Times* (February 1, 1978).

15. S. Cameron, "Added Value Plan for Distributing ICI's Wealth," *Financial Times* (January 7, 1977).

16. Vickers da Costa, *Testing for Success* (London: Mimeo, 1979).

17. M. Renshall, R. Allan, and K. Nicholson, *Added Value in External Financial Reporting* (London: Institute of Chartered Accountants in England and Wales, 1979).

18. Morley, *The Value Added Statement.*

19. Cox, *Value Added.*

20. Gray and Maunders, *Added Value Reporting.*

21. Michael F. Morley, "The Value Added Statement in Britain," *Accounting Review* (July 1979), p. 626.

22. Ibid., p. 628.

23. Michael F. Morley, "The Value Added Statement: A British Innovation," *Chartered Accountant Magazine* (May 1978), p. 33.

24. B. A. Rutherford, "Published Statements of Value Added: A Survey of Three Years' Experience," *Accounting and Business Research* (Winter 1980), p. 23.

25. Morley, *The Value Added Statement,* p. 87.

26. Accounting Standards Steering Committee, *The Corporate Report,* p. 50.

27. Rutherford, "Published Statements of Value Added," p. 28.

28. Morley, "The Value Added Statement: A British Innovation," p. 32.

29. Morley, "The Value Added Statement in Britain," p. 621.

30. Ibid.

31. Ibid., p. 622.

32. Cox, *Value Added,* pp. 67-82.

33. Gokul Sinha, *Value Added Income* (Calcutta: Book World, 1983), pp. 130-37.

34. K. T. Maunders, "The Decision Relevance of Value Added Reports," in *Frontiers of International Accounting: An Anthology,* ed. Frederick D. Choi and Gerhard G. Mueller (Ann Arbor, Mich.: UMI Research Press, 1985), p. 241.

35. Morley, "The Value Added Statement in Britain," p. 623.

36. M. F. Morley, "Value Added Reporting," in *Developments in Financial Reporting,* ed. Thomas A. Lee (London: Philip Allan, 1981), p. 259.

37. Maunders, "The Decision Relevance of Value Added Reports," pp. 225-45.

38. Ibid., p. 229.

39. Morley, "The Value Added Statement in Britain," p. 624.

40. R. R. Gilchrist, *Managing for Profit: The Value Added Concept* (London: Allen and Unwin, 1971).
41. Morley, "The Value Added Statement: A British Innovation," p. 30.
42. Rutherford, "Published Statements of Value Added," p. 52.
43. Morley, *The Value Added Statement,* p. 141.
44. da Costa, *Testing for Success.*
45. Rutherford, "Published Statements of Value Added," p. 17.
46. Ibid.
47. Ibid., p. 23.

SELECTED BIBLIOGRAPHY

Accounting Standards Steering Committee, *The Corporate Report* (London: Accounting Standards Steering Committee, 1975).

Ball, R. J., "The Use of Value Added in Measuring Managerial Efficiency," *Business Ratios* (Summer 1968), pp. 5-11.

Beattie, D. M., "Value Added and Return on Capital as Measures of Managerial Efficiency," *Journal of Business Finance* (Summer 1970), pp. 22-28.

Bentley, Trevor, "Value Added and Contribution," *Management Accounting* (March 1981), pp. 17-21.

Burchell, Stuart, Colin Clubb, and Anthony G. Hopwood, "Accounting and Its Social Context: Towards a History of Value Added in the United Kingdom," *Accounting, Organizations and Society,* 10, no. 4 (1985), pp. 381-413.

Chua, K. C., "The Use of Value Added in Productivity Measurement," in *Productivity-Measurement and Achievement,* Proceedings of Accountancy (Victoria: University of Wellington, 1977).

Cox, Bernard, *Value Added: An Appreciation for the Accountant Concerned with Industry* (London: Heinemann, 1978).

Cruns, R. P., "Added-Value: The Roots Run Deep into Colonial and Early America," *Accounting Historian Journal* (Fall 1982), pp. 25-42.

Dewhurst, James, "Assessing Business Performance," *Accountant* 188 (March 3, 1983), pp. 17-18.

Egginton, D. A., "In Defense of Profit Measurement: Some Limitations of Cash Flow and Value Added as Performance Measures for External Reporting," *Accounting and Business Research* (Spring 1984), pp. 99-110.

Foley, B. J., and K. T. Maunders, *Accounting Information Disclosure and Collective Bargaining* (London: Macmillan, 1977).

Gilchrist, R. R., *Managing for Profit: The Value Added Concept* (London: Allen and Unwin, 1971).

Gray, Sidney J., and K. T. Maunders, "Recent Developments in Value Added Disclosures," *Certified Accountant* (August 1979), pp. 225-36.

______, "Recent Developments in Value Added Reporting," *Certified Accountant* (August 1979), pp. 229-36.

______, *Value Added Reporting: Uses and Measurement* (London: Association of Certified Accountants, 1980).

McLead, Charles C., "Use of Value Added," *Bests Review* (January 1984), pp. 80-84.

McLeay, Stuart, "Value Added: A Comparative Study," *Accounting, Organizations and Society* 8, no. 1 (1983), pp. 31-56.

McSweeney, Brendan, "Irish Answer to Value Added Statements," *World Accounting Report* (July 1983), pp. 11-12.

Maunders, K. T., "The Decision Relevance of Value Added Reports," in *Frontiers of International Accounting: An Anthology*, ed. Frederick D. Choi and Gerhard G. Mueller (Ann Arbor, Mich.: UMI Research Press, 1985), pp. 225-45.

Morley, Michael F., "Value Added Reporting," in *Developments in Financial Reporting*, ed. Thomas A. Lee (London: Philip Allan, 1981), pp. 251-69.

______. *The Value Added Statement* (London: Gee & Co. for the Institute of Chartered Accountants of Scotland, 1978).

______, "The Value Added Statement: A British Innovation," *Chartered Accountant Magazine* (May 1978), pp. 31-34.

______. "The Value Added Statement in Britain," *Accounting Review* (July 1979), pp. 618-89.

Pendrill, David, "Introducing a Newcomer: The Value Added Statement," *Accountancy* (December 1977), pp. 92-94.

Purdy, Derek E., "Value Added Statement: The Case Is Not Yet Proven," *Accountancy* (September 1981), pp. 113-14.

Renshall, Michael, Richard Allan, and Keith Nicholson, *Added Value in External Financial Reporting* (London: Institute of Chartered Accountants in England and Wales, 1979).

Rutherford, B. A., "Easing the CCA Transition in Value Added Statements," *Accountancy* 93 (May 1983), pp. 121-22.

______, "Five Fallacies about Value Added," *Management Accounting* (September 1981), pp. 31-33.

______, "Published Statements of Value Added: A Survey of Three Years' Experience," *Accounting and Business Review* (Winter 1980), pp. 15-28.

______, "Value Added as a Focus of Attention for Financial Reporting: Some Conceptual Problems," *Accounting and Business Research* (Summer 1972), pp. 215-20.

Sinha, Gokul, *Value Added Income* (Calcutta: Book World, 1983).

Woolf, Emile, "Case of Added Value," *Accountants* (March 3, 1983), pp. 13-16.

______, "Time to Scrap the P&L Account?" *Accountancy* (August 1981), pp. 93-95.

2

EMPLOYEE REPORTING

While the question of the final identity of users of financial reports continues to plague the accounting world, it is a well-accepted fact in the literature and in practice that employees deserve to be considered as important users of financial reports during their recruitment, their years of employment, and prior to their retirement. Unions as representative of employees also qualify as important users of accounting information especially with the purpose of finding convincing arguments for their collective-bargaining positions. With the emergence of employees and unions as potential users of accounting information, it also appears, and for a good many reasons, that the annual report to shareholders is not the all-inclusive document suitable for all unions. The solution lies in the production of a special report to employees and unions. This solution has been accepted in a lot of country members of the Organization of Economic Cooperation and Development, including the United States, West Germany, Canada, France, Denmark, Norway, Sweden, and the United Kingdom. The idea has been accepted not only operationally but conceptually. For example, in the United Kingdom, the *Corporate Report* identifies employees as a user group of published company annual reports.[1] Therefore, the objective of this chapter is to review the literature on employee reporting with the purpose of providing answers on the factors influencing the phenomenon, the information needs of employees and unions, the content of this special report, and the role of the accountant.

FACTORS INFLUENCING EMPLOYEE REPORTING

This section elaborates on the factors influencing employee reporting. Because different factors apply for employees and unions, each will be

reviewed spearately. In fact, a sample employment report, included as an appendix to the *Corporate Report*, showed quantitative data under the following headings:

1. Number employed (analyzed in various ways);
2. Location of employment;
3. Age distribution of permanent work force;
4. Hours worked during the year (analyzed);
5. Employee costs;
6. Pension information;
7. Education and Training (including costs);
8. Recognized trade unions;
9. Additional information (race relations, health and safety statistics etc.); and
10. Employment ratios.[2]

Similarly, in Canada, the Canadian Institute of Chartered Accountants published a research study in June 1980 entitled *Corporate Reporting: Its Future Evolution.*[3] The report identified explicitly employees (past, present, and future) as users of corporate reports.

Factors Influencing Disclosure to Employees

Firms do have a continuous communication process with employees through various media including plant-level discussions, quality circles, audiovisual presentations, and in-house journals and notices. The purpose of the formal employees' annual report is to provide an integrative and exhaustive report rather than a piecemeal approach. The same point is argued as follows:

> It must be a report, capable of satisfying additional information needs of employees, rather than simply suplicating information already provided through alternative internal channels, or providing unwanted information. Unless the preparers of an annual report to employees can identify a genuine information void left by other internal communication media, and can justifiably believe that such a report can fill this void, then the report has no real justification.[4]

The literature has identified various aims and reasons for reporting to employees. A survey of the literature on financial reporting to employees between 1919 and 1979 identified the following reasons: (a) heralding changes, (b) presenting management propaganda, (c) promoting interest in understanding of company affairs and performance, (d) explaining management decisions, (e) explaining the relationship between employees, management, and shareholders, (f) explaining the objectives of the

company, (g) facilitating greater employee participation, (h) responding to legislative or union pressure, (i) building company image, (j) meeting information requirements peculiar to employees, (k) responding to management fear of wage demands, strikes, and competitive disadvantages, and (l) promoting a higher degree of employee interest.[5] The same survey shows that the level of interest in reporting to employees reached a higher level when the following four socioeconomic factors were also present: (a) the use of new technology in the workplace, (b) increased mergers in the corporate sector, (c) the emergence of antiunion sentiment, and (d) fears of economic recessions.[6] It seems that management may have increased the level of employee reporting in reaction to the potential consequence of each of these factors or a combination of these factors. N. R. Lewis, L. D. Parker, and P. Sutcliffe, the authors of the survey, speculated that management may have hoped to

1. allay fears of lost rank, skill or employment through technological advances;
2. counter fears of "bigness," monopoly power, employee relocation and loss of identity through corporate mergers;
3. take advantage of community anti-union sentiments by bypassing union communication channels (reporting directly to employees), emphasizing management prerogatives and the need to control wages and associated costs and generally weakening the unions' potential to disrupt operations; and
4. prepare employees for hard times, confirm or dispel rumors of imminent company failure, allay fears of unemployment and urge employees to greater efforts in difficult economic times.[7]

Dennis Taylor, Laurie Webb, and Les McGinley identified the following personal benefits which management might attempt to seek for itself by providing an annual report to employees in addition to using the conventional management-employee communication media: (a) building a favorable employee impression of the management group, (b) reducing the resistance of employees to changes initiated by management, and (c) providing a useful response to union pressure for more corporate financial information from management.[8] They also identified the following personal benefits which might accrue to employees with employee reporting: (a) having the basis for deciding whether to continue employment with the company or an organization section of the company; (b) having the basis for assessing the relative position of the employees within the corporate structure, particularly in terms of getting a "fair go"; and (c) understanding the image of the company, as a basis for deciding at a personal level whether to identify with this image.[9]

Finally, B. J. Foley and K. T. Maunders identified arguments supporting disclosure directly to employees: (a) feedback of information to employees will improve job performance via learning effects and also serve to increase

motivation; (b) the role of employee reporting is crucial to effective worker participation which will contribute to the efficiency of the company; (c) the fundamental change in the nature of the firm and its "social responsibility" legitimizes employee reporting; (d) employee reporting may be seen by some employers as a possible way of resurrecting the concept of joint consultation as a means of avoiding unionization; (e) finally, the socialist tradition with its ultimate objective of changing the basis of ownerships and the control of resources sees employee reporting as a step to increase "workers' control" and develop "workers' self confidence."[10] According to Foley and Maunders, the case for employee reporting using the socialist argument rests on two fundamental principles:

1. That it is a technique which helps employees to establish greater democratization of decision making in industry;
2. That is may usefully act as a check on those aspects of the market system which result in adverse external effects in the form of pollution and environmental degradation.[11]

Factors Influencing Disclosure to Unions

P. F. Pope and D. A. Peel rely on the rational expectations hypothesis to argue the desirability of disclosure to unions.[12] Basically, the argument goes that in the absence of a certain piece of information, the unions will form an expectation about it which, on the average, will be unbiased. If the forecast is biased, the variance of the forecasts carries with it a cost due to the possible difference of opinion between the union and management. Therefore, disclosure of the information by management would reduce the variance and eliminate the forecast error. The interests of management should be in a more liberal disclosure policy to unions. "The bargaining process is not costless since it involves the commitment of considerable managerial resources. If a more liberal disclosure policy is adopted the differences in initial perceptions will be reduced immediately, confidence in outcomes will be increased, and the length of the subsequent negotiations will decrease."[13] Thus the disclosure of information can be expected to affect the bargaining process to the relative advantage of both labor and management. Foley and Maunders identified two major arguments favoring greater disclosure of company information to trade unions: a means of shifting bargaining power from management to union negotiators, and a necessary condition if integrative bargaining is to develop.[14] The same point had been made earlier by R. B. McKersie and L. C. Hunter as follows:

The more information the parties share, the better the problem-solving is apt to function. Some companies still feel reluctant to reveal the "inner-workings" of the enterprise. Such hesitation makes the definition of problems, the development of

alternatives and the selection of solutions difficult to execute. Without basis data and the overture of trust that is involved in sharing sensitive information, problem-solving cannot be effective and attitudes will remain frozen.[15]

James A. Craft identified some specific factors that will influence the needs of a firm to disclose information to the union in collective bargaining.[16]

1. The discretion management enjoys regarding information disclosure beyond that required by the law which is related to its bargaining power vis-à-vis the union. More specifically, Craft reasons:

   > If management has substantial bargaining power, it will usually enjoy much discretion regarding disclosure of financial and other management information. It can obtain a settlement favorable to itself in any case, and the amount and type of disclosure will be determined by management's objectives and its relationship with the union.[17]

2. The independence an organization enjoys in collective-bargaining decision making, with a more independent employer feeling greater pressures for disclosure because of the increased need to justify a negotiating position arising from the absence of specific settlement or general pattern to be followed.
3. The nature of the collective-bargaining relationship with the union, with little incentive to disclose beyond that which is required by the law in relationships characterized by extensive conflict and with strong incentive to fully inform the union by providing nonselective disclosures in cooperative relationships between the union and management.
4. The political stability of the union with strong leadership creating a situation for more opportunities for disclosure in collective bargaining, in addition to what is required by law or accepted and supported by management.
5. The level of sophistication of union leaders and membership regarding financial accounting and related information, with higher sophistication leading to better disclosure.

Not all the arguments are in favor of disclosure of information to unions. Foley and Maunders cite the following arguments:

1. Lack of expertise and training in financial accounting of most union negotiators and particularly shop stewards can result in misunderstanding, mistrust, and damage to the bargaining process.
2. The disclosure of information will strengthen the bargaining position of shop stewards and trade unions, leading to more aggressive bargaining and earlier pay settlements in those cases where industrial relations are already in poor conditions.
3. The disclosure of sensitive information to unions—especially when the information deals with cost structure, efficiency indicators, pricing policy, and future development plans—may reach competitors.

4. The disclosure of information to unions presents a problem of confidentiality where the rights of shareholders are concerned, especially if these shareholders have not been consulted.
5. The disclosure of information to unions may negatively affect management's right to manage as it hinders the legitimacy of managerial authority.
6. The disclosure of information to unions rather than contributing to a better industrial relations atmosphere may lead to *"greater militancy and more inflationary trade union wage demands."*[18]

INFORMATION NEEDS IN EMPLOYEE REPORTING

Information Needs of Employees

Employee reporting is concerned with the provision of information that is useful to the decisions. Relevance of the information is naturally important to guard the credibility of the information with employees. Two approaches may be used: the consumer sovereignty approach and/or the decision-oriented approach. The consumer sovereignty approach consists of merging the information needs of employees and evaluating the present disclosures to correct any discrepancies. This approach may suffer from the failure of employees to determine the appropriate information needed and from their tendency to demand information similar to what is currently available.

The decision-oriented approach focuses on defining the decision models of the employees and determining the information needs in terms of the decision models' variables and parameters. Those models are either deductive or descriptive. Deductive models are subject to a number of limitations. These have been identified by David Cooper and Simon Essex as follows:

1. The difficulty and lack of an operational single measure of utility
2. The difficulty of summarizing and synthesizing individual and inconsistent desires into a practical bargaining strategy
3. The constantly changing values of the probabilities of the identified outcomes, the utility associated with each outcome, and the range of alternative actions specified in the basic subjective expected utility maximization model
4. The cognitive limitations and the limited information processing capabilities of individual employees[19]

Descriptive models focus on a correct portrayal of the real world and decision making, taking into account the idea that individuals and organizations are intentionally rational but limited by the complexity of the environment in which they operate. Various authors have provided descriptive models of employee decision making with the aim of identifying their information needs. Cooper and Essex provided a model entering the shop steward's role, decision models, and information needs. Exhibit 2.1 provides their summary of shop steward role, decision models, and

information needs. Various authors identified employee need for information as evidenced by demands or suggested needs. Exhibit 2.2 provides a detailed list of types of information which have been either suggested by an author as potentially useful to employees or observed as employee demands by an author.[20] Lewis, Parker, and Sutcliffe identified the following employee decisions: (a) acceptance or rejection of entity offer of retaining/relocation/promotion/new position, (b) level of productivity, (c) job satisfaction, stay or leave, retirement planning, (d) personal investment, saving levels, insurance (non-entity superannuation), employee shares, debentures in entity, (e) union membership or nonmembership, (f) level of involvement of member, and (g) personal expenditure: general organization's products, new products.[21] Exhibit 2.3 provides the information deemed useful to those decisions.

Four major categories of information needs of employees are identified by Foley and Maunders: (a) financial and economic information relating to job security, (b) information on working conditions, (c) information on achievement and performance indicators, and (d) information on equity or fairness in the distribution of economic reward.[22]

Finally, N. H. Cuthbert and A. Whitaker suggest the following information as potentially useful to shop stewards:

1. Individual plant operating accounts, particularly relating to levels of profitability.
2. Details of the costing process:
   2.1. The type of costing system used and their impact on cost structure.
   2.2. How these affect returns at the level of a given plant.
3. Budgets and the variances produced.
4. The transfer pricing system (already a major topic in international trade union circles in respect of the policies of multinational corporations).
5. Stock levels.
6. State of the Order Book.[23]

Disclosure Policy in Labor Relations

Craft suggests a disclosure policy in labor relations conceptualized in terms of the extent of information disclosed to the union and the usefulness of the information to the union in dealing with specific collective-bargaining issues and questions.[24] The extent of information to unions ranges from low to high. What results are five disclosure policies in collective bargaining as shown in Exhibit 2.4. They are basically (1) limited disclosure, (2) selective disclosure, (3) judgmental disclosure, (4) ineffective disclosure, and (5) complete disclosure. *Selective disclosure, limited disclosure, ineffective disclosure,* and *complete disclosure* are definable in terms of either high or low or both the extent of information disclosed and the usefulness of the information to the union. *Judgmental disclosure* policy refers to the decision

Exhibit 2.1

Summary of Shop Steward's Role, Decision Models, and Information Needs

Role	Decisions	Information	
Union duties	Inter-union disputes	Membership of all unions in enterprise	
	Grievances	Grievance procedures in enterprise	
		Grievance records including results	
	Recruitment	Type of member (age, sex)	
		Density of membership in enterprise	
		Current wage and wage structure	
	Subscriptions	Union membership in enterprise	
		Outstanding dues	
Pay bargaining	Amount of claim	Future cash flows of enterprise	Ability to pay
		Current and future performance of enterprise	Ability to pay
		Contribution per employee – current and expected	Ability to pay
		Labour productivity	Ability to pay
		Cost structure of plant	Ability to pay
		Current pay structure – current and expected	Minimum acceptable
		Value added – current and expected	Minimum acceptable
		Members' cost of living – current and expected	Minimum acceptable
		Changes in nature of job – current and expected	Minimum acceptable
		Agreements of similar workers in plant and locality	Minimum acceptable
	Contest claim	Support from other unions	
		Local unemployment levels	
		Demand for product	
		Current stock levels	
		Union density	
Management of the enterprise	Demand extra safety expenditure	Accident and compensation record of enterprise	
		Noise and toxity levels	
		Safety of new machinery and working methods	
	Economic viability of enterprise	Liquidity	Of enterprise in the future
		Cash Flows	Of enterprise in the future
		Profitability	Of enterprise in the future
		Investment plans	Of enterprise in the future
		Labour and capital ratios	Of enterprise in the future
		Mergers and takeovers proposed	Of enterprise in the future
	Contest closures	Job opportunities in locality	
		Age structure	
	Extent of job satisfaction	Extent 'motivating' factors available	
		Absenteeism	
		Changes to work methods and organisation planned	

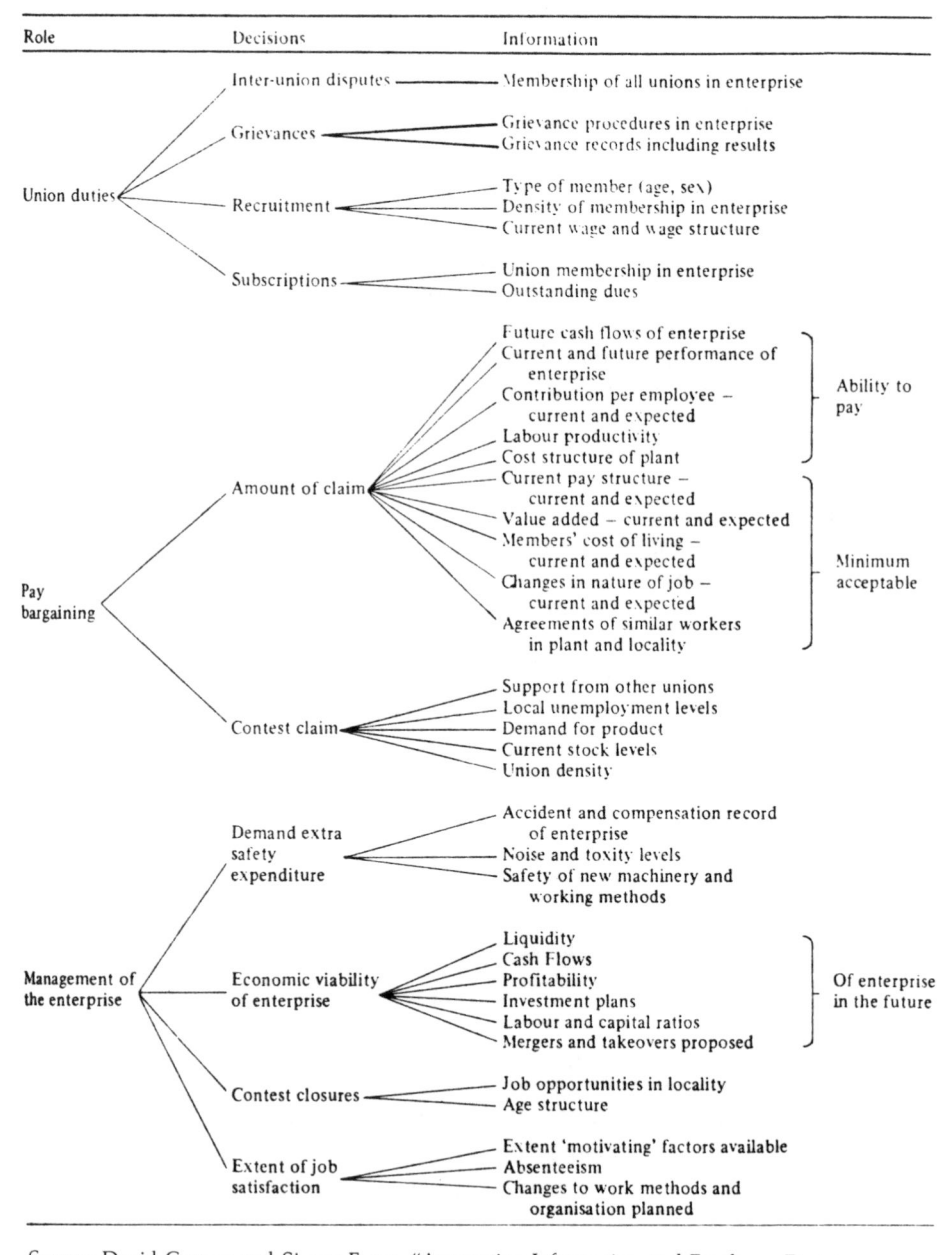

Source: David Cooper and Simon Essex, "Accounting Information and Employee Decision Making," *Accounting, Organizations and Society* 2, no. 3 (1977), p. 209. Reprinted with permission.

Exhibit 2.2
Employee Need for Information as Evidenced by Demands or Suggested Needs

---

Presented below are types of information which have been either suggested by an author as potentially useful to employees or observed as employee demands by an author. Information types are grouped according to the publication in which they were discussed.

Information on productivity and efficiency data at plant level; manpower plans; benefits; intragroup payments; transfer prices; company's future plans. (Lafferty, 1977)

Pricing policy, especially transfer prices; advice re imminent collapse; social auditing (Swedish style). (Jenkins, 1975)

Future employment levels and work conditions; plans for expansion or contraction; effects of technological changes; traning schemes; health and safety practices; pay conditions; terms of employment of various groups including managers; contribution made by employees in different plants and divisions; is adequate provision being made for pension payments?; can company afford higher wages?; can company succeed against competition?; is the company's overall product/cost/price structure right?. (Thompson, 1975)

Costings; performance indicators; manpower statistics. (Miller, 1975)

Details of past, present and planned capital spending; unit costs of inputs (operating costs and overheads); details of sources and uses of funds; changes in value of fixed assets and trade investments; details of individuals' earnings and hours. (GMWU, 1976)

Performance detail of their own particular unit, be it factory, department, or company. (Holmes, 1977)

Matters directly affecting their own work and conditions on the shop floor; information about future developments. (ICAEW, 1976)

Performance, pay prospects. (ICMA, 1978)

Reporting on health and safety of the workplace; reporting on the effect of productivity bargaining and the monitoring of profit-sharing schemes; reporting on planning, agreements made between entity and government and the effect of these on job security; reporting on current and alternative distributions of income and the effect these have on the efficient allocation of resources; reporting for the purpose of negotiating a wage settlement. (Climo, 1976)

State of the order book; sales campaigns; exports; contracts entered; proposed capital expenditure and the reasons for it; fixed assets; the state of the cash flow; employment figures; changes in working practices and manpower requirements; productivity and proposed acquisition and disposals of segments of the company together with details of reasons for decisions taken; production, selling and distribution costs; costs of machinery; cost of management; costs of materials; health and safety costs and benefits; customer complaints; information re conduct of industrial relations; information on future plans. (Jones, 1975)

Exhibit 2.2 *(continued)*

Production and marketing plans; difficulties likely to be met; research and development activity; future capital investment plans in terms of profit and equity; new facilities and the influence of these on employment and deployment of labor; information on success against previous objectives and identification of reasons for failure; changes in operating costs; details of cash flow situations; analysis of profit/loss generation; profit compared with sales and its disposition; capital employed performance; stock policy; plant utilization; overtime; absenteeism; sickness; etc. (Gogarty, 1975)

Monetary rewards; promotion opportunities; stability of employment; justice in distribution of rewards; identification with company's image. (Taylor et al., 1979)

Individual plant spending accounts, particularly relating to levels of profitability; details of costing process; the types of costing system used and their impact on cost structure; how these affect returns at the level of the given plant; budgets and variances produced; the transfer pricing systems; stock levels; state of the order book. (Cuthbert and Whitaker, 1977)

Local factory and departmental accounts, cost structures, forecasts, and budgets. (ICAEW and IPM, 1978)

Company's safety records; investment plans; product performance; employee benefits; pension rights; progress with factory plans; outlook for future. (Martin, 1977)

Source: N. R. Lewis, L. D. Parker, and P. Sutcliffe, "Financial Reporting to Employees: Towards a Research Framework," *Accounting and Business Research* (Summer 1984), pp. 237-38. Reprinted with permission.

Exhibit 2.3
Table of Possible Employee Decisions and Information Useful to Those Decisions

Employee Decisions	**Information Useful**
Acceptance or rejection of entity offer of retraining/relocation/promotion/new position.	Profile of entity employees: age, sex, volume changes, location, hierarchical/job type levels. Degree of employee welfare provisions. Management policy/attitudes. Technology changes. Capital or labour intensive comparisons. New business developments. Expansion or contraction plans.
Level of productivity.	Wage levels, perquisites, advancement possibilities, attitude of remote/close management, budgetary proposals, imminent technological changes, safety of new machinery, working methods,

Exhibit 2.3 *(continued)*

	accident and compensation record of entity, noise and toxicity levels, employee contribution to output, levels of workers in associated plants, product demand, stock level, cost structure of area/section/plant/division.
Job satisfaction. Stay or leave. Retirement planning.	Pension availability, contribution levels, and performance. Merger or takeover likelihood. Profitability, sales volumes, production volumes, cash flows, liquidity, labour and capital ratios, job opportunities in entity. Future manpower plans and technological changes. New products or ventures planned.
Personal investment. Saving levels, insurance (non-entity superannuation), employee shares, debentures in entity.	Likely or occurring takeovers or mergers. Profitability, liquidity, sales projections, new products, or ventures, expansion or contraction plans. Employee pension fund availability and performance.
Union membership or non-membership; level of involvement if member.	Industrial relations statistics. Management policy/attitudes. Open or closed shop. Corporate social responsibility attitudes. Attitudes of management re profit-seeking versus cost-cutting. Expansion, contraction, relocation, new technologies, retraining plans. Employee welfare provisions—canteens, health and safety bonus schemes. Employment terms and wages levels. Profitability, liquidity.
Personal expenditure: General Organization's products New products	Product knowledge of entity and its associated companies. New products. Employee purchase schemes. Product safety, performance and environment effects. Mergers and takeover developments. Wage levels. Liquidity. Gearing. Sales volumes. Profitability.

Source: N. R. Lewis, L. D. Parker, and P. Sutcliffe, "Financial Reporting to Employees: Towards a Research Framework," *Accounting and Business Research* (Summer 1984), pp. 238-39. Reprinted with permission.

Exhibit 2.4
Disclosure Policies in Collective Bargaining

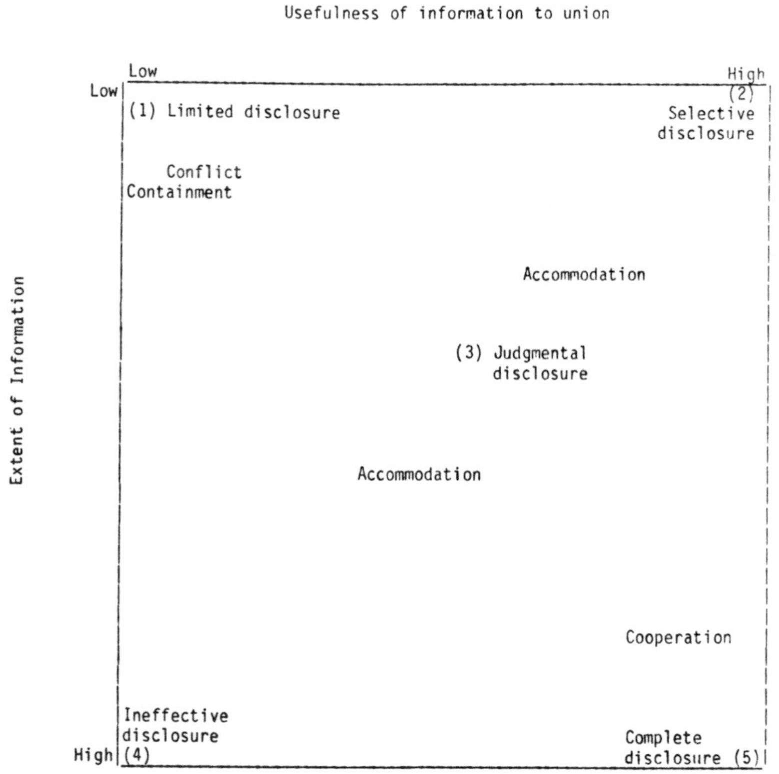

Source: James A. Craft, "Information Disclosure and the Role of the Accountant in Collective Bargaining," *Accounting, Organizations and Society* 6, no. 1 (1981), p. 101. Reprinted with permission.

of management to choose information for disclosure with broader objectives than simply conforming to the law and substantiating its own bargaining position. More specifically, "The information management does provide is chosen to help the union bargain within a meaningful framework, but due to cost and collection problems, may not be as detailed and specific as the union might desire."[25]

CONTENT OF THE EMPLOYEE REPORT

The content of the report to employees has not been standardized yet. Consequently, the alternatives available vary in the level of qualification and sophistication. A survey of the relevant literature revealed the

following report contents: (a) employee relationships, (b) future prospects (firm and employee), (c) statement of value added, (d) corporate-government relations, (e) corporate objectives, (f) cash flow, (g) where money came from and where it went, (h) profit and loss, (i) balance sheet, (j) social balance sheet, (k) break-even chart, (l) role of profits, (m) personnel related information, (n) chairman's address, and (o) competitions to encourage readership.[26]

Similarly, the dissemination of the information varied. The same survey identified the following techniques used: (a) mailed directly to employees, (b) report issued plus a management meeting, (c) letter format, (d) newspapers, (e) slides and films, (f) radio, (g) notice boards, (h) video tapes, (i) pay packets, (j) a request, (k) through supervisors, (l) financial training, and (m) integration with total communication network.[27]

To be read and accepted by employees, the employee report should at all cost avoid offending the employees. Richard Martin has identified some of the pitfalls to avoid:

Don't be patronizing.

Aim at the above average employee. It is better for some not to be interested than for those who are interested to feel they are being treated like children.

Avoid "them" and "us" language. Refer to *our* business and what *we* own.

Don't try to avoid the word profit—no business can survive unless it makes a profit.

When mentioning "extraordinary items," specify them.

Avoid the use of bowler hats and cloth caps in illustrations.

Don't discuss politics because you won't convince those with other views—you simply widen the rift.

Don't be afraid to repeat the message from year to year if it's worth it, it won't be remembered and there are always new employees.

Avoid jargon: use simple straightforward language but make sure it is not capable of misinterpretation or thought to be advertising or propaganda.

The report must be informative and motivational; it should provoke inquiry, explanation and subsequent action.

The report should encourage pride in the company's products and services.

Charts should be simple and product related if possible.

Problems in the company should not be ignored but discussed openly and solutions proposed.

Personnel problems can be included but debate this aspect carefully beforehand. Headmasterly tickings-off should be avoided as they cause resentment. If the problem is very large, such as lateness, pilferism or absenteeism, it is difficult to ignore but must obviously be handled with tact. One major company produced an employee report concentrating on this subject with considerable candour; it discussed recruitment, labour turnover, absenteeism, days lost through strikes and lay-offs and the company's safety record.[28]

Naturally, employees may well be required to learn some of the accounting jargon used in accounting reports. Such education is essential if the disclosure of employee information is going to be effective.

ROLE OF THE ACCOUNTANT IN EMPLOYEE REPORTING

Employee reporting presents a unique opportunity for accountants to expand their expertise beyond conventional accounting information, to investigate the information needs of unions and employees and to provide new information of relevance to employees and unions. Some authors went even further by calling for a management bargaining team role for the cost accountant.[29] Firms, however, differ in terms of the role of the accountant and the data they use to evaluate labor contract proposals:

> There are Type A firms that use primarily demographic data but make little use of either accounting or other financial data; Type B firms that use primarily demographic and accounting data; and Type C firms that use all these kinds of data. Demographic data are used to describe the vital statistics of an employee population, e.g., number of dependents, rates of pay, and years of service. Accounting data are used to describe information that can usually be obtained from payroll records, e.g., amounts paid in direct wages, overtime-premiums, military leave pay, vacation pay, holiday pay, etc. Other financial data are used to describe internal economic data that are not directly related to payroll costs. They would include information, such as past or estimated future revenues, production volume, product mix, and non-labor costs that are normally found in a corporate budget or profit report.[30]

Given these divergences, the Controllership Foundation suggested seven ways for the accountant to present accounting information for use in collective bargaining.

1. By compiling in advance a "fact book" or a series of tables and reports, but without concerning himself directly with the actual negotiations.
2. By acting as a consultant to the company negotiator, before and during the bargaining sessions—but again without becoming directly involved.
3. By obtaining close cooperation between his deputies and those of the negotiator to guide the presentation of facts for bargaining.
4. By serving as a member of a negotiating committee which attends all sessions, but not presenting any facts himself.
5. By making himself available for such presentations of facts as the negotiator desires.
6. By taking charge of the actual presentation of factual material, with the negotiator retaining control of the company's argument and the ultimate terms of agreement.
7. By forming special committees or task forces to collect, analyze and interpret data on certain provisions of the collective bargaining agreement.[31]

Craft also examined the role of the accountant in collective bargaining by presenting a conceptual framework in terms of the accountant's relationship to the parties in collective bargaining and the degree of his involvement in the labor relations process.[32] The relationship varies from neutral to partisan and the degree of the involvement from low to moderate/high. The resulting framework illustrates roles for the accountant in collective bargaining, as shown in Exhibit 2.5. The appropriate role of the accountant, given the range of alternatives, is made contingent on other factors including disclosure policy, qualifications and interest of the accountant, and role of financial issues in negotiations.

Exhibit 2.5
Illustrative Roles for the Accountant in Collective Bargaining

Relationship to Parties	Degree of involvement in labor relations process: Low	Degree of involvement in labor relations process: Moderate/High
Partisan	(1) No role (2) Preparation of information at negotiator special request I	(1) Preparation of bargaining facts and assist bargaining team (2) Member of negotiating team (3) Chief negotiator II
Neutral	(1) Audit data presented by management in collective bargaining III	(1) Consultant with access to company financial information to assist union (2) Facilitator, mediator, and/or teacher assist both parties to understand, use, interpret financial information; teach what should be used and how to use it IV

Source: James A. Craft, "Information Disclosure and the Role of the Accountant in Collective Bargaining," *Accounting, Organizations and Society* 6, no. 1 (1981), p. 104.

FUTURE RESEARCH IN EMPLOYEE REPORTING

The review of the literature in this chapter shows a general consensus among researchers that information should be reported to employees and unions in a separate report, giving definite benefits for both unions and employees on one hand and firms and managers on the other hand. It appears, however, from the same review that a lot of remaining questions are unanswered equally with regard to the identity of the user groups, the information needs, the content and format of the report, and the behavioral and/or market impact that may follow such disclosure. To guide such research, Lewis, Parker, and Sutcliffe provided a research design that identifies the required empirical tests and the corresponding propositions.[33] They are shown in Exhibits 2.6 and 2.7. Empirical evidence in each of these propositions will provide more answers to the challenging subject of employee reporting.

NOTES

1. Accounting Standards Steering Committee, *The Corporate Report* (London: Accounting Standards Steering Committee, 1975), p. 200.
2. Ibid., pp. 88-91.
3. Edward Stamp, *Corporate Reporting: Its Future Evolution* (Toronto: Canadian Institute of Chartered Accountants, 1980).
4. Dennis Taylor, Laurie Webb, and Les McGinley, "Annual Reports to Employees: The Challenge to the Corporate Accountant," *Chartered Accountant in Australia* (May 1979), p. 33.
5. N. R. Lewis, L. D. Parker, and P. Sutcliffe, "Financial Reporting to Employees: The Pattern of Development 1919 to 1979," *Accounting, Organizations and Society* (June 1984), p. 278.
6. Ibid., p. 281.
7. Ibid.
8. Taylor, Webb, and McGinley, "Annual Reports to Employees," p. 35.
9. Ibid., p. 36.
10. B. J. Foley and K. T. Maunders, *Accounting Information Disclosure and Collective Bargaining* (London: Macmillan, 1977), pp. 27-34.
11. Ibid., p. 34.
12. P. F. Pope and D. A. Peel, "Information Disclosure to Employees and Rational Expectations," *Journal of Business Finance and Accounting* (Spring 1981), pp. 139-46.
13. Ibid., p. 142.
14. Foley and Maunders, *Accounting Information Disclosure*, pp. 39-40.
15. L. C. Hunter and R. B. McKersie, *Pay Productivity and Collective Bargaining* (London: Macmillan, 1973), p. 173.
16. James A. Craft, "Information Disclosure and the Role of the Accountant in Collective Bargaining," *Accounting, Organizations and Society* 6, no. 1 (1981), pp. 99-101.

Exhibit 2.6

A Narrative Flowchart of Required Empirical Tests

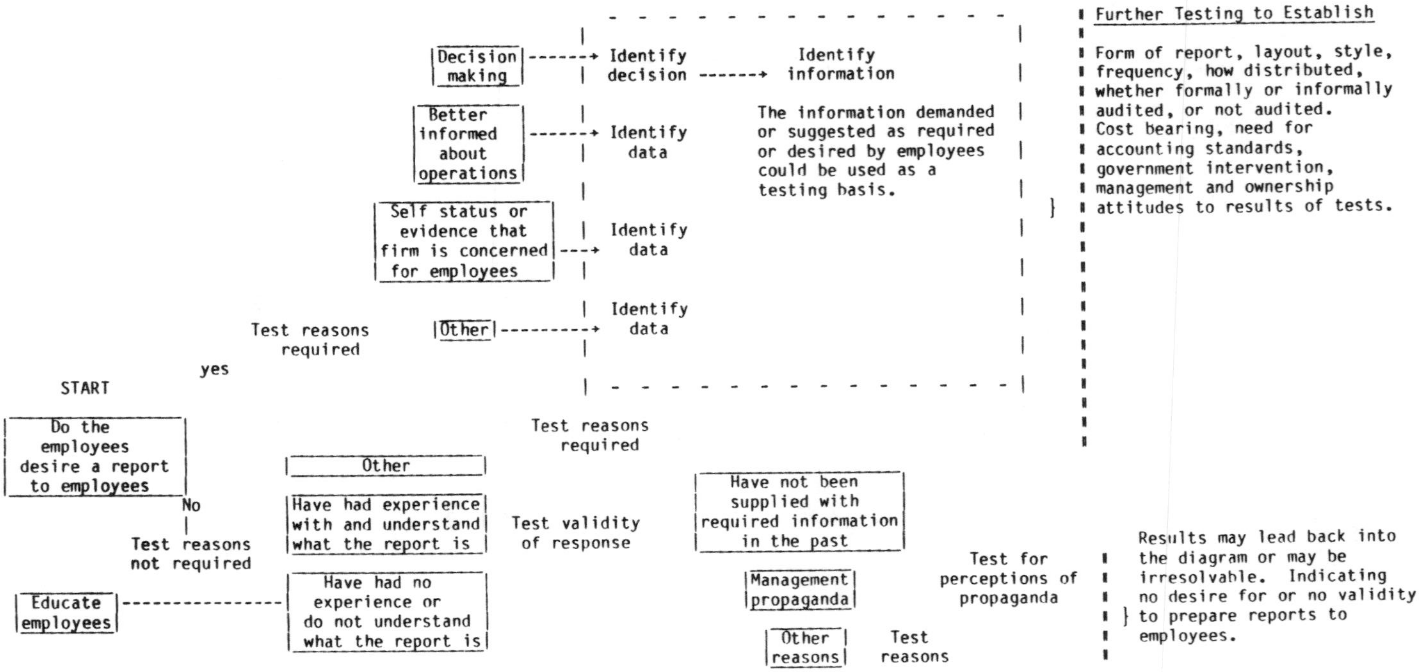

Source: N. R. Lewis, L. D. Parker, and P. Sutcliffe, "Financial Reporting to Employees: Towards a Research Framework," *Accounting and Business Research* (Summer 1984), p. 233. Reprinted with permission.

Exhibit 2.7
A Flowchart of Propositions

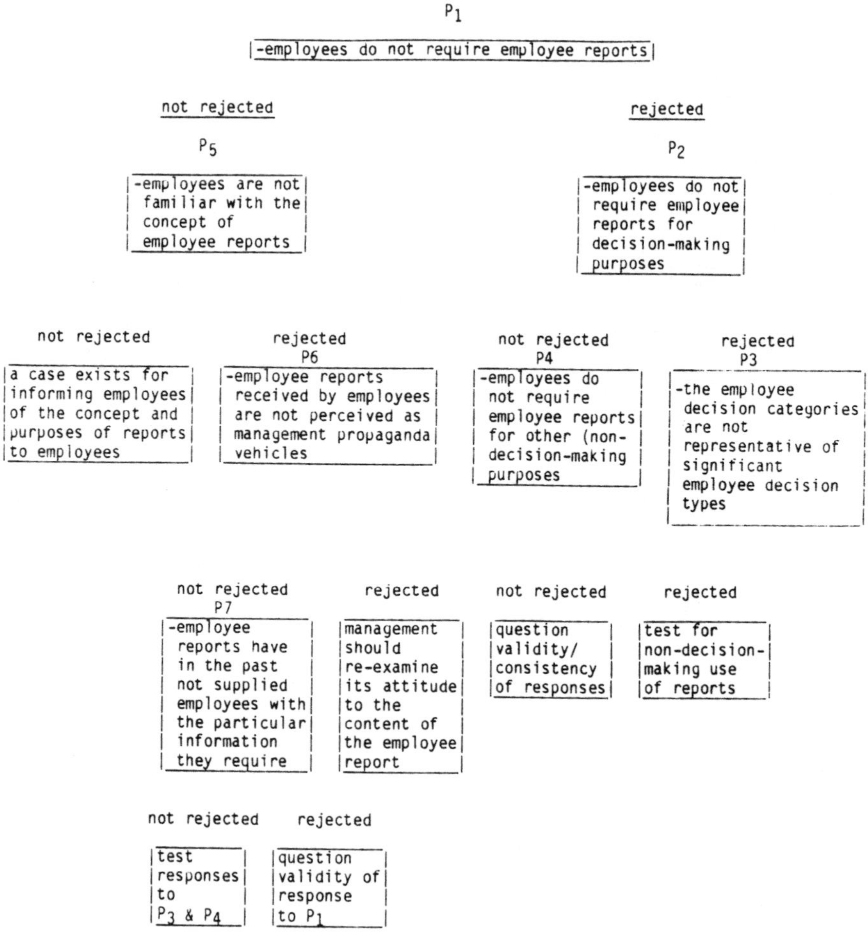

Source: N. R. Lewis, L. D. Parker, and P. Sutcliffe, "Financial Reporting to Employees: Towards a Research Framework," *Accounting and Business Research* (Summer 1984), p. 234. Reprinted with permission.

17. Ibid., p. 99.
18. Foley and Maunders, *Accounting Information Disclosure,* pp. 43-50.
19. David Cooper and Simon Essex, "Accounting Information and Employee Decision Making," *Accounting, Organizations and Society* 2, no. 3 (1977), pp. 202-6.
20. N. R. Lewis, L. D. Parker, and P. Sutcliffe, "Financial Reporting to Employees: Towards a Research Framework," *Accounting and Business Research* (Summer 1984), pp. 237-38.
21. Ibid., pp. 238-39.
22. Foley and Maunders, *Accounting Information Disclosure,* p. 39.
23. N. H. Cuthbert and A. Whitaker, "Disclosure of Information and Collective Bargaining: A Reexamination," *Journal of Business Finance and Accounting* 4, no. 3 (1977), p. 374.
24. Craft, "Role of the Accountant in Collective Bargaining," pp. 101-2.
25. Ibid., p. 102.
26. Lewis, Parker, and Sutcliffe, "Financial Reporting to Employees: The Pattern of Development 1919 to 1979," p. 278.
27. Ibid., p. 279.
28. Richard Martin, "Providing the Employee Report," *Management Accounting* (September 1977), p. 342.
29. Lee C. Shaw, "Company Labor Policy—and the Accountant's Part," *NACA Bulletin* (March 1954), p. 865; Robert E. Hess, "Labor Unions Look at Accountants," *Management Accounting* (October 1967), p. 60; Harold H. Jack, "The Accountant's Role in Labor Relations," *Management Accounting* (October 1970), p. 60; Michael F. Granof, "Financial Evaluation of Labor Contracts," *Management Accounting* (July 1973), p. 42.
30. Granof, "Financial Evaluation of Labor Contracts," p. 42.
31. Earl Brooks, N. Arnold Tolls, and Richard F. Dean, *Providing Facts and Figures for Collective Bargaining: The Controller's Role* (New York: Controllership Foundation, 1950), p. 26.
32. Craft, "Role of the Accountant in Collective Bargaining," pp. 103-6.
33. Lewis, Parker, and Sutcliffe, "Financial Reporting to Employees: Towards a Research Framework," pp. 233-34.

SELECTED BIBLIOGRAPHY

Carlsberg, B. V., and A.J.B. Hope, ed., *Current Issues in Accounting* (London: Philip Allan, 1977).

Climo, T., "The Role of the Accountant in Industrial Relations," *Accountant* (December 16, 1976), p. 702.

Cooper, D., and S. Essex, "Accounting Information and Employee Decision Making," *Accounting, Organizations and Society* 12, no. 3 (1977), pp. 201-17.

Craft, J. A., "Information Disclosure and the Role of the Accountant in Collective Bargaining," *Accounting, Organizations and Society* 6, no. 1 (1981), pp. 97-107.

______, "A Reply to Maunders and Foley," *Accounting, Organizations and Society* 9, no. 1 (1984), pp. 107-8.

Cuthbert, N. H., and A. Whitaker, "Disclosure of Information and Collective Bargaining: A Reexamination," *Journal of Business Finance and Accounting* 4, no. 3 (1977), pp. 373-78.

Dale, Ernest, *Sources of Economic Information for Collective Bargaining* (New York: American Management Association, 1950).

Foley, B. J. and K. T. Maunders, *Accounting Information Disclosure and Collective Bargaining* (London: Macmillan, 1977).

General and Municipal Workers Union (U.K.), *Law at work* (London: GAWU, 1976).

Gogarty, J. P., "What Employees Expect to be Told," *Management Accounting* (United Kingdom) (November 1975), pp. 359-60.

Granof, Michael F., "Financial Evaluation of Labor Contracts," *Management Accounting* (July 1973), p. 42.

Holmes, G., "How UK Companies Report," *Accountancy* (November 1977), p. 66.

Horwitz, B., and R. Shalahang, "Published Corporate Accounting Data and General Wage Increases of the Firm," *Accounting Review* (April 1971), pp. 243-52.

Hussey, R., *Employees and the Employee Report* (London: Touche Ross, 1978).

Hussey, R., and R. J. Craig, *Keeping Employees Informed* (Sydney, Australia: Butterworth, 1982).

Institute of Chartered Accountants in England and in Wales, *The Reporting of Company Financial Results to Employees* (London, December 1976).

Institute of Chartered Accountants in England and in Wales and the Institute of Personnel Management, *Assisting Employees in the Understanding and Use of Financial Information* (London, 1978).

Institute of Cost and Management Accountants, "Presentation of Information," (December 1978).

Jack, Harold H., "The Accountant's Role in Labor Relations," *Management Accounting* (October 1970), p. 60.

Jackson-Cox, J., J. E. Thirkell, and J. McQueeney, "The Disclosure of Company Information to Trade Unions: The Relevance of the ACAS Code of Practice on Disclosure," *Accounting, Organizations and Society* (June 1984), pp. 253-73.

Jenkins, C., "A Trade Unionist's Viewpoint on Financial Information Requirements," *Management Accounting* (November 1975), p. 359.

Jones, D. M. C., "Designing Accounts to Inform More Effectively," *Management Accounting* (1975), p. 359.

Lafferty, M., "A Landmark for Union and the City," *Financial Times* (July 26, 1977), p. 13.

Lewis, N. R., L. D. Parker, and P. Sutcliffe, "Financial Reporting: The Pattern of Development 1919 to 1979," *Accounting, Organizations and Society* 9 (June 1984), pp. 275-85.

———, "Financial Reporting to Employees: Towards a Research Framework," *Accounting and Business Research* (Summer 1984), pp. 229-39.

Martin, R., "Providing an Employee Report," *Management Accounting* (September 1977), pp. 341-48.

Maunders, Keith T., "Employee Reporting," in *Developments in Financial Reporting*, ed. Thomas A. Lee (London: Philip Allan, 1981), pp. 171-95.

Maunders, Keith T., and B. J. Foley, "Accounting Information, Employees and

Collective Bargaining," *Journal of Business Finance and Accounting* (Spring 1974), pp. 109-27.

______, "How Much Should We Tell Trade Unions?" *Accounting Age* (February 22, 1974), pp. 340-46.

Miller, J., "Financial Information for Employees," *Accountant* (May 29, 1975), p. 690.

Palmer, John R., *The Use of Accounting Information in Labor Negotiations* (New York: National Association of Accountants, 1977).

Parker, L. D., "Financial Reporting to Corporate Employees: A Growing Practice in Australia," *Chartered Accountant in Australia* (March 1977), pp. 5-9.

Pope, P. F., and D. A. Peel, "Information Disclosure to Employees and Rational Expectations," *Journal of Business Finance and Accounting* (Spring 1981), pp. 139-46.

Taylor, Dennis, Laurie Webb, and Les McGinley, "Annual Reports to Employees: The Challenge to the Corporate Accountant," *Chartered Accountant in Australia* (May 1979), pp. 33-39.

Thompson, S., "Involving a Financial Policy and Strategy which Includes Consideration of Employees Information Needs," *Management Accounting* (November 1975), p. 360.

3

VALUE-ADDED TAXATION

Value-added taxation (VAT) is being used by most European countries, generating about half of the tax revenues of France and Norway and in excess of 25% of all revenues for West Germany. In the United States the present federal structure, composed primarily of corporate and individual income taxation and payroll taxes, has been questioned as being sometimes inferior to VAT, generating in the process a continuous debate about the feasibility and desirability of a VAT in the United States. In addition to the United States most other countries are seriously considering a VAT similar to the European method as a necessary way to promote economic growth, stability, and productivity. Accordingly, this chapter elaborates on the major facets of the debates surrounding the feasibility and desirability of VAT as an alternative to other types of taxes.

HISTORY OF VAT

The value-added tax is not a new idea. The roots run deep into colonial and early America. Robert P. Crum showed that the concepts of ad valorem, transaction basis, indirect levy, multistep collection, and transaction of net product were present during that early period.[1] The combination of these factors existed in the form of the value-added tax.

The American economists' early embrace of statistical, economic, and business analysis, and the development of a formula for computing the gross national product (GNP), led economists and fiscal experts to think of using the GNP as a tax base. The idea was more easily supportable than implementable as the European countries jumped on the bandwagon first. France adopted VAT in 1954, 13 years before the European community

recommended its adoption by its members. The creation of the European Economic Community (EEC) following the Treaty of Rome (March 25, 1957) spurred the need for a tax harmonization among the member countries. The Newmark Report called for such harmonization and the eventual acceptance by all members of all-stage value-added tax systems. It specifically called for replacing the gross turnover tax systems with systems of value-tax. Two directives dated April 11, 1967, called for the implementation of the value-added tax systems. And after more delays from Belgium and Italy all the EEC countries adopted the system. Outside the EEC, Scandinavian countries—like Denmark in 1967, Sweden in 1969, and Norway in 1970—followed suit.

DEFINITION AND COMPUTATION

The VAT is basically the tax on the value added by the firm in the course of its operations. The value added, as was stated in chapter 1, can be defined by using either the subtractive method as the difference of the sales and purchases or the additive method as the sum of the wages, rent, interest, and profits. Because of its practicality the subtractive method is generally favored for the computation of VAT in European countries. The calculation of VAT is, as a result, a double process involving a tax on a firm's sales and a credit received by the firm for the VAT paid on its purchases. Exhibits 3.1 and 3.2 show the computation for a retailer and wholesaler.

Exhibit 3.1 uses the subtractive method to compute the value added. In that case the value added due ($500) is computed as the difference between the value added due on sales ($1,000) and the VAT credit on purchases ($500). Assume a simple tax rate; the VAT in this case could be directly obtained by taxing the tax base of $5,000 by 10%, resulting in a $500 VAT.

Exhibit 3.1
Computation of the Value-Added Tax for a Retailer

Profit and Loss Statement		VAT computed at 10%
Sales	$10,000	+ $1,000 VAT debit on Sales
Less Purchases	5,000	- 500 VAT credit on Purchases
Value Added	5,000	$ 500 VAT net due.
Less labor and other costs	2,000	
Profit before tax	3,000	

Exhibit 3.2
Computation of the Value-Added Tax for a Manufacturer, Wholesaler, and Retailer

		VAT Computed at 10%		
	Profit and Loss Statement	VAT Computation	Net VAT due at each stage	Cumulative VAT due to the Government
Manufacturer				
Sales	$10,000	$1,000		
Less Purchases	- 0	0		
Value Added	$10,000	$1,000	$1,000	
Less Other Costs	5,000			
Profit	$ 5,000			$1,000
Wholesaler				
Sales	$30,000	$3,000		
Less Purchases	10,000	- 1,000		
Value Added	20,000	$2,000	$2,000	
Less Other Costs	7,000			
Profit	3,000			$3,000
Retailer				
Sales	$50,000	$5,000		
Less Purchases	30,000	3,000		
Value Added	$20,000	$2,000	$2,000	
Less Other Costs	10,000			$5,000
Profit	10,000			
Price to Consumer	$50,000	$5,000		$55,000
Value Added	$50,000			

Exhibit 3.2 uses the subtractive method to compute the value added throughout the chain of production and distribution formed by the manufacturer, wholesaler, and retailer. The VAT due at each stage is $1,000 for the manufacturer, $2,000 for the wholesaler, and $2,000 for the retailer.

Exhibit 3.3 shows the computation of VAT among the subtractive, the additive, and the invoice method.

Exhibit 3.3
Alternative Methods of Value-Added Tax Computation for 10% VAT Rate (Consumption-Type VAT Base)

Method	Firm A	Firm B	Firm C	Consumer
1. Subtraction Method:				
Net Sales	$300	$500	$700	
Less:				
Purchases	-0-	300	500	
Capital Acq'n	100	50	-0-	
Net VAT Base	$200	$150	$200	$700
VAT @ 10%	$ 20	$ 15	$ 20	$ 70
2. Addition Method:				
Payments to Productive Factors:				
Payroll/Int. Rent	$200	$100	$100	
Profit	100	100	100	
Total Payments	$300	$200	$200	
Less:				
Change in Inv.	-0-	-0-	-0-	
Cap. Acquisition	100	50	-0-	
Net VAT @ Base	$200	$150	$200	$700
VAT @ 10%	$ 20	$ 15	$ 20	$ 70
3. Invoice Method:				
Invoiced VAT On Sales	$ 30	$ 50	$ 70	
Less:				
Invoiced VAT On Purchases	10	$ 35	50	$ 70
Net VAT Due	$ 20	$ 15	$ 20	$ 70

VAT COLLECTION METHODS

There are two possible VAT collection methods, the cash-collection or tax-credit method and the invoice-collection or additive method.

The cash-collection or tax-credit method recognizes VAT liability in sales and VAT credits on purchases at the time of cash payment. Under this method the VAT must be determined and shown separately on all merchandise invoices. One of its advantages is that it is self-policing:

A merchant (manufacturer, wholesaler, or retailer) collects the VAT on his sales, as with any other sales tax. He then pays the taxing authority that amount minus any allowable offsets. (The allowable offsets are the VAT paid by the merchant on purchases.) Thus, the individual's net tax due is determined on the basis of and traceable to sales and purchase invoices. Any buyer of goods therefore has a direct interest in ensuring that the amount of VAT charged and reported by his supplier is correct, as that charge becomes his tax credit. This system relies less on voluntary compliance than does an income tax system.[2]

The invoice-collection or additive method recognizes VAT liability on sales and VAT credits on purchases at the time of invoicing. It is similar to the Michigan business tax, the only American VAT where the same result is achieved by having taxpayers add up the individual components of their value added: compensation paid, depreciation, depletion, and other capital cost recovery allowances; taxable income (other than dividends received); and interest, rent, and royalties paid in excess of interest; and rent and royalties received. They then deduct purchases of investment goods.

TYPES OF VAT: CONSUMPTION, INCOME, AND GROSS PRODUCT

Because the purchases may include both purchases of goods and purchases of capital assets, the alternative methods of treating purchases of capital assets generate three possible types of VAT, namely, the consumption type, the income type, and the gross product type.

Under the consumption type, the VAT credit or purchases include both purchases of goods and capital assets. It is labeled as consumption-type VAT because the economic base of VAT is total private consumption. Under the income type, the VAT credit on purchases includes both the purchase of goods and the amortization value of the capital assets for the year. It is labeled as income-type VAT because the economic base of VAT is net national income.

Under the gross product type, the VAT credit on purchases includes only the purchase of goods and does not include any credit for capital assets (in total or in part). It is called the gross product type because the economic base is the open national product, which is equivalent to consumption plus investment. Exhibit 3.4 illustrates the computation of VAT for the three types, consumption, income, and gross national product.

OTHER CHARACTERISTICS OF VAT

The examples used up to now assume that a single rate is being used and no adjustments are made. In fact, most existing VAT systems include at least one of the following adjustments:

1. Multiple rates applicable to different categories of goods.
2. Specific exemptions from VAT to include, for example, (a) exemption of separated products, (b) exemption of products for political or social reasons, (c) exemption given to certain retailers, and (d) the exclusion of some stages in the production-distribution process.[3]
3. Reduced taxable base.

Exhibit 3.4
Value-Added Transactions and Alternative Tax Bases

Facts:	Firm A	Firm B	Firm C	Consumer
Sales	$300	$500	$700	
Input Purchases	-0-	300	500	
Value-Added	$300	$200	$200	
Labor/Rent/ Interest	200	100	100	
Profit	$100	$100	$100	
Capital Acq. (5-Yr. Life)	$100	$ 50	-0-	
Fraction of Value Added	3/7	2/7	2/7	
Alternative VAT Bases				
1. Consumption Type VAT				
Sales	$300	$500	$700	
Less:				
Purchases	-0-	300	500	
Capital Acq'n	100	50	-0-	
Net VAT Base	$200	$150	$200	$700
2. Income Type VAT				
Sales	$300	$500	$700	
Less:				
Purchases	-0-	300	500	
Depreciation on Cap. Acq.	20	10	-0-	
Net VAT Base	$280	$190	$200	$700
3. Gross Product Type VAT				
Sales	$300	$500	$700	
Less:				
Purchases	-0-	300	500	
Net VAT Base	$300	$200	$200	$700

With regard to the exemptions, we may include items of consumption that are intrinsically difficult to tax under VAT or any other consumption tax, such as domestic services and expenditures abroad by Americans. The most important services difficult to tax under VAT are the services of financial intermediaries, including insurance companies. The following quote illustrates the difficulty:

> *Banks, insurance companies, and other financial institutions are exempt* from the Danish value-added tax simply, it is said, because of the difficulty of applying to them the concept of total sales and total purchases. Interest as such is of course not subject to the consumption-type of value-added tax; but "interest" as a payment for services rendered by a bank free of direct charge (e.g., free checkbook and checking services) is in principle taxable. Such a service would have to be given an imputed value, and divided into that part rendered to business firms and that part rendered to households, so that the tax levied on the service rendered to firms could be taken by those firms as a credit against the tax on their own sales. An approximate solution would be to tax the financial institution on its payroll, and divide this tax between the two groups of customers on some relevant basis, perhaps number of checks handled, but Denmark has been unwilling to attempt this or any other rough substitute. Meanwhile the exclusion of these financial institutions from the value-added tax system has caused some difficulty. The banks have set up a cooperative electronic data processing institute to perform services for the smaller banks, but these services are held taxable, and the small banks get no tax credit, being themselves exempt. The larger banks perform their own EDP [electronic data processing] services, and pay no tax on that value added.[4]

Some suggest retail sales tax as an alternative to VAT. There are fundamental differences between VAT and the retail sales tax although both of them are consumption taxes. While VAT is collected at every level of the business process, the retail sales tax is only levied at the point of final sale. There are also administrative and political differences underlying the comparison between the sales retail tax and VAT. First, VAT requires more paperwork than a national sales tax. Second, the evasion is more difficult under VAT given that under VAT evasion would be limited to the level of production where it occurred, while under a retail sales tax, the whole potential tax revenue is eliminated. Finally, most states have a sales tax and would not welcome the addition by the government of a VAT.

MAJOR ADVANTAGES ATTRIBUTED TO VAT

1. The VAT system will be easy to administer with its reliance on the invoices generated in the normal course of business which will give the IRS all the information needed to compute the tax due.

2. The pure VAT, with all goods and services subject to the same rate, will be economically neutral in the sense that no sector of the economy will be favored over any other.

3. The VAT may restore an edge in international trade, since the tax would be rebated on American exports and imposed on imports. In effect, under the General Agreement on Tariffs and Trade (GATT), indirect taxes like VAT, excise, and commodity tax, can be rebated on exports and levied on imports, while direct taxes, like income taxes, cannot. Because most trading partners of the United States levy a large percentage of their revenues through indirect taxes like VAT, it creates an inequity in the tax structure allowing them to enjoy a tax holiday while American exports are double-taxed. A VAT system may help correct the situation by helping domestic exports and by making domestic products more competitive with imports.

4. Because VAT taxes only consume income, they may encourage savings. Higher savings would reduce the adverse effects on domestic competitiveness by reducing the flow of foreign capital in the United States and thereby lowering the value of the dollar.

5. VAT would be noninflationary if it is a net tax increase but a replacement tax that will restructure taxes that are currently inefficient and inequitable.

6. Use of VAT would alleviate the underground economy because it provides incentives for more participants to stay in the system to obtain credits for their import taxes. While this advantage has not been proven empirically, the European experience seems to contradict it. For example:

> The underground economy does exist under a VAT. For example, it is not uncommon for a European home owner dealing with tradesmen such as painters, plumbers and carpenters, to be given a choice between a price with the VAT included or a lower price without a VAT. The reason this practice can be profitable under the VAT is that typically, in labor intensive activities, the input tax incurred by the business person may be relatively small. Accordingly, only a small number of taxable transactions need to be entered into to insure that the VAT collected is sufficient to offset credits for VAT paid. Once this balance is achieved, service can be offered "underground," free of VAT, with no adverse tax consequences to the business and with possibly highly favorable results because of the competitive advantage gained from the lower prices. Although the principal audit problems arise at the retail level, more complex avoidance schemes involving chains of selling and purchasing can be devised.[5]

7. When compared with other types of taxes, VAT appears to be the most neutral toward businesses of all types. Exhibit 3.5 summarizes the impacts of alternative taxes on industries with different characteristics.

Exhibit 3.5

Differential Impact of Various Possible Changes in the U.S. Tax Structure

Characteristic of industries	VAT	Higher corporate income tax rates	Elimination of investment credit and reduction in depreciation allowances	Increased taxes on capital gains of individuals	Surtax on individual income taxes	Reduction in deductions allowed on individual income taxes	Increased payroll taxes	Increased business property taxes	Increase in residential property taxes
1. Largely incorporated	0	-	-	-/+	+	0	0	0	0
1a. Largely unincorporated	0	+	+	-	-	0	0	0	0
2. High debt/equity ratio	0	+	+	+	0(+)*	0	0	0	0
2a. Low debt/equity ratio	0	-	-	-	0(-)*	0	0	0	0
3. High return on equity (or on sales)	0/+	-	_	-(equity) 0 (sales)	0/+(-)*	0/+(0)*	0/+	0/+	0/+
4. High capital-intensiveness	0/+	-	-	0	0/-(+)*	0/+	+	-	0/+
4a. High labor-intensiveness	0/-	+	+	0	0/-(+)*	0/-	-	+	0/-
5. Sizeable assets in land	0/+	0	+	-	0	0/-	0	-	-/0/+
6. Sizeable assets in buildings	-/0/+	0	-	-	0/-	0/-	0/-	-	-/0
7. Industry-wide collective bargaining or strong labor unions	-	0	0	0	-	-	-	0	-

Exhibit 3.5 *(continued)*

Characteristic of industries	VAT	Higher corporate income tax rates	Elimination of investment credit and reduction in depreciation allowances	Increased taxes on capital gains of individuals	Surtax on individual income taxes	Reduction in deductions allowed on individual income taxes	Increased payroll taxes	Increased business property taxes	Increase in residential property taxes
8. Diversified sources of purchase	+	+/0†	+/0†	0	0/+	0	+	+/0†	0/+
9. High import cost component	0/+	+/0†	+/0†	0	0/+	0	+	0/+	0/+
10. High elasticity in demand for industry's product	-	0/-	0/-	0/-	-	-	-	0/-	-
10a. Low elasticity in demand for industry's products	+	0/+	0/+	0/+	+	+	+	0/+	+
11. High product substitutability (high cross-elasticity)	-/0	-/0†	-/0†	0/-	0/-	-	-	0/-	-/0
12. Intense price competition	-/0	-/+	-/+	0/-	0/-	-	-	-/0	-/0
13. Diversified markets	+	0/+	0/+	0	+	+	+	0/+	+
14. Producers of capital goods	+/-	-	-	-	0/-	+/-	+/-	-/0	-/0/+

15. Industries doing much exporting	0/-/+	-/0†	-/0†	0/-	+/0/-	0/+/-	-	0	0/-
16. Industries competing with imports	0/-	-/0†	-/0†	0/-	0/-	0/-	-	0	0/-

\+ = Industries aided directly by a proportionately lower tax burden or indirectly by a relative increase in profits, a comparatively smaller reduction in sales, or a relatively smaller increase in costs vis-à-vis industries with the opposite characteristic.

0 = Impact would be neutral between industries with opposite characteristics.

— = Industries hurt directly by a proportionately higher tax burden or indirectly by a relative decrease in profits, a comparatively larger reduction in sales, or a relatively larger increase in costs vis-à-vis industries with the opposite characteristic.

*Sign in parenthesis indicates impact on unincorporated firms with the indicated characteristic.

†The effect of the tax change would be neutral only if the tax were not shifted at all to customers.

Note: To produce equal revenues only a low rate VAT would have to be imposed, while substantial increases in the rates of either the corporate income tax (CIT) or the individual income tax (IIT) would be required. for example, the CIT would have to be raised from 48 percent to roughly 63 percent to generate the additional revenues produced by a 3 percent VAT (minus revenues lost by compensating changes in the IIT). The higher rates would mean that the impact of the CIT might in many cases be greater than the impact of the VAT. Although a 12 percent surcharge on the individual income tax would be needed to raise the additional revenues produced by a 3 percent VAT, the higher IIT rate might not have quite the dampening effect on consumer demand as the low VAT vecause the IIT is a more progressive tax.

Source: D. T. Smith, J. B. Webber, and C. M. Cerf, *What You Should Know about the Value Added Tax* (Homewood, Ill.: Dow Jones-Irwin, 1973), p. 137. Reprinted with permission.

8. VAT has been assumed to contribute to a drastic increase in inflation because it raises prices at each level. According to Alan Tait, data on prices can show the effects of the introduction of VAT in four ways:

- There may be a single upward shift in the consumer price index clearly associated with the period when the tax was introduced, but with an unchanged, or little changed, rate of increase in prices, if the tax increases government revenue and if traders pass forward the increase. This is called the shift case. If inflation is defined as a continuing general increase in prices, the tax that results in a once-and-for-all price change cannot be inflationary by itself.
- There may be an increase in the rate of change of the index, as a result of the introduction of the tax. This is called the acceleration case.
- The acceleration may be combined with a shift in the overall price level. This is referred to as the shift plus acceleration case.
- There may be no discernible effects at all, if the tax substitutes perfectly for the one it replaces or if the authorities can offset any accompanying pressures to increase prices.[6]

In fact, using data and circumstantial evidence, the analysis of 31 countries using VAT showed that the introduction of the tax need not be inflationary. In the case of accelerated inflation, the cause was more often than not apparently due to expansionary wage and credit policies.[7] Another argument refuting the inflationary effect of a VAT goes as follows: "An all-round use in consumer prices not accompanied by an increase in money incomes will force consumers to restrict their demands for some goods or services, and this will tend to bring prices down to their previous level."[8]

9. One of the advantages of VAT is that under the system the tax burden is being shifted forward from stage to stage all the way up to the consumer, thus creating the usual characterization of VAT as a tax on consumption. Questions are generally raised about the realism of such an assumption: "how much weight should be given to special situations of highly depressed markets that force taxpayers at some preconsumption stage to absorb part of the tax to avoid curtailing demand on the part of their customers?"[9]

10. One advantage of VAT comes from the borderline adjustments (BTA) on goods entering international trade where it is customary to rebate any VAT previously collected on exports and apply VAT to the imports. The mechanisms if adopted by the United States would go as follows:

> In the case of imports, the VAT would be applied, at the same rate applicable to value added in domestic production, to the full value of the imports as reported to the Custom Bureau as the imports entered customs. In the case of exports, the U.S. exporter would deduct the invoice value of export sales from his total net sales and receipts before deducting his purchases from other businesses in arriving at his taxable value added, assuming the subtraction method is used for computing the tax. Under the invoice method the taxpayer has no VAT liability on his export sales and claims a credit for all of the VAT shown on his purchase invoices.[10]

11. The matter of evasion is important when considering the adoption of a tax system. The VAT system is considered efficient at reducing some of the tax evasion taking place under other systems. For one thing, if VAT is evaded at the retail stage where it is the most unbearable, the government would have at least collected it in earlier stages. If the "credit" method of tax deduction is used, the VAT system acts as a self-policing mechanism. Under such a system at each stage one actor specifies to the other the VAT he or she had paid and wants to recoup. The invoice serves as evidence of the exact amount to be paid. The relative burdens of record that VAT requires, where firms must keep tax records with respect to their purchases as well as their sales, act as a hindrance to any evasion schemes.

MAJOR DISADVANTAGES ATTRIBUTED TO VAT

1. The VAT is perceived as regressive and likely to affect lower-income groups and bigger families that spend a bigger share of their income. This feature may be corrected if a higher VAT rate on luxury goods is levied and food and pharmaceuticals are exempted, making VAT more progressive.

2. It could contribute to a drastic increase in inflation because it raises prices at each level. The impact could be, however, reduced by the appropriate combination of fiscal and monetary policy.

3. It will disturb some of the states which rely on retail sales taxes and which may resent the federal government's intrusion into their domain. VAT, because of similarity to sales tax, will allow the government to cut into states' favorable revenue source and that may handicap the states at a crucial moment.

4. VAT coupled with cuts in personal and corporation income taxes would have no effect in aggregate exports even though the income tax cuts would induce companies to lower prices. Henry J. Aaron, a senior fellow at the Brookings Institution, explains as follows:

> Initially, all exporters and import-competing companies would tend to sell more, but in a world of flexible exchange rates, a drop in the prices of American exports and import-competing goods would cause the dollar to appreciate, since foreign demand for dollars to buy American goods would increase and American demand for foreign currencies to buy imports would decrease. The appreciation of the dollar would substantially offset the price cuts. Companies that cut their prices by more than the average would tend to gain market share, those that cut prices less would tend to lose share. But the aggregate effect would be negligible. So, if one looks only at trade, replacing part of the personal and corporation income taxes with a B.T.T. would have little or no effects on our companies' capacity to meet foreign competition.[11]

5. Limited merit is given the argument that VAT will improve American exports, and thus its exchange position. Witness the following quotation:

The corporate income tax reduces our competitive position in world markets only to the extent that the tax is shifted forward in higher export prices. Even for domestic sales, that tax shifting remains doubtful, and it is less likely that the tax is shifted at all to export prices. To the extent that the corporation tax is shifted, removal of the tax would initially improve our export position. This can be done as effectively by devaluation of the dollar. However, the present foreign exchange value of the dollar reflects any shifted elements of the corporate tax and the value may be slightly lower than it would be if the tax did not exist. Furthermore, other countries use corporate income taxes in addition to value added taxes, they normally do not replace the former by the latter. These foreign corporate taxes are roughly comparable to those of the United States government. Essentially, the American firms are now at a disadvantage even to the extent that the corporation tax is shifted, and if the United States would replace its corporate tax by a value added tax, retaliation almost certainly would follow. It is important to note that one of our chief competitors in the world market, Japan, does not employ a value added tax.[12]

6. One of the disadvantages of VAT is its assumed regressivity given that consumption as a percentage of income falls as income rises. Then VAT would take a larger proportion of the income of the poor than of the rich. This leads proponents of VAT to suggest that various exceptions or exemptions from VAT be allowed and that various output classes such as food, clothing, shelter, and health care be excluded. Some, however, would argue that the view that VAT is a consumption tax is, at best, only partially correct. The argument goes as follows:

People are likely to reduce their consumption *and* their saving in equal proportions in response to the VAT, thus shifting the burden of the tax back to the producers—to those supplying production inputs. The VAT may appropriately be seen as burdening consumption insofar as revenues are used to finance government activities the products of which offered less satisfaction than those which would have been consumed in the absence of the tax. But in this sense, there is no way of telling whether the VAT burdens consumption more or less than any other tax producing the same amount of tax revenues. Nor is there any a priori basis for determining whether this sort of consumption burden is heavier on the poor than on the affluent.[13]

THE POTENTIAL FOR VAT IN THE UNITED STATES

How Much Longer Can We Stand the Federal Debt?

The federal debt is reaching enormous proportions. With the same trend continuing there will be about $2.25 of debt for each dollar of GNP by 1995. When one examines overall debt relationship to GNP, the picture shows an accelerating speed in the growth of debt relative to GNP. Trying to rely on foreigners to continue to finance the federal deficit at a rate of about $100

billion a year is a false solution with serious consequences. People's attitudes towards financial leverage add to the problem. This is reflected in the increase in leverage buyouts and corporate takeovers financed with the so-called junk bonds ($18 billion in 1985); in second mortgages outstanding, from $40 billion in 1981 to $150 billion in 1985; and in consumer debt, with credit cards going from $75 million in 1982 to $100 million now.

Are we mortgaging the future of our children? The obvious remedy is lowering the federal deficit and changing the attitudes of all including the federal government toward debt. This calls for a revision of a tax code which includes obvious and powerful incentives for debt accumulations both at the corporation and household levels. With the federal budget deficit going toward the gigantic figure of $220 billion plus, the supply-side notion that tax cuts generate rising revenues sounds ludicrous. As put by Yale University professor William D. Nordhaus, Arthur B. Laffer's theories are no more than "economic laetrile," after the cance drug that most doctors scoff at. The notion that the United States could cut tax rates across the board and bring more money in is at best absurd. The notion still made Laffer the intellectual godfather of the tax-cut movement.

What's Next after the Gramm-Rudman Act?

The Gramm-Rudman Act is a nonbinding congressional budget resolution, which sets annual receipts and spending targets into a binding law subject to approval or veto by the president. It requires a lowering of the federal deficit to $144 billion from the actual $290 billion. It mandates a balanced federal budget by 1991. There is a challenge to the constitutionality of the law in the courts, on the basis that it transfers the power to appropriating funds from the legislative to the executive branch, but a counterchallenge claims that Congress cannot bring suit because it has not been "personally adversely affected." So the act is a reality of the times. The arithmetic of the Gramm-Rudman Act calls for a tax hike as a way out. What alternatives are available is the question of interest. Three alternatives that seem capable of drawing some support from those eager to reduce the deficit in line with the Gramm-Rudman Act are a broad-based oil excise tax, higher excise taxes, and value-added taxes.

The energy tax would take the form of a comprehensive oil tax combining an excise on all crude oil, imported or domestic, with an increased duty on imports of petroleum products. The brunt would be felt by energy-intensive industries, including chemicals, electric utilities, heavy manufacturing, and transportation. At a rate of $5 per barrel, the scheme would secure $30 billion a year for revenues.

The higher excise tax could be levied on alcoholic beverages, tobacco products, long-distance telephone calls, and airline tickets. Around $10 billion a year would be raised as revenues.

The value-added tax as a tax imposed at each stage of production could raise more than $90 billion a year with a 7% rate. It will be, by far, the simplest and most uniform way to raise enormous amounts of revenues.

The Business Transfer Tax (BTT)

Tax reform is on the minds of most legislators. The objectives are generally to motivate savings and provide capital for growth. For example, Delaware Republican senator William V. Roth suggests the following objectives:

- Level the playing field in international trade by connecting the inequities that allow Japanese and European products to compete in the world market with sizeable tax advantages.
- Increase the savings potential of Individual Retirement Accounts by allowing full I.R.A. benefits for spouses, by introducing super-savings accounts that allow up to $6,000 in tax-deferred savings for families and by maintaining current law governing 401(K) pension plans.
- Stimulate industry and employment both by increasing savings and by introducing a system that would allow businesses to immediately write-off half of their expenditures on new equipment the first year and depreciate the remainder according to President Reagan's capital-cost recovery system.
- Reduce the corporate tax rate to 33 percent, 13 percentage points lower than current law and 3 percentage points lower than the provision in the House-passed resolution.[14]

To do so, Roth proposes a Business Transfer Tax, a VAT-like tax on all stages of production and distribution. However, unlike a full VAT, a BTT would not tax retail markups. Both would use the estimated $90 billion or more a year that a 7% BTT would bring to pay for a big cut in income taxes, while retaining most credits and deductions including the investment-tax credits and generous depreciation allowances. Forty percent of the BTT would be paid by foreign companies. Much like the European and Japanese tax system acceptable under the GATT, the tax would be rebated on American exports and imposed on imports.

CONCLUSIONS

VAT appears as an interesting alternative to corporate and individual income taxes in the United States. It has curved its advantages and limitations. From the discussion in this chapter, the advantages seem to outweigh the limitations. In addition, VAT has been successfully imple-

mented in most European countries. For the sake of a worldwide tax harmonization, VAT appears a practical and efficient tool. What is needed in those countries that have not yet adopted VAT is some bold attempt to change the status quo and convince entrenched interest groups of the feasibility and the desirability of a system deemed to become accepted worldwide as a revenue raiser and a necessary way to promote economic growth, stability, and productivity.

NOTES

1. Robert P. Crum, "Value-Added Taxation: The Roots Run Deep into Colonial and Early America," *Accounting Historians Journal* (Fall 1982), pp. 25-42.

2. P. M. Reckers and H. L. Bates, "Ready for VAT?" *Financial Executive* (February 1980), p. 25.

3. Dan Throop Smith, James B. Webber, and Carol M. Cerf, *What You Should Know about the Value Added Tax* (Homewood, Ill.: Dow Jones-Irwin, 1973), p. 8.

4. Carl S. Shoup, "Experience with Value-Added Tax in Denmark, and Prospects in Sweden," *Finanzarchiv* (March 1969), p. 245.

5. Paul R. McDaniel, "A Value Added Tax for the United States? Some Preliminary Reflections," *Journal of Corporation Law* (Fall 1980), p. 29.

6. Alan Tait, "Is the Introduction of a Value-Added Tax Inflationary?," *Finance and Development* (June 1981), p. 42.

7. Ibid., p. 42.

8. Eric Schiff, *Value-Added Taxation in Europe,* Foreign Affairs Studies (Washington, D. C.: American Enterprise Institute for Public Policy Research, 1973), p. 22.

9. Ibid., p. 23.

10. Norman B. Ture, "Economics of the Value Added Tax," in *Value Added Tax: Two Views,* by Charles E. McLure, Jr., and Norman B. Ture (Washington, D.C.: American Enterprise Institute for Public Policy Research, 1972), p. 77.

11. Henry J. Aaron, "How a V.A.T. Would Hurt Our Exports," *New York Times* (March 23, 1986), p. 2F.

12. John F. Due, "Economics of the Value Added Tax," *Journal of Corporation Law* (Fall 1980), p. 71.

13. Norman B. Ture, "The Basic Economics of a United States VAT," *Journal of Corporation Law* (Fall 1980), p. 59.

14. William V. Roth, "Why We Need to Tax Consumption," *New York Times* (March 23, 1986), p. 2F.

SELECTED BIBLIOGRAPHY

Aaron, Henry J., ed., *The Value-Added Tax: Lessons from Europe* (Washington, D.C.: Brookings Institution, 1981).

Brecher, Stephen M., Donald W. Moore, Michael M. Hoyle, and Peter G. B. Trasker, *The Economic Impact of the Introduction of VAT* (Morristown, N.J.:

Research Foundation of the Financial Executives Institute, 1982).

Brown, Ray L., "Management Accountants: Are You Ready for VAT?" *Management Accounting* (November 1981), pp. 40-42, 44, 52.

Calkins, Hugh, "Role of the Value-Added Tax in the Developing United States Tax System," *Journal of Corporation Law* (Fall 1980), pp. 83-102.

Campet, C., *Influence of Sales Taxes on Productivity* (Paris: European Productivity Agency of the Organization for European Economic Cooperation, 1958).

Carlson, George N., "Value-Added Tax: Appraisal and Outlook," *Journal of Corporation Law* (Fall 1980), pp. 37-47.

Crum, Robert P., "Value-Added Taxation: The Roots Run Deep into Colonial and Early America," *Accounting Historians Journal* (Fall 1982), pp. 25-42.

Curtis, John E., "Legislative Perspective on the Value added Tax," *Tax Management International Journal* (June 1980), pp. 7-9, 16.

Dickinson, J. A., "Adding Value Can Be Fun," *Management Accounting* (November 1979), pp. 52-53.

Dresch, Stephen, P., An-Loh Lin, David K. Stout, and Milton L. Godfrey, *Substituting a Value-Added Tax for the Corporate Income Tax: First Round Analysis* (Cambridge, Mass.: Ballinger, 1977).

Due, John F., "Economics of the Value Added Tax," *Journal of Corporation Law* (Fall 1980), pp. 61-81.

———, "Universality and Neutrality of the Value Added Tax Reexamined," *Taxes—The Tax Magazine* (July 1977), pp. 469-75.

Foley, B. J., and K. T. Maunders, *Accounting Information Disclosure and Collective Bargaining* (London: Macmillan, 1977).

Godwin, Michael, "VAT—Compliance Costs to the Independent Retailer," *Accountancy* (England) (September 1976), pp. 48-50, 52, 54-56, 58, 60.

Kirchhofer, John D., "Value-Added Tax: Proposed Use in the U.S. and Possible Effects on CPA's," *Georgia Journal of Taxation* (Spring 1980), pp. 171-88.

Laffer, Arthur B., "International Impact of a Value-Added Tax," *Journal of Corporation Law* (Fall 1980), pp. 119-25.

Landers, Mathew P., "Motivations Behind VAT Proposals," *Tax Executive* (October 1979), pp. 13-20.

Lindholm, Richard W., *The Economics of VAT: Preserving Efficiency, Capitalism, and Social Progress* (Lexington, Mass.: Lexington Books, 1980).

———, "Origin of the Value-Added Tax," *Journal of Corporation Law* (Fall 1980), pp. 11-14.

———, "VAT Designed for the United States," *Tax Executive* (October 1970), pp. 13-20.

McDaniel, Paul R., "A Value Added Tax For the United States) Some Preliminary Reflections," *Journal of Corporation Law* (Fall 1980), pp. 15-36.

McKee, Thomas E., "Value-Added Taxation: New Federal Revenue Source or New Federal Headache?" *Atlanta Economic Review* (January-February 1975), pp. 14-17.

McLure, Charles E., "Administrative Considerations in the Design of Regional Tax Incentives," *National Tax Journal* (June 1980), pp. 177-88.

———, "State and Federal Relations in the Taxation of Value Added," *Journal of Corporation Law* (Fall 1980), pp. 127-39.

McLure, Charles E., Jr., and Norman B. Ture, *Value Added Tax: Two Views* (Washington, D.C.: American Enterprise Institute for Public Policy Research, 1972).

Messere, Ken, "Defense of Present Border Tax Adjustment Practices," *National Tax Journal* (December 1979), pp. 481-92.

Murray, Bart R., "Value Added Tax and the United States," *Tax Adviser* (September 1979), pp. 546-49.

Norris, Alf, *Value Added Tax: A Tax on the Consumer* (London: Fabian Society, 1970).

Parker, Seth K., "Compliance Costs of the Value-Added Tax," *Taxes—The Tax Magazine* (June 1976), pp. 369-80.

Prest, A. R., *Value Added Taxation: The Experience of the United Kingdom* (Washington, D. C.: American Enterprise Institute for Public Policy Research, 1980).

Reckers, Philip M. J., and H. L. Bates, "Ready for Vat?" *Financial Executive* (February 1980), pp. 24-26, 28.

Rutherford, B. A., "Value Added as a Focus of Attention for Financial Reporting: Some Conceptual Problems," *Accounting and Business Research* (England) (Summer 1977), pp. 215-20.

Sanford, C. T., M. R. Godwin, P. J. W. Hardwick, and M. I. Butterworth, *Costs and Benefits of VAT* (London: Heinemann, 1981).

Schiff, Eric, *Value-Added Taxation in Europe* (Washington, D.C.: American Enterprise Institute for Public Policy Research, 1973).

Smith, Dan Throop, James B. Webber, and Carol M. Cerf, *What You Should Know about the Value Added Tax* (Homewood, Ill.: Dow Jones-Irwin 1973).

Storrer, Philip P., "Tax Reform and a Proposal: The Value Added Tax," *Taxes—The Tax Magazine* (October 1978), pp. 629-34.

Sullivan, Clara K., *The Tax on Value Added* (New York: Columbia University Press, 1966).

Symonds, Edward, "Very Potent Revenue Source," *Accountant* (January 24, 1980), pp. 111-13.

Tait, Alan, "Is the Introduction of a Value-Added Tax Inflationary?" *Finance and Development* (June 1981), pp. 38-42.

"Tax Division Study Examines If VAT Is Applicable in U.S.," *Journal of Accountancy* (February 1976), pp. 22, 24.

Ture, Norman B., "The Basic Economics of a United States VAT," *Journal of Corporation Law* (Fall 1980), pp. 49-60.

Wagner, Richard E., et al., *Perspective on Tax Reform, Death Taxes, Tax Loopholes, and the Value Added Tax* (New York: Praeger, 1974).

Waldauer, Charles, "Comment on the Variable Rate Value-Added Tax as an Anti-Inflation Fiscal Stabilizer," *National Tax Journal* (March 1981), pp. 131-32.

Wetzler, James W., "Role of a Value Added Tax in Financing Social Security," *National Tax Journal* (September 1979), pp. 334-44.

White, Daniel L., "Variable Rate Value Added Tax as an Anti-Inflation Fiscal Stabilizer," *National Tax Journal* (June 1980), pp. 227-32.

______, "Variable Rate Value Added Tax as an Anti-Inflation Fiscal Stabilizer," *National Tax Journal* (March 1981), p. 133.

4

COMPARATIVE MANAGEMENT AND ACCOUNTING RESEARCH

International business is an old phenomenon, present throughout the centuries. R. D. Robinson has identified four eras characterized by a particular business emphasis; the commercial era (1500-1850), motivated by personal fortune seeking; the explorative era (1850-1914), motivated by empire building; the concessionary era (1914-1945), motivated by protectionism; and the national era (1945-1970), motivated by market development.[1] One may add the international or multinational era (1970-1987), motivated by competition among multinationals. As the corporate world became more and more interrelated and international, increased multinational operation was followed by increased analysis from different cultures and increased multiculturalism. This led to the development of a cross-cultural perspective in management and comparative management research. Therefore, the objective of this chapter is to cover the development and scope of comparative management research and report on its potential impact on accounting practice and research.

THE CONCEPT OF CULTURE

Societies present similarities and differences in their cultural patterns. The culture of people is shaping them as well as it is being shaped by them. It may be, as an interpretive tool, constraining people to less than an objective understanding of some cultures and greater misunderstanding of other cultures. As H. C. Triandis points out, people from other cultures tend to appear strange, peculiar, or often crazy.[2] In a sense, culture controls human behavior in a nonrational[3] and often persistent way.[4]

The concept of culture is also an illusive one. No consensus exists on the definition of culture. After reviewing more than 150 years' uses of the concept, Alfred L. Kroeber and Clyde Kluckhohn proposed the following definition:

> Culture consists of patterns, explicit and implicit, of and for behavior acquired and transmitted by symbols, constituting the distinctive achievements of human groups, including their embodiments in articrafts; the essential core of culture consists of traditional (i.d., historically derived and selected) ideas and especially their attached values; culture systems may on the one hand be considered as products of action, on the other as conditioning elements of future action.[5]

The distinctive achievements constituting culture include both physical objects (or physical culture), which are man-made, and subjective objects (or subjective culture), which are the subjective responses to what is man-made. This last point was made by Triandis et al., who elaborate on the concept as follows:

> *Subjective culture* refers to variables that are attributes of the cognitive structures of groups of people. The *analysis* of subjective culture refers to variables extracted from consistencies of their responses and results in a kind of "map" drawn by a scientist which outlines the subjective culture of a particular group. In short, when we observe consistent responses to classes of stimuli that have some quality in common, we assume that some "mediators" (attitudes, norms, values, etc.) are responsible for their consistencies. It is the cognitive structures which "mediate" between stimuli and responses in different cultural settings that we wish to study.[6]

Subjective culture refers to the cognitive structures used by individuals in their information processing in a particular world setting. Understanding how these cognitive structures affect the information processing of individuals from different cultures is one of the objectives of cross-cultural research.

CROSS-CULTURAL RESEARCH AND COMPARATIVE MANAGEMENT

The basic objective of cross-cultural research is to test the generalizability of psychological laws in order to understand whatever cultural differences are observed. J. W. Berry provides the following explanation:

> Cross-cultural psychology seeks to comprehend the systematic covariation between cultural and behavioral variables. Included within the term *cultural* are ecological and societal variables, and within the term *behavioral* are inferred variables. Thus the purpose is to understand how two systems, at the levels of group- and individual-analyses, relate to each other. Ideally, of course, more than covariation is sought; under some conditions *causal* relations may be inferred as well.[7]

Cross-cultural research was in fact started by cultural anthropologists trying to understand culture; it later attracted the interest of other social scientists in general and international business researchers in particular. Comparative management is therefore a subject of cross-cultural research aimed at understanding the cultural environments of international business.

The issues examined include (1) attitudes and values, (2) attitude change, (3) conflict resolution and ethocentricity, (4) decision making and bargaining, (5) economics, (6) education, creativity, and intelligence, (7) efficiency and productivity, (8) international business, (9) interpersonal behavior, (10) labor, (11) language and communication, (12) leadership, (13) management development, (14) motivation and achievement, (15) national character and stereotypes, (16) occupational prestige, (17) organizational structure, (18) perception, (19) personality, (20) personnel selection and testing, (21) satisfaction, (22) social and technical change, and (23) training for cross-cultural contacts.[8] These variables, generally the dependent variables, are supposedly influenced by culture, the independent variable.

Three approaches have characterized comparative management, the universalist approach, the economic cluster approach, and the cultural cluster approach.[9]

The universalist or cultural universals approach was aimed at finding the universals common to all clusters, the common denominator of cultures. In an article first published in 1952, anthropologist Clyde Kluckhohn argued for a cultural universals approach:

> In principle . . . there is a generalized framework that underlies the more apparent and striking facts of cultural relativity. All cultures constitute so many somewhat distinctive answers to essentially the same questions posed by human biology and by the generalities of the human situation. . . . Every society's patterns for living must provide approved and sanctioned ways of dealing with such universal circumstances as the existence of two sexes; the helplessness of infants; the need for satisfaction of the elementary biological requirements such as food, warmth, and sex; the presence of individuals of different ages and of different physical and other capacities.[10]

An example of an exhaustive list of "cultural universals" provided by G. P. Murdock is shown in Exhibit 4.1.[11] This approach obviously stresses the similarities rather than the differences among cultures and has limited impact on cooperative management research.

The value systems approach classifies cultures by focusing on differences in their value systems as major cultural variables. Basically, people of a culture, faced with basic human problems, develop value systems to define how the problems can best be solved. A precise anthropological definition of value is proposed by Kluckhohn: "A value is a conception, explicit or implicit, distinctive of an individual or characteristic of a group, of the

Exhibit 4.1
Cultural Universals

age grading	inheritance rules
athletic sports	joking
bodily adornment	kingroups
calendar	kinship nomenclature
cleanliness training	language
community organization	law
cooking	luck superstitions
cooperative labor	magic
cosmology	marriage
courtship	mealtimes
dancing	medicine
decorative art	modesty concerning natural functions
divination	mourning
division of labor	music
dream interpretation	mythology
education	numerals
eschatology	obstetrics
ethics	penal sanctions
ethnobotany	personal names
etiquette	population policy
faith healing	postnatal care
family	pregnancy usages
feasting	property rights
fire making	propitiation of supernatural beings
folklore	puberty customs
food taboos	religious rituals
funeral rites	residence rules
games	sexual restrictions
gestures	soul concepts
gift giving	status differentiation
government	surgery
greetings	tool making
hairstyles	trade
hospitality	visting
housing hygiene	weaning
incest taboos	weather control

Source: G. P. Murdock, "The Common Denominator of Cultures," in *The Science of Man in the World Crises,* ed. Ralph Linton (New York: Columbia University Press, 1945), p. 77. Reprinted with permission.

desirable which influences the selection from available modes, means and ends of actions."[12]

Similarly, a definition that runs through contemporary theoretical approaches to values is proposed by G. McLaughlin:

> Values (1) are not directly observable, (2) have cognitive, affective, and connotative elements, (3) do not operate independently of the biological organization or social field. . . . Values are conceived of as (4) referring to standards of the desirable rather than to the desired, (5) hierarchically organized in the personality system, and (6) relevant to actual behavior as a function of personal commitment and situational factors.[13]

Cross-cultural research shows that value systems differ from one culture to another and that "value profits" can be developed for various cultures. Various instruments have been used for cross-cultural research, including

1. G. W. Allport, P. E. Vernon, and G. A. Lindzey's values, which classify human ideas and activities as theoretical, economic, aesthetic, political, and religious,[14]
2. C. W. Morris's ways to live, which measures values as philosophical orientations about ways to live,[15]
3. F. R. Kluckhohn and F. L. Strodtbeck's value theory, which focuses on existential and evaluative beliefs,[16]
4. Irving Sarnoff's human value index, which views values as "values of aggrandizement" to be reflected in wealth, prestige, and power, and as "values of realization" to be reflected in humanitarian, egalitarian, aesthetic, and intellectual areas,[17] and
5. Milton Rokeach's value survey, which classifies eighteen values as terminal and eighteen values as instrumental.[18]

The value systems approach led to results supporting the existence of different cultural value systems with impact on behavior.

Finally, the systems approach to corporate management research focuses on the subsystems defining a given culture. For example, P. R. Harris and R. T. Moran identified eight such subsystems: kinship, education, economy, politics, religion, association, health, and recreation.[19] Others attempted to cluster countries on attitudinal dimensions by defining the country rather than culture as the unit of analysis. A review of the literature identified eight cluster studies.[20] These included Mason Haire, E. E. Ghiselli, and L. W. Porter,[21] D. Sirota and J. M. Greenwood,[22] Simcha Ronen and A. I. Kraut,[23] Geert Hofstede,[24] R. W. Griffeth, P. W. Horn, A. DeNisi, and W. Kirchner,[25] S. G. Redding,[26] and M. K. Badawy.[27]

The objective of these clustering studies is to show that certain aspects of employee attitude and behavior can be generalized to a particular society and that the differences between these aspects are explainable by cultural

or national differences. Several variables were examined in these studies: work goal importance; need deficiency, fulfillment, and job satisfaction; managerial and organizational variables; and work role and interpersonal orientation. The writers tended to cluster geographically, linguistically, and religiously which was expected as they are not independent, but the studies also tended to cluster on the basis of technological development. These clusters when synthesized included the Anglo cluster, the Germanic and Nordic cluster, the Latin European cluster, the Latin American cluster, the Near Eastern cluster, the Far Eastern cluster, and the Arab cluster. Some of these clusters were, however, ill-defined in these studies. Despite the limitations inherent in any type of cross-cultural research, the clustering approach provides a worthwhile step toward theoretical development. As stated by Simcha Ronen and Oded Shenkar:

> The clusters produced in the present synthesis can be used as a general framework of reference for theoreticians and practitioners. Researchers in the future should put these clusters to continuous empirical testing. They should be concerned, however, not only with the predictive qualities of clustering, but also with its promotion of theoretical development. Rather than just inquire about the nature of differences in employee work goals, future researchers should proceed to investigate the underlying cultural and social traits that may produce these differences.[28]

APPROACHES TO RESEARCHING CROSS-CULTURAL MANAGEMENT STUDIES

Cross-cultural management studies have been found to vary in their assumptions about universality, in their ways of dealing with similarity and differences, and in the methodologies used. In a methodological review of the literature Nancy Adler delineated six approaches to researching cross-cultural management issues: (a) *parochial,* which focuses on one country, resulting in single-country studies, (b) *ethnocentric,* which replicates one-country research in foreign countries, resulting in second-culture replication studies, (c) *polycentric,* which conducts research in foreign countries, resulting in studies conducted in many cultures, (d) *comparative,* which focuses on differences in various cultures, resulting in studies contrasting organizations across cultures, (e) *geocentric* which investigates organizations operating in more than one culture, resulting in international management studies, and (f) *synergistic,* which focuses on creating universality, resulting in cross-cultural management studies.[29] The main characteristics of the six types of cross-cultural management research are summarized in Exhibit 4.2. Exhibit 4.3 delineates the universal from the particular, and Exhibit 4.4 presents the methodological issues in comparative management research.

Exhibit 4.2
Types of Cross-Cultural Management Research

Title	Culture	Approach to Similarity and Difference	Approach to Universality	Types of Study	Primary Question	Main Methodological Issues
PAROCHIAL RESEARCH	Single culture studies	Assumed similarity	Assumed universality	Domestic management studies	What is the behavior of people like in work organizations? Study is only applicable to management in one culture and yet it is assumed to be applicable to management in many cultures.	*Traditional methodologies:* All of the traditional methodological issues concerning design, sampling instrumentation, analysis and interpretation without reference to culture.
ETHNO-CENTRIC RESEARCH	Second culture studies	Search for similarity	Questioned universality	Replication in foreign cultures of domestic management studies	Can we use home country theories abroad? Can this theory which is applicable to organizations in Culture A be extended to organizations in Culture B?	*Standardization and translation:* How can management research be standardized across cultures? How can instruments be literally translated? Replication should be identical to original study with the exception of language.

Exhibit 4.2 *(continued)*

Title	Culture	Approach to Similarity and Difference	Approach to Universality	Types of Study	Primary Question	Main Methodological Issues
POLYCENTRIC RESEARCH	Studies in many cultures	Search for similarity and difference	Denied universality	Individual studies of organizations in specific foreign cultures	How do you managers manage and employees behave in country X? What is the pattern of organizational relationships in country X?	*Description:* How can country X's organizations be studied without either using home country theories or models and without using obtrusive measures? Focus is on inductive methods and unobtrusive measures.
COMPARATIVE RESEARCH	Intercultural Management	Search for both similarity and differences	Emergent universality	Studies comparing organizations in many foreign cultures	How are the management and employee styles similar and different across cultures? Which theories hold across cultures and which do not?	*Equivalence:* Is the methodology equivalent at each stage in the research process? Are the meanings of key concepts defined equivalently? Has the research been designed such that the samples, instrumentation,

Title	Culture	Approach to Similarity and Difference	Approach to Universality	Types of Study	Primary Question	Main Methodological Issues
						administration, analysis, and interpretation are equivalent with reference to the cultures included?
GEOCENTRIC RESEARCH	International management studies	Search for similarity	Extended universality	Studies of multinational organizations	How do multinational organizations function?	*Geographic Dispersion:* All of the traditional methodological questions are relevant with the added complexity of geographical distance. Translation is often less of a problem since most MNOs have a common language across all countries in which they operate. The primary question is to develop an approach for studying the

Exhibit 4.2 *(continued)*

Title	Culture	Approach to Similarity and Difference	Approach to Universality	Types of Study	Primary Question	Main Methodological Issues
						complexity of a large organization. Culture is frequently ignored.
SYNERGISTIC RESEARCH	Intercultural management studies	Use of similarities and differences as a resource	Created universality	Studies of intercultural interaction within work settings	How can the intercultural interaction within domestic or international organization be managed? How can organizations create structures and processes which will be effective in working with members of all cultures?	*Interaction models and integrating processes:* What are effective ways to study cross-cultural interaction within organizational settings? How can universal and culturally specific patterns of management be distinguished? What is the appropriate balance between culturally specific and universal processes within one organization? How can the proactive use of cultural differences to create universally accepted organizational patterns be studied?

Source: Nancy J. Adler, "A Typology of Management Studies Involving Culture," *Journal of International Business Studies* (Fall 1983), pp. 30-31. Reprinted with permission.

Exhibit 4.3
Differentiating the Universal from the Particular

Terms Denoting Cultural Uniqueness	Terms Denoting Universality
Culturally Specific	*Culturally General*
Emic: Sounds which are specific to a particular language.	*Etic:* Sounds which are similar in all languages.
Particular	*Universal*
Idiographic: Descriptive of the uniqueness of the individual.	*Nomothetic:* Laws describing behavior of groups of individuals.
Polycentric: Cultures must be understood in their own terms.	*Geocentric:* Search for universal, pancultural laws of human behavior.
Within culture: Studies behavior from within the culture to discover whatever structure it might have. Both the antecedents and the consequences of the behavior are found within the culture.	*Across cultures:* Emphasizes the most general description of social phenomena with concepts that are culture free. Structure of observation is created by the scientists.
Culturally contingent: The studied behavior is dependent on the particular culture in which it is embedded.	*Culturally independent:* The studied behavior is not related to or influenced by the particular culture in which it is embedded.
Difference emphasized	*Similarity emphasized*
Universality denied	*Universality central and accepted*
Unique	*Pancultural*

Source: Nancy J. Adler, "A Typology of Management Studies Involving Culture," *Journal of International Business Studies* (Fall 1983), p. 36. Reprinted with permission.

Exhibit 4.4
Methodological Issues in Comparative Management Research

Methodological Issue	Description
PURPOSE of Comparative Management Research	To develop equivalent theories of social behavior within work settings in cultures around the world.
FUNDAMENTAL DILEMMAS confronted in all Comparative Management Research	WHAT IS CULTURE? - What is the definition of culture? - Can country be used as a surrogate definition for culture? - Should domestic (within country) populations be assumed to be multicultural or culturally homogeneous? - Culture should be used as an independent or as a dependent variable, but not as a residual variable.
	CULTURALLY SPECIFIC VERSUS UNIVERSAL ASPECTS OF ORGANIZATIONAL BEHAVIOR - Which aspects of organizational behavior vary across culture and which are constant regardless of culture? - When is culture a contingency? - When is culture--as an independent variable--not related to the dependent variable or theory of interest? When is a theory culture-free?
	MENTAL PROGRAMMING OF THE RESEARCHER AS A CULTURAL BEING In order to design, conduct and interpret research from each culture's perspective--and not strictly from a single culture or ethnocentric perspective--research teams should be multicultural.

Methodological Issue	Description
	IDENTICAL VERSUS EQUIVALENT APPROACHES TO CROSS-CULTURAL RESEARCH At a sufficiently high level of abstraction, research topics, concepts, and approaches should be identical. At lower levels of abstractions, the operationalization of the concepts and approaches should not be identical, but should be culturally equivalent. THREATS TO INTERPRETATION: Interaction Between Cultural Variables and the Research Topic and Approach - Cultural and research variables interact. The interaction can confound results and render them uninterpretable. - Multiple approaches and multiple methods are needed to understand interaction effects.
RESEARCH TOPIC	At the highest level of abstraction, the research topic (that is, the research question or theory being tested) should be identical across cultures. The conceptual and methodological approaches to researching that topic should be equivalent across cultures. Across cultures, the topic should be: - Conceptually equivalent. The definition of the concept should have the same meaning in each culture. - Equally important. The phenomenon should be equally modal or marginal in each culture. - Equally appropriate. For example, the topic should be equally appropriate regarding political and religious sensitivities in each culture.

Exhibit 4.4 *(continued)*

Methodological Issue	Description

SAMPLING	Sampling issues involve size of sample, selection of cultures, representative versus matched samples, and the independence of samples.
	- *Size of sample.* The number of cultures selected should be large enough to:
	  - Randomize variance on non-matched variables.
	  - Eliminate rival hypotheses.
	  Studies with insufficient numbers of cultures (that is, 2 or 3) should be treated as pilot studies.
	- *Selection of cultures.* The selection of cultures should be based on theoretical dimensions of the research, not on the opportunistic availability of access to particular cultures.
	- *Representative versus matched samples.* Is the research goal to have samples which are representative of each culture or is it to have matched samples which are equivalent on key theoretical dimensions across cultures? Matched samples should be functionally, not literally, equivalent.
	- *Independence of samples.* Given the interrelatedness of the industrialized world, culturally, politically, and geographically independent samples in management research are generally neither feasible nor desirable.

TRANSLATION	*Equivalence of language.* The language used in each version of the research--instrumentation and administration--should be equivalent across cultures, not literally identical.
	- *Wording.* The wording of items and instructions should:
	  - Use a common vocabulary (such as high frequency words).
	  - Avoid idiomatic expressions.

Methodological Issue	Description
	- Use equivalent grammar and syntax.
	- Use plain, short sentences.
	- Include redundancy.
	- *Method of translation.* Recognizing the Whorfian hypothesis, the translation technique should aim at equivalence, not at literal translations.
	- *Whorfian hypothesis.* Different cultural and linguistic backgrounds lead to different ways of perceiving the world. Unless their linguistic backgrounds are similar or can be calibrated, people who speak 2 different languages will not perceive the world in the same way.
	- *Translation techniques.* To achieve equivalent translations, the material should be:
	- Back-translated. Translated and then back-translated into the original language using a good bilingual target population, or
	- Translated by an expert. Translated independently by excellent bilingual translators who are (1) familiar with the linguistic and cultural backgrounds in both cultures, (2) familiar with the subject matter of the research, and (3) translating into his or her native language.
MEASUREMENT AND INSTRU-MENTATION	*Equivalence of instrumentation.* Are the test items, scaling, instrumentation and experimental manipulations equivalent across cultures?
	- *Equivalent variables.* Across cultures, are the items or measures conceptually equivalent, equally reliable and equally valid? Have indigenous measures been created to operationalize conceptually equivalent variables? Are

Exhibit 4.4 *(continued)*

Methodological Issue	Description
	variables based on equally salient conceptual dimensions? - *Equivalent scaling.* Differences in means are uninterpretable unless measured on equivalent scales which have been developed individually in each culture. - *Equivalent procedures.* Researcher must use the same or equivalent procedures in each culture to develop scales, or similar patterns of correlations. Items must have similar patterns of correlations within each culture. - *Equivalence of language.* See translation above. - *Equivalence of experimental manipulations.* Interaction between experimental and cultural variables can confound interpretation. Therefore experimental manipulations must be equivalent across cultures.
ADMINISTRATION	*Equivalence of administration.* The research settings, instructions, and timing should be equivalent, not identical, across cultures. *Equivalance of response.* Given that observation changes that which is observed (Heinsenberg effect), the influence of the research on the subjects should be equivalent across cultures. The research should be designed and administered in such a way that the responses to the stimuli and to the situation are similar across cultures on such dimensions as: - *Familiarity.* Subject should have equal familiarity with test instruments, format, and the social situation of the research. - *Psychological response.* Subjects should have similar levels of anxiety and other psychological responses in the test situation.

Methodological Issue	Description
	- *Experimenter effect.* The extent to which the researchers communicate their preferred hypotheses to subjects--both verbally and nonverbally--should be equivalent across cultures.
	- *Demand characteristics.* The extent to which subjects attempt to discover the researcher's hypotheses and thereafter attempt to help (usually) or hinder the research varies across cultures based on such things as (1) sensitivity to various topics (sex, religion, politics) and (2) the courtesy bias.
	- *Characteristics of the person conducting the research.* Depending on the culture, there can be a difference in response (respectfulness, indifference, hospitality) to such characteristics of the research administrator as: - Gender - Race - Origin: from an economically developed or developing country - Status relative to subjects: high versus low - Foreigner versus citizen
	- *Characteristics of the presentation.* The response of the subjects can vary in reaction to the: - Introduction of the research - Introduction and characteristics of the presenter - Task instructions - Closing remarks - Timing of the presentation and data collection - Setting of the presentation and data collection

Exhibit 4.4 *(continued)*

Methodological Issue	Description
	The goal in comparative management research is to have the administration and experimental conditions equivalent, not standardized in each culture. The approach to conducting the research may be identical, but the ways in which it is operationalized will vary from culture to culture.
ANALYSIS	*Multivariate techniques.* Comparative research studies are complex. Univariate statistical techniques are generally inappropriate. *Ecological fallacy.* The problem in comparative research is that cultures are often treated and categorized as if they were individuals. Cultures are not individuals; they are wholes, and their internal logic cannot be understood in terms used for personality dynamics of individuals [Hofstede 1980]. The ecological fallacy is the confusing of country or cultural level (ecological) correlations with individual correlations. The reverse ecological fallacy is the confusing of individual correlations with ecological/cultural correlations.

Source: Nancy J. Adler, "A Typology of Management Studies Involving Culture," *Journal of International Business Studies* (Fall 1983), pp. 37-40. Reprinted with permission.

METHODOLOGIES IN RESEARCHING CROSS-CULTURAL MANAGEMENT ISSUES

Two typologies were used to classify and analyze international business and comparative management research. Hans Schöllhammer referred to five approaches: (a) conceptualizing, (b) synthesizing, (c) descriptive, (d) analytical-interpretive, and (e) generalizing-normative.[30] J. J. Boddewyn and R. Nath referred to three categories: (a) descriptive, (b) conceptual, and (c) hypothesis testing.[31] An examination of the three methodologies follows.

DESCRIPTIVE STUDIES

The descriptive studies in cross-cultural management are generally exploratory in nature and rely on specific data collection methods such as interviews, case collection, and survey techniques. They tend to report the results of a study focusing on a particular research question. These questions deal with matters such as (a) financial issues focusing on the use of corporate finance techniques, financial control systems, or capital budgeting techniques; (b) personnel issues focusing on the selection, compensation, and development of international executives, job satisfaction of managers, or such topics as managerial attitudes, leadership, and motivation in organizations; and (c) other functional areas issues, namely, marketing, production, or accounting. The findings of these studies are rarely generalizable and are constrained by various limitations. Witness the following comment:

> A critical analysis of a large number of empirical research studies in international business that can be placed into the "descriptive" category leads one to the conclusion that these studies are generally one-dimensional, i.e., narrow in scope, and they tend to be based on a relatively small sample from which the *empirical data* are derived. In addition, the information in most cases is gathered by means of questionnaire surveys among a randomly selected sample. In general, these descriptive studies are not directed toward the reputation or confirmation of specific hypotheses and thus their potential contribution to theory development is impaired.[32]

Conceptual Studies

The conceptual studies are aimed at *deductively* building a conceptual framework and/or a model of comparative management.

The first example of a conceptual study was provided by Frederick H. Harbison and Charles A. Myers's attempt to construct a framework for comparing management in the industrial world.[33] The analysis compares managers from three dimensions: (a) management as a resource, and the extent of its use, (b) management as a system of authority (dictatorial, paternalistic, constitutional, or democratic), and (c) management as a class

or elite (patriarchal, political, or professional). The situations in twelve of the countries were compared using secondary sources and interviews.

The second example of a conceptual study was provided by Richard N. Farmer and Barry N. Richman's conceptual model of comparative management[34] (see Exhibit 4.5). The model postulates that external constraints (educational, sociological, legal, political, and economic) *affect* elements of the management process, such as planning, organizing, staffing, directing, controlling, and policy-making, which also *affect* management and managerial effectiveness, therefore *determining* firm efficiency and system efficiency.

The third example, provided by Howard Perlmutter, classifies multinational corporations on the basis of the attitudes taken by their top management toward multinational business policies; ethnocentric (home-country oriented), polycentric (host-country oriented), and geocentric (world oriented).[35] He deduced that (a) performance evaluation in a

Exhibit 4.5
Farmer and Richman Model

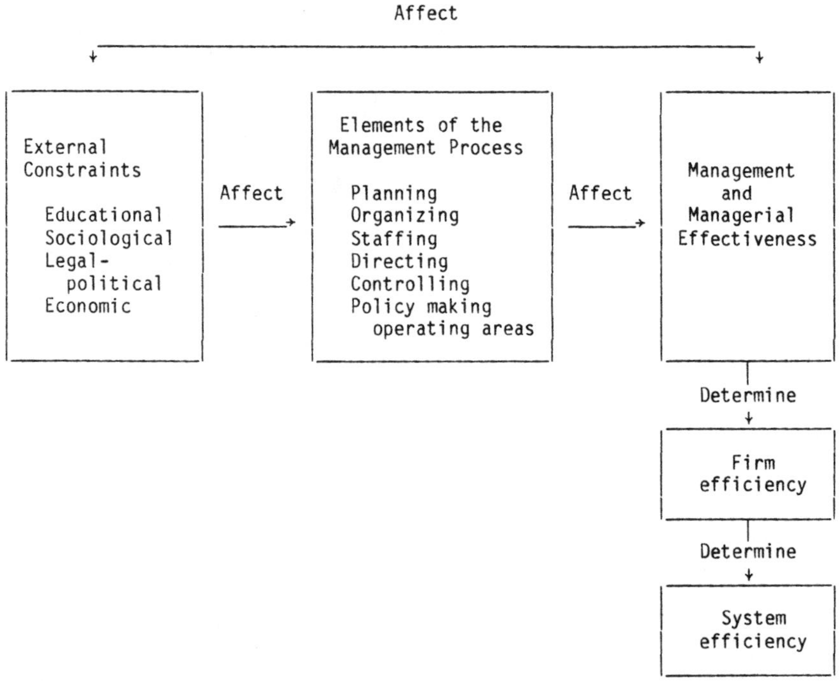

Source: R. N. Farmer and B. M. Richman, *Comparative Management and Economic Progress* (Homewood, Ill.: Irwin, 1965), p. 35. Reprinted with permission.

centralized ethnocentric firm will be tightly controlled by the parent company, while in a decentralized polycentric or geocentric company it will be less controlled by the parent company, and (b) because more conflict situations arise in ethnocentric and polycentric cases than in geocentric cases, organizational effectiveness in the geocentric cases is maximized.

The fourth example, provided by Anant R. Negandhi and S. Benjamin Prasad, views management and enterprise effectiveness (the effectiveness of the economic system as a whole) as the result of specific management practices (planning, organizing, staffing, motivating and directing, and controlling) which in turn are considered to be determined by both management philosophy (management attitudes toward employees, consumers, suppliers, stockholders, government, and community) and environmental factors (socioeconomic, educational, political, legal, and cultural).[36] (See Exhibit 4.6.) When applying the model to American subsidiaries in Argentina, Brazil, India, the Philippines, and Uruguay, along with local firms, Negandhi and Prasad found that (a) managers in American subsidiaries were more likely to debate than managers in locally owned firms, and (b) there was little difference between their managerial styles and effectiveness.[37] To test the Farmer and Richman model against that of

Exhibit 4.6
Comparative Management Construct: Negandhi and Prasad Model

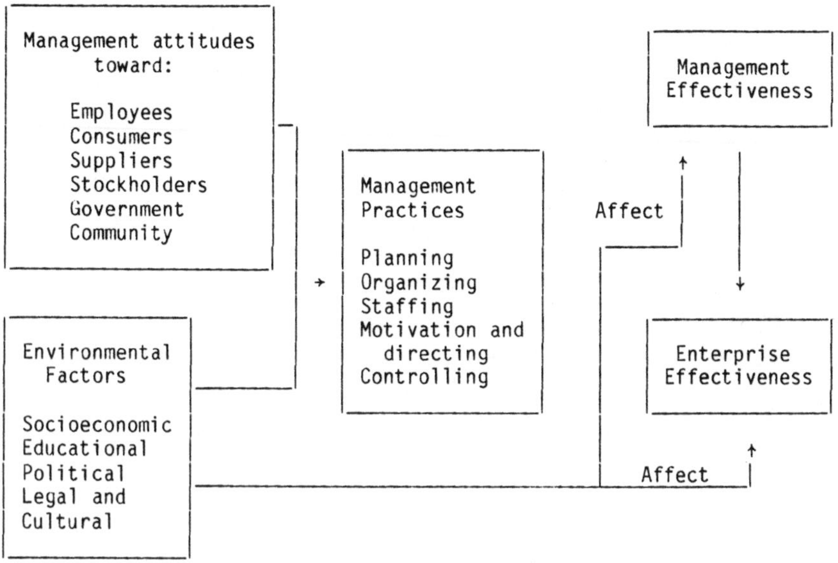

Source: A. R. Negandhi and S. B. Prasad, *Comparative Management* (New York: Appleton-Century-Crofts, 1971), p. 73. Reprinted with permission.

Negandhi and Prasad model, the study by L. Kelley and R. Worthley[38] compared similarities and differences in the managerial attitudes of Japanese, Caucasian American, and Japanese-American managers working in financial institutions, given that previous research by H. H. Kitano[39] had suggested that Japanese-Americans in Hawaii were attached to Japanese attitudes and values. Kelley and Worthley's study supported Farmer and Richman's thesis on the role of culture in shaping managerial attitudes but did not find that managerial philosophy is an important variable. In fact, it may act as an important independent variable in the role of culture in shaping managerial attitudes. Ronen emphasizes the point as follows:

> We suggest that managerial philosophy may be important and that philosophy and culture may not necessarily coincide to the extent that philosopy well into the prevailing culture, both variables should yield similar behavioral consequences. To the extent that philosophy does not fit in with the prevailing culture, the impact of culture may diminish. Culture may be the primary variable from a theoretical standpoint, but its impact depends on precisely this fit. The Farmer and Richman and Negandhi and Prasad model may thus *complement* each other—the relative importance of either model may be expected to vary from country to country.[40]

Hypothesis-Testing Studies

These studies were first structured around specific hypotheses then conducted after the securing of adequate data to test whether what is postulated is, in fact, true. The result is definitely a more rigorous effect than in the descriptive studies. They may be classified as either analytical-interpretive studies aimed at classifying, explaining, and evaluating new general knowledge given established hypotheses and existing, related research findings, or generalizing-normative studies aimed at drawing generalizations from empirical results. An evaluation of these studies led to the following points:[41]

1. The cross-cultural comparisons led to the development of some conceptual models.
2. Comparative management research highlighted the role of the environment.
3. Most studies of foreign management systems (or parts thereof) are not explicitly comparative.
4. There was also an uneven coverage of actors, processes, structures, and functions in the comparative studies of management systems.
5. A lack of rigor characterizes many of the studies.
6. The research has provided some valid generalizations although findings are apt to be more tentative and suggestive than conclusive.

Methodological problems have also been raised. For example, F. Kenneth Berrien points to four of them: (a) the comparability of respondents or subject samples, (b) the ethnic influences on research questions, (c) the comparability of research instruments, and (d) the circumstances under which ethnically detached or culturally bound interpretations may be justified.[42]

Ronen pointed to ten factors that may affect the international validity of the experimental results in cross-cultural research; (a) emic versus etic distinction, (b) problems of instrumentation—construction and validation, (c) data collection techniques, (d) sampling design issues, (e) data analysis, (f) problems of translation/stimulus equivalence, (g) static group comparisons, (h) lack of knowledge of others' way of seeing things, (i) problems of resolving contradictory findings, and (j) administrative problems.[43]

To avoid some of these problems Berrien proposed a strategy for cross-cultural research and stated the following:

> The best cross-cultural research is that which 1) engages the collaborative efforts of two or more investigators of different countries, who are 2) strongly supported by institutions in their respected countries, to 3) address researchable problems of a common concern not only to the science of psychology, but 4) relevant to the social problems of our time. Such collaborative enterprises would begin with 5) the joint definition of problems, 6) employ comparable methods, 7) pool data that would be "owned" by the collaborators jointly who are free to 8) report their own interpretations to their own constituents, but 9) are obligated to strive for interpretations acceptable to a world community of scholars.[44]

Other shortcomings of cross-cultural research include the following:

1. The absence of a theoretical base;
2. The presence of ethnocentrism;
3. Heavy reliance on convenience samples;
4. Overemphasis on cultural variance;
5. Studies limited to one nation rather than being truly comparative;
6. Problems of linguistic meanings, failing to take into account the limitations of language in conveying equivalent meanings in two or more languages;
7. The assumption that important factors in one nation have equal value in another nation;
8. The use of a single research method, in general questionnaires;
9. The limitations of cross-sectional studies, providing an image of reality that is confined to one point in time;
10. The lack of data to support conclusions;
11. The bias toward studying large corporations;

12. The rare instances of using samples of employees and managers across hierarchical levels across nations;
13. The failure to state and test a priori hypotheses;
14. The overemphasis on studying attitudes rather than behavior;
15. The unbalance in terms of areas-of-the-world studies, with critical ignorance of the Third World;
16. The failure to articulate cultural and other explanations.[45]

ACCOUNTING RESEARCH OF RELEVANCE TO CROSS-CULTURAL RESEARCH

One anthropological study relevant to cultural relativism in accounting explores the degree to which accounting systems influence perceptions of opportunities by comparing the local view of business possibilities derived from the native system of accounts in Cuanago, a Tarascan village in Mexico, with more formal accounting methods.[46] In this study, J. Acheson found that while the native accounting system, a crude cash-flow-based system, does not permanently block responsiveness to opportunities where they exist; it confuses, however, the view of opportunities, leading to many poor business decisions, and hence plays a critical role in influencing further business decisions.

Research on cultural relativism in accounting is in its infancy and has not yet reached a high level of theoretical and methodological rigor. Various accounting issues have been examined. First, the issue of whether the same accounting information may be perceived differently by different cultural groups was examined by Gilles Chevalier using French Canadians and English Canadians.[47] Perceptions were found not to differ with regard to the importance of conventional published financial information, which had been expected to differ with the French Canadians placing more importance on additional and nonconventional information such as data on human resources, earnings forecasts, and management philosophy.

Chevalier's subjects were essentially students from the Francophone and Anglophone sections of Canada. Other groups examined, however, include investors and financial analysts from various cultural settings. L. S. Chang and K. S. Most investigated the uses of financial statements by individual investors, institutional investors, and financial analysts from three countries—the United States, the United Kingdom, and New Zealand—all of which have large capital markets and well-organized stock exchanges which tend to function in a similar manner.[48] The results showed a strong belief in the importance of corporate annual reports as a source of information for investment decisions and a stronger belief that the most important parts of the corporate annual report for this purpose were those pertaining to the

financial data. The study also examined the composition of the three financial user groups and found the institutional investors and financial analysts comprised homogeneous groups while the individual investors were a diverse group.

Because the decisions of most investors in any country are greatly influenced by the opinions held by financial analysts, Ahmed Belkaoui, Alfred Kahl, and Josette Peyrard examined the differential needs of financial analysts in Canada, the United States, and Europe.[49] Any differences in perception were hypothesized to be primarily due to the differences in the European and American methods of investing. The European approach has been more debt-oriented, with analysis concentrated on the balance sheet. In brief, the method requires the preparation of three reports: profit and loss account, financing table, and balance sheet. These reports are presented in vertical form highlighting a set of totals and subtotals deemed to be of interest to the financial analysts. The reports offer a convenient means of achieving European comparisons of European accounting information. In contrast, the American method is oriented more toward equity investment, the income statement, and corporate earning power. As expected, the study demonstrates that there is a high degree of consensus by North American financial analysts on the informational items of value to equity investors, but there is quite a divergence of opinion when the North Americans are compared with their European counterparts. This divergence was attributed to institutional differences in the accounting and investment environments of Europe and North America, as well as to differences in outlook, with Europeans more interested in balance sheet information while North Americans tended to be more concerned about the income statement.

In addition, two hypotheses on the impact of the cultural environment and individual value orientations on financial disclosures were developed by B. Jaggi.[50]

Hypothesis 1: The reliability of disclosures in financial statements is likely to differ with differences in the value orientations of managers from different countries. Accounting principles and procedures will vary to respond to the needs of individual countries and to ensure reliability in a given set of cultural environments.

Hypothesis 2: As a result of the prevailing cultural environment in the developing countries, the reliability of financial disclosure is not expected to be high unless legal disclosure standards are set.[51]

Without empirically testing these two important hypotheses, Jaggi goes on to suggest that the procedures for developing accounting principles should be modified to suit the cultural environments.

LINGUISTIC-RELATIVISM RESEARCH OF RELEVANCE TO CROSS-CULTURAL RESEARCH

The Nature of Linguistic Relativism

Because language mediates our worldview, it plays a central role in the development of cognition and perception. Individuals, as they learn a language, acquire not only a store of lexical and grammatical characteristics but also a linguistic mode of cognition and perception.

Anthropologists have always emphasized the role of language in their studies of culture. Edward Sapir's investigations of the linguistic symbolism of a given culture view language both as an instrument and as communication of thought. A given language predisposes its users to a distinct belief. The idea that language is an active determinant of thought forms the basis of the principle of linguistic relativism. According to the Whorfian version of the principle, ways of speaking are reflections of metaphysics of a culture. These metaphysics constitute the unstated premises which shape the perception and thought of those who participate in that culture and predispose them to a given method of perception.

J. A. Fishman's work is an attempt to systematize this set of assumptions, known as the "Sapir-Whorf Hypothesis."[52] Fishman's fourfold analytical scheme (Exhibit 4.7) distinguishes between two levels of language (lexical and grammatical) and two types of behavior (linguistic and nonlinguistic). The lexical level refers to all words which compose a language. Languages differ in the number of terms they possess to describe phenomena. *Grammatical level* refers to the manner in which the structural units of a language are organized. *Linguistic behavior* refers to choices among words. *Nonlinguistic behavior* refers to choices among objects. These distinctions are clarified in the following explanation of the cells in Exhibit 4.7.

1. Cell 1 posits a relationship between the lexical properties of a language and the speaker's linguistic behavior. Linguistic behavior, the choice of words for describing a particular phenomenon, differs from one language to another.
2. Cell 2 posits a relationship between the lexical properties of a language and the nonlinguistic behavior of the users of that language. This refers to the idea that speakers of a language that makes certain lexical distinctions will be able to perform tasks better and more rapidly than speakers of languages that do not make such distinctions.[53]
3. Cell 3 posits a relationship between grammatical characteristics and linguistic behavior. This refers to the idea that speakers of a language with specific grammatical rules acquire a worldview quite different from that of speakers of languages that do not employ such rules.[54]
4. Cell 4 posits a relationship between grammatical characteristics and nonlinguistic behavior. This refers to the idea that speakers of a language with certain grammatical characteristics will perform nonlinguistic tasks differently from speakers of languages that do not have these characteristics.[55]

Exhibit 4.7
Fishman's Schematic Systematization of the Sapir-Whorf Hypothesis

Data of Language Characteristics	Data of Cognitive Behavior	
	Language Data ("Cultural Themes")	Nonlinguistic Data
Lexical or "Semantic" Characteristics	Level 1	Level 2
Grammatical Characteristics	Level 3	Level 4

Accounting as a Language

Accounting has been often called the language of business. It is one means of communicating information about a business. What makes accounting a language? To answer this question, let us look at the possible parallels existing between accounting and language. There are two components to a language, namely, symbols and grammatical rules. Thus, the recognition of accounting as a language rests on the identification of these two components as the two levels of language. It may be argued that the symbols or lexical characteristics of any language are its identifiable "meaningful" units or words. These symbols are linguistic objects used to identify particular concepts. Symbolic representations do exist in accounting. For example, D. L. McDonald identifies numerals and words, and debits and credits, as the only symbols respectively accepted and unique to the accounting discipline.[56] It may also be argued that the grammatical rules of any language refer to its existing syntactical arrangements. Such rules exist in accounting. They refer to the general set of procedures used for the creation of all financial data for the business. T. H. Jain establishes the following parallel between grammatical rules and accounting rules:

The CPA (the expert in accounting) certifies the correctness of the application of the accounting rules as does an accomplished speaker of a language for the grammatical

correctness of the sentence. Accounting rules formalize the structure of accounting in the same way as grammar formalizes the inherent structure of a natural language.[57]

Given the existence of the components identified—symbols and grammatical rules—accounting may be defined a priori as a language. Consequently, according to the Sapir-Whorf Hypothesis, both its lexical and grammatical characteristics will shape the worldview held by users of accounting: that accounting influences thinking.

Accounting Research of Relevance to Linguistic Relativism

Ahmed Belkaoui argues that accounting is a language and, according to the Sapir-Whorf Hypothesis, its lexical characteristics and grammatical rules will affect the linguistic and nonlinguistic behavior of users. Four propositions derived from the linguistic-relativism paradigm were introduced to conceptually integrate research findings on the impact of accounting information on the user's behavior.

1. The users that make certain lexical distinctions in accounting are enabled to talk and/or solve problems that cannot be solved by users that do not.
2. The users that make certain lexical distinctions in accounting are enabled to perform (nonlinguistic) tasks more rapidly or more completely than those users that do not.
3. The users that posses the accounting (grammatical) rules are predisposed to different managerial styles or emphasis than those that do not.
4. The accounting techniques may tend to facilitate or render more difficult various (nonlinguistic) managerial behaviors on the part of users.[58]

These propositions were empirically tested and verified in two studies pointing to the importance of linguistic considerations in the use of accounting information and in international standards setting.[59]

Within the linguistic-relativism school, the role of language is emphasized as a mediator and shaper of the environment. This would imply that accounting language may predispose "users" to a given method of perception and behavior.[60] Furthermore, the affiliation of users with different professional organizations or communities with their distinct interaction networks may create different accounting language repertoires. Accountants from different professional groups may use different linguistic codes because of different organizational constraints and objectives. At worst, a confounding lack of communication may emerge. Using a "sociolinguistic thesis," Belkaoui empirically shows that various affiliations in accounting create different linguistic repertoires or codes for intragroup or intergroup communications.[61] The sociolinguistic construct was used to

justify the possible lack of consensus on the meaning of the accounting concepts. As a result, specific issues identified which need further research include (a) the presence and the nature of the "institutional language" within each accounting professional group, (b) the presence of a profession-linked linguistic code in the accounting field composed of a "formal language" and a "public language," and (c) a test of whether the public language is understood by users of public data (for example, financial analysts) and whether the formal language is understood by users of formal data (for example, students).[62]

Other studies investigated the linguistic effects of accounting data and techniques without relying on the linguistic-relativism thesis or the sociolinguistic thesis. Instead, they focus on the difference in the intragroup and intergroup communication of accounting data or techniques among the users and producers of accounting data. To prove these differences the studies relied on various techniques including a semantic differential technique,[63] the antecedent-consequent technique,[64] multidimensional scaling techniques,[65] and the Cloze procedure.[66]

CONCLUSIONS

The field of comparative management research promises to provide useful answers to those involved in international business by providing empirical findings and conceptual frameworks for understanding differences in management practices resulting from cultural differences. To date the research produced suffers from a lack of theoretical grounding and methodological anomalies. It is, however, the normal state for an emerging field to face a period of insecurity characterized by debates, criticisms, and theories striving for dominance. What will probably emerge from this situation are more established, competing paradigms to guide the future comparative management research. Although accounting has not yet fully jumped on this bandwagon, there are attempts to link either culture or language to some of the accounting behaviors or phenomena. It is urgent that the accounting discipline put cultural and linguistic relativism on the agenda as the cross-cultural differences may affect the various stages surrounding the accounting datum, namely, preparation, classification, recording, communication, verification, and/or use.

NOTES

1. R. D. Robinson, *International Business Policy* (New York: Holt, Rinehart and Winston, 1964).
2. H. C. Triandis, *Interpersonal Behavior* (Monterey, Calif.: Brooks/Cole, 1977).
3. Geert Hofstede, *Culture's Consequences: International Differences in Work Related Values* (Beverly Hills, Calif.: Sage, 1980).

4. E. T. Hall, *The Silent Language* (Greenwich, Conn.: Fawcett, 1959).

5. A. L. Kroeber and Clyde Kluckhohn, *Culture: A Critical Review of Concepts and Definitions* (Cambridge, Mass.: Harvard University Press, 1952), p. 81.

6. H. C. Triandis et al., eds., *The Analysis of Subjective Culture* (New York: Wiley, 1972), p. 3.

7. J. W. Berry, "An Ecological Approach to Cross-Cultural Psychology," *Netherlands Journal of Psychology* 30 (1973), pp. 379-92.

8. Karlene H. Roberts, "On Looking at an Elephant," *Psychological Bulletin* 74, no. 5 (1970), p. 329.

9. Clyde Kluckhohn, "Universal Categories of Culture," in *Anthropology Today*, ed. S. Tax (Chicago: Chicago University Press, 1962), pp. 317-18.

10. Ibid.

11. B. P. Murdock, "Common Denominator of Cultures," in *The Science of Man in the World Crises,* ed. R. Linton (New York: Columbia University Press, 1945), p. 77.

12. Clyde Kluckhohn, "Values and Value-Orientations in the Theory of Actions: As Exploration in Definition and Classification," in *Towards a General Theory of Action,* ed. T. Parsons and E. A. Shils (Cambridge, Mass.: Harvard University Press, 1951), p. 395.

13. G. McLaughlin, "Values in Behavioral Science," *Journal of Religion and Health* (1965), p. 16.

14. G. W. Allport, P. E. Vernon, and G. A. Lindzey, *Study of Values* (Boston: Houghton Mifflin, 1960).

15. C. W. Morris, *Varieties of Human Value* (Chicago: University of Chicago Press, 1956).

16. F. R. Kluckhohn and F. L. Strodtbeck, *Variations in Value Orientations* (Westport, Conn.: Greenwood Press, 1961).

17. Irving Sarnoff, *Society with Tears* (Secaucus, N.J.: Citadel Press, 1960).

18. Milton Rokeach, *The Nature of Human Values* (New York: Free Press, 1973).

19. P. R. Harris and R. T. Moran, *Managing Cultural Differences* (Houston: Gulf Publishing, 1979).

20. Simcha Ronen and Oded Shenkar, "Clustering Countries on Attitudinal Dimensions: A Review and Synthesis," *Academy of Management Review* 10, no. 3 (1985), pp. 435-54.

21. Mason Haire, E. E. Ghiselli, and L. W. Porter, *Managerial Thinking: An International Study* (New York: Wiley, 1966).

22. D. Sirota and J. M. Greenwood, "Understand Your Overseas Work Force," *Harvard Business Review* 49, no. 1 (1971), pp. 53-60.

23. Simcha Ronen and A. I. Kraut, "Similarities among Countries Based on Employee Work Values and Attitudes," *Columbia Journal of World Business* 12, no. 2 (1977), pp. 89-96.

24. Geert Hofstede, "Nationality and Espoused Values of Managers," *Journal of Applied Psychology* 61, no. 2 (1976), pp. 148-55; idem, *Culture's Consequences.*

25. R. W. Griffeth, P. W. Horn, A. DeNisi, and W. Kirchner, "A Multivariate of Managerial Attitudes, Beliefs and Behavior in England and France," Paper presented at the 40th Annual Meeting of the Academy of Management, Detroit, August 1980.

26. S. G. Redding, "Some Perceptions of Psychological Needs among Managers in South-East Asia," Paper presented at the Third International Conference at the

International Association for Cross-Cultural Psychology, Tilburg, Holland, July 1976.

27. M. K. Badawy, "Managerial Attitudes and Need Orientations of Mid-Eastern Executives: An Empirical Cross-Cultural Analysis," Paper presented at the 39th Annual Meeting of the Academy of Management, Atlanta, Ga., August 1979.

28. Ronen and Shenkar, "Clustering Countries on Attitudinal Dimensions," p. 453.

29. Nancy J. Adler, "A Typology of Management Studies Involving Culture," *Journal of International Business Studies* (Fall 1983), pp. 29-47.

30. Hans Schöllhammer, "Strategies and Methodologies in International Business and Comparative Management Research," *Management International Review* (1973), pp. 6-32.

31. J. J. Boddewyn and R. Nath, "Comparative Management Studies: An Assessment," *Management International Review* 10 (1970), pp. 3-11.

32. Schöllhammer, "Strategies and Methodologies," p. 6.

33. Frederick H. Harbison and Charles A. Myers, *Management in the Industrial World: An International Study* (New York: McGraw-Hill, 1959).

34. Richard N. Farmer and Barry M. Richman, "A Model for Research in Comparative Management," *California Management Review* (Winter 1964), pp. 55-68; Richard N. Farmer and Barry M. Richman, *Comparative Management and Economic Progress* (Homewood, Ill.: R. D. Irwin, 1965).

35. Howard V. Perlmutter, "The Tortuous Evolution of the Multinational Corporation," *Columbia Journal of World Business* (January-February 1969), pp. 9-18.

36. Anant R. Negandhi and S. Benjamin Prasad, *Comparative Management* (New York: Appleton-Century-Crofts, 1971).

37. Ibid.

38. L. Kelley and R. Worthley, "The Role of Culture in Comparative Management: A Cross-Cultural Perspective," *Academy of Management Journal* 24, no. 1 (1981), pp. 164-73.

39. H. H. Kitano, *Japanese Americans: Evolution of a Subculture* (New York: Prentice-Hall, 1968).

40. Simcha Ronen, *Comparative and Multinational Management* (New York: Wiley, 1986).

41. Boddewyn and Nath, "Comparative Management Studies," pp. 5-8.

42. F. Kenneth Berrien, "Methodological and Related Problems in Cross-Cultural Research," *International Journal of Psychology* 2 (1967), pp. 33-43.

43. Ronen, *Comparative and Multinational Management,* p. 47.

44. F. K. Berrien, "A Super-Ego for Cross-Cultural Research," *International Journal of Psychology* 5 (1970), pp. 33-34.

45. Richard Peterson, "Future Directions in Comparative Management Research: Where We Have Been and Where We Should Be Going," *International Management Newsletter* (Fall 1986), pp. 6-8.

46. J. Acheson, "Accounting Concepts and Economic Opportunities in a Tarascan Village: Emic and Etic Views," *Human Organization* (Spring 1972), pp. 83-91.

47. Gilles Chevalier, "Should Accounting Practices Be Universal?" *CA Magazine* (July 1977), pp. 47-50.

48. L. S. Chang and K. S. Most, "An International Comparison of Investor Uses

of Financial Statements," *International Journal of Accounting Education and Research* (Fall 1981), pp. 43-60.

49. Ahmed Belkaoui, Alfred L. Kahl, and Josette Peyrard, "Information Needs of Financial Analysts: An International Comparison," *International Journal of Accounting Education and Research* (Fall 1977), pp. 19-27.

50. B. Jaggi, "The Impact of the Cultural Environment on Financial Disclosure," *International Journal of Accounting Education and Research* (January 1975), pp. 75-84.

51. Ibid., p. 83.

52. J. A. Fishman, "A Systematization of the Whorfian Hypotesis," *Behavioral Science* (1960), pp. 323-35.

53. E. H. Lenneberg, "Cognitions in Ethnolinguistics," *Language* (1973), pp. 463-71; R. W. Brown and E. H. Lenneberg, "A Study in Language and Cognition," *Journal of Abnormal and Social Psychology* (1954), pp. 454-62; D. L. Lantz, "Language and Cognition Revisited," *Journal of Abnormal and Social Psychology* (1953), pp. 545-62.

54. H. Hoijer, "Cultural Implications of the Navaho Linguistic Categories," *Language* (1951), pp. 111-20; S. Erwin-Tripp, "Sociolinguistics," in *Advances in Experimental Social Psychology*, ed. L. Berkovitz (New York: Academic Press, 1969), pp. 91-165.

55. J. B. Carol and J. B. Casagrande, "The Functions of Language Classification in Behavior," in *Readings in Social Psychology*, ed. E. E. Macoby, T. M. Newcomb, and E. L. Hartley, 3d ed. (New York: Holt, Rinehart and Winston, 1958).

56. D. L. McDonald, *Comparative Accounting Theory* (Reading, Mass.: Addison-Wesley, 1972).

57. T. H. Jain, "Alternative Methods of Accounting and Decision Making: A Psycholinguistic Analysis," *Accounting Review* (January 1973), p. 101.

58. Ahmed Belkaoui, "Linguistic Relativity in Accounting," *Accounting, Organizations and Society* (October 1978), pp. 97-104.

59. Ibid., p. 103.

60. Ahmed Belkaoui, "The Impact of Socio-Economic Accounting Statements on the Investment Decision: An Empirical Study," *Accounting, Organizations and Society* (September 1980), pp. 263-84; Janice Belkaoui and Ahmed Belkaoui, "Bilingualism and the Perception of Professional Concepts," *Journal of Psycholinguistic Research* 12, no. 2 (1983), pp. 111-27.

61. Ahmed Belkaoui, "The Interprofessional Linguistic Communication of Accounting Concepts: An Experiment in Sociolinguistics," *Journal of Accounting Research* (Autumn 1980), pp. 362-74.

62. Ibid., p. 371.

63. A. Haried, "The Semantic Dimensions of Financial Statements," *Journal of Accounting Research* (Autumn 1979), pp. 376-91; B. Oliver, "The Semantic Differential: A Device for Measuring the Interprofessional Communication of Selected Accounting Concepts," *Journal of Accounting Research* (Autumn 1974), pp. 299-316; E. Flamholtz and E. Cook, "Cognitive Meaning and Its Role in Accounting Change: A Field Study," *Accounting, Organizations and Society* (October 1978), pp. 115-39.

64. A. Haried, "Measurement of Meaning in Financial Reports," *Journal of Accounting Research* (Spring 1973), pp. 117-45.

65. R. Libby, "Bankers' and Auditors' Perceptions of the Message Communicated by the Audit Report," *Journal of Accounting Research* (Spring 1973), pp. 99-122.

66. A. Adelberg, "A Methodology for Measuring the Understandability of Financial Report Messages," *Journal of Accounting Research* (Autumn 1979), pp. 565-92.

SELECTED BIBLIOGRAPHY

Acheson, J., "Accounting Concepts and Economic Opportunities in a Tarascan Village: Emic and Etic Views," *Human Organization* (Spring 1972), pp. 83-91.

Adler, N. J., "Cross-Cultural Management Research: The Ostrich and the Trend," *Academy of Management Review* (1983), pp. 226-32.

______, "Cultural Synergy: The Management of Cross-Cultural Organizations," in *Trends and Issues in OD: Current Theory and Practice*, ed. W. W. Burke and L. D. Goodstein (San Diego, Calif.: University Associates, 1980).

______, "A Typology of Management Studies Involving Culture," *Journal of International Business Studies* (Fall 1983), pp. 29-47.

______, "Understanding the Ways of Understanding: Cross-Cultural Methodology Reviewed," in *Comparative Management: Essays in Contemporary Thought*, ed. R. N. Farmer (Greenwich, Conn.: JAI Press, 1982).

Adler, N. J., and J. de VillaFranca, "Epistemological Foundations of a Symposium Process; A Framework for Understanding Culturally Diverse Organizations," *International Studies of Management and Organization* (Winter 1982-1983), pp. 7-22.

Ajiferuke, N., and J. J. Boddewyn, "Culture and Other Explanatory Variables in Comparative Management Studies," *Academy of Management Journal* (1970), pp. 53-165.

______, "Socioeconomic Indicators in Comparative Management," *Administrative Science Quarterly* (1970), pp. 453-58.

Al-Issa, I., ed., *Culture and Psychology* (Baltimore: University Park Press, 1982).

Allport, G. W., P. E. Vernon, and G. A. Lindzey, *Study of Values* (Boston: Houghton Mifflin, 1960).

Almaney, A., "Intercultural Communication and the MNC Executive," *Columbia Journal of World Business* (October 1974), pp. 23-28.

Aplander, G. G., "Drift to Authoritarianism: The Changing Managerial Styles of the U.S. Executives Overseas," *Journal of International Business Studies* (June 1973), pp. 1-14.

______, "Foreign MBA: Potential Managers for American International Corporations," *Journal of International Business Studies* (March 1973), pp. 1-13.

______, "Multinational Corporations: Homebase Affiliate Relations," *California Management Review* (Spring 1978), pp. 47-56.

Aronoff, J., *Psychological Needs and Cultural Systems* (New York: Van Nostrand, 1967).

Arpan, J. S., D. A. Ricks, and D. J. Patton, "The Meaning of Miscues Made By Multinationals," *Management International Review* (March 1974), pp. 3-11.

Asante, M. K., E. Newmark, and C. A. Blake, eds., *Handbook of Intercultural Communication* (London: Sage, 1979).

Badawy, M. K., "Managerial Attitudes and Need Orientations of Mid-Eastern Executives: An Empirical Cross-Cultural Analysis," Paper presented at the

39th Annual Meeting of the Academy of Management, (Atlanta, Ga., August 1979).

______, "Styles of Mideastern Managers," *California Management Review* (August 1980), pp. 51-58.

Baker, J. C., and J. M. Ivancevich, "The American Executives Abroad: Systematic, Haphazard, or Chaotic?" *California Management Review* (October 1971), pp. 39-44.

Ballon, R. J., "Non Western Work Organization," *Asia Pacific Journal of Management* (September 1983), pp. 1-4.

Barrett, G. V., and R. M. Bass, "Cross-Cultural Issues in Industrial and Organization Psychology," in *Handbook of Industrial and Organizational Psychology*, ed. M. Dunnette (Chicago: Rand McNally, 1976), pp. 1639-86.

Basche, J. R., and M. Duerr, *Experiences with Foreign Production Work Forces* (New York: Conference Board, 1975).

Bass, B. M., "Leadership in Different Cultures," in *Stogdill's Handbook of Leadership*, ed. B. M. Bass (New York: Free Press, 1981), pp. 522-49.

Bass, B. M., and P. C. Burger, *Assessment of Managers: An International Comparison* (New York: Free Press, 1979).

Behrman, J. N., *National Interests and the Multinational Enterprise* (Englewood Cliffs, N.J.: Prentice-Hall, 1970).

Belkaoui, Ahmed, "Economic, Political and Civil Indicators and Reporting and Disclosure Adequacy," *Journal of Accounting and Public Policy* 2 (Fall 1983), pp. 207-20.

______, "The Interprofessional Linguistic Communication of Accounting Concepts: An Experiment in Sociolinguistics," *Journal of Accounting Research* (Autumn 1980), pp. 362-74.

Belkaoui, Ahmed, Alfred Kahl, and Josette Peyrard, "Information Needs of Financial Analysts: An International Comparison," *International Journal of Accounting Education and Research* (Fall 1977), pp. 19-27.

Belkaoui, Janice, and Ahmed Belkaoui, "Bilingualism and the Perception of Professional Concepts," *Journal of Psycholinguistic Research* 12, no. 2 (1983), pp. 111-27.

Bendix, R., "Contributions of the Comparative Approach," in *Comparative maagement and Marketing*, ed. J. Boddewyn (Glenview, Ill.: Scott Foresman, 1969), pp. 10-13.

Boddewyn, J. J., ed., *Comparative Management and Marketing* (Glenview, Ill.: Scott Foresman, 1969).

______, *European Industrial Managers: West and East* (White Plains, N.Y.: International Arts and Sciences Press, 1976).

Bourgeois, L. J. III, and M. Boltvinik, "OD in Cross Cultural Settings: Latin America," *California Management Review* (Spring 1981), pp. 75-81.

Brislin, R. W., *Cross Cultural Encounters: Face to Face Interaction* (Elmsford, N.Y.: Pergamon, 1981).

Brislin, R. W., S. Bochner, and W. J. Lonner, *Cross Cultural Perspectives on Learning* (New York: Wiley, 1975).

Brooke, M. Z., and H. L. Remmers, *International Management and Business Policy* (Boston: Houghton Mifflin, 1978).

Brown, E., and L. Sechrest, "Experiments in Cross Cultural Research," in *Handbook of Cross Cultural Psychology: Methodology*, vol. 2, ed. H. C. Triandis and J.

W. Berry (Boston: Allyn & Bacon, 1980), pp. 297-318.

Brown, J. L., and R. Schneck, "Structural Comparison Between Canadian and American Industrial Organizations," *Administrative Science Quarterly* (March 1979), pp. 24-47.

Chang, L. S., and K. S. Most, "An International Comparison of Investor Uses of Financial Statements," *International Journal of Accounting Education and Research* (Fall 1981)), pp. 43-60.

Chevalier, G., "Should Accounting Practices Be Universal?" *CA Magazine* (July 1977), pp. 47-50.

Child, J., "Culture, Contingency and Capitalism in the Cross National Study of Organizations," in *Research in Organizational Behavior,* vol. 3, ed. L. L. Cummings and B. M. Staw (Greenwich, Conn.: JAI Press, 1981), pp. 303-56.

Child, J., and A. Kieser, "Organization and Managerial Roles in British and West German Companies: An Examination of the Culture-Free Thesis," in *Organizations Alike and Unlike,* ed. C. J. Lammers and D. J. Hickson (London: Routledge & Kegan Paul, 1979), Ch. 13.

Clee, G. H., and W. M. Sachtjen, "Organizing a Worldwide Business," *Harvard Business Review* (November-December 1964), pp. 55-67.

Cole, M., J. Gay, and D. Sharp. *The Cultural Context of Learning and Thinking* (New York: Basic Books, 1971).

Condon, J. C., and F. S. Yousef, *An Introduction to Intercultural Communication* (Indianapolis: Bobbs-Merrill, 1975).

Cuttman, A. W., and H. R. Knudson, eds., *Management Problems in International Environments* (Englewood Cliffs, N.J.: Prentice-Hall, 1972).

Davidson, A. J., J. Jaccard, J. Triandis, J. Morales, and R. Diaz-Guerrero, "Cross-Cultural Model Testing: Toward a Solution of the Emic-Etic Dilemma," *International Journal of Psychology* 11 (1976), pp. 1-13.

Davis, S. M., "Basic Structures of Multinational Corporations," in *Managing and Organizing Multinational Corporations* (Elmsford, N.Y.: Pergamon, 1979).

______, *Comparative Management: Organizational and Cultural Perspectives* (Englewood Cliffs, N.J.: Prentice-Hall, 1971).

______, *Managing and Organizing Multinational Corporations* (Elmsford, N.Y.: Pergamon, 1979).

De la Torre, J., and B. Toyne, "Cross-national Managerial Interaction: A Conceptual Model," *Academy of Management Review* (July 1978), pp. 462-74.

Deutscher, I., "Asking Questions Cross-Culturally: Some Problems of Linguistic Comparability," in *Institutions and the Person,* ed. H. Becker, B. Goer, D. Reisman, and R. Weiss (Chicago: Aldine, 1968).

DeVos, G. A., "Achievement and Innovation in Culture and Personality," in *The Study of Personality: An Interdisciplinary Approach,* ed. E. Norbeck, D. Price-Williams, and W. M. McCord (New York; Holt, Rinehart and Winston, 1968).

DeVos, T., *U.S. Multinationals and Worker Participation in Management: The American Experience in the European Country* (Westport, Conn.: Greenwood Press, 1981).

Doz, Y. L., and C. K. Prahalad, "Headquarters Influence and Strategic Control in MNCs," *Sloan Management Review* (Fall 1981), pp. 15-29.

______, "How MNCs Cope with Host Government Intervention," *Harvard Business Review* (March-April 1980), p. 58.

Duerr, M. G., and J. M. Roach, "Organization and Control in European Multinational Corporation," in *Managing and Organizing the Multinational Corporation*, ed. S. M. Davis (Elmsford, N.Y.: Pergamon, 1979), pp. 341-52.

Dyaz, G. P., and H. T. Thanheiser, *The Emerging European Enterprises: Strategy and Structure in French and German Industry* (London: Macmillan, 1976).

Dymsza, W. A., and A. R. Negandhi, "Introduction to Cross Cultural Management Issues," *Journal of International Business Studies* (Fall 1983), pp. 15-16.

Edgerton, R. B., and L. L. Langness, *Methods and Styles in the Study of Culture* (San Francisco: Chandler and Sharp, 1974).

Elder, J. W., "Comparative Cross National Methodology," *Annual Review of Sociology* (1976), pp. 209-30.

England, G. W., "Managers and Their Value Systems: A Five Country Comparative Study," *Columbia Journal of World Business* (Summer 1978), pp. 35-44.

England, G. W., and R. Lee, "Organizational Goals and Expected Behavior among American, Japanese and Korean Managers: A Comparative Study," *Academy of Management Journal* (December 1971), pp. 425-38.

England, G. W., and A. R. Negandhi, "National Context and Technology as Determinant of Employee's Perceptions," in *Organizational Functioning in a Cross-Cultural Perspective*, ed. G. W. England, A. R. Negandhi, and B. Wilpert (Kent, Ohio: Kent State University Press, 1979), pp. 175-90.

Farmer, R. N., and J. V. Lombardi, eds., *Readings in International Business* (Bloomington, Ind.: Cedarwood Press, 1983).

Farmer, R. N., and B. M. Richman, *Comparative Management and Economic Progress* (Homewood, Ill.: R. D. Irwin, 1965).

______, "A Model for Research in Comparative Management," *California Management Review* (Winter 1964), pp. 55-68.

Fayerweather, J., "A Conceptual Scheme of the Interactions of the Multinational Firm: International Issues," *Journal of Business Administration* (Fall 1975), pp. 67-89.

______, *The Executive Overseas* (Syracuse, N.Y.: Syracuse University Press, 1959).

______, *International Business Policy and Administration* (New York: International Executive, 1976).

Fayol, H., *General and Industrial Management* (London: Pitman, 1949).

Ford, D. L., Jr., "Cultural Influences on Organizational Behavior," in *Organization and People: Readings, Cases and Exercises*, ed. J. B. Ritchie and P. Thompson (New York: West, 1976).

Frank, Werner G., "An Empirical Analysis of International Accounting Principles," *Journal of Accounting Research* (Autumn 1979), pp. 539-605.

Franko, L. G., *The European Multinationals: A Renewed Challenge to American and British Big Business* (Stamford, Conn.: Greylock, 1976).

______, *Joint Ventures Survival in Multinational Corporation* (New York: Praeger, 1971).

Freemantle, D., "Foreign Assignments: A Recruiter's Nightmare," *Personnel Management* (October 1978), pp. 33-37.

Gabriel, P., "MNCs in the Third World: Is Conflict Unavoidable?" *Harvard Business Review* (July-August 1977), p. 50.

Geertz, C., "Thick Description: Towards an Interpretative Theory of Culture," in *The Interpretation of Cultures* (New York: Basic Books, 1973).

Gladwin, T. N., *Environment, Planning and the Multinational Corporation* (Greenwich, Conn.: JAI Press, 1977).

Gladwin, T. N., and V. Terpstra, Introduction to *The Cultural Environment of International Business*, ed. V. Terpstra (Cincinnati: Southwestern, 1978), pp. x-xxiv.

Glynn, L., "Multinationals in the World of Nations," in *The Multinational Enterprise in Transition*, ed. P. O. Grub, F. Ghadar, and D. Khambata (Princeton, N.J.: Darwin Press, 1984).

Gordon, L. V., *Survey of Interpersonal Values: Revised Manual* (Chicago: Science Research Associates, 1976).

______, *Survey of Personal Values: Manual* (Chicago: Science Research Associates, 1967).

Graham, W. K., and K. H. Roberts, *Comparative Studies in Organizational Behavior* (New York: Holt, Rinehart and Winston, 1972).

Granick, D., "International Differences in Executive Reward Systems: Extent, Explanation and Significance," *Columbia Journal of World Business* (Summer 1978), pp. 45-55.

______, *Managerial Comparisons of Four Developed Countries: France, Britain, US and Russia* (Cambridge, Mass.: MIT Press, 1972).

Graves, D., "The Impact of Culture Upon Managerial Attitudes, Beliefs and Behavior in England and France," in *Management Research: A Cross Cultural Perspective*, ed. D. Graves (San Francisco: Jossey-Bass, 1973), pp. 282-304.

Grosset, S., *Management: European and American Styles* (Belmont, Calif.: Wadsworth, 1970).

Grub, P. D., F. Khadar, and D. Khambata, eds., *The Multinational Enterprise in Transition* (Princeton, N.J.: Darwin Press, 1984).

Gruenfeld, L. W., "Field Dependence and Field Independence as a Framework for the Study of Task and Social Orientations in Organizational Leadership," in *Management Research: A Cross Cultural Perspective*, ed. D. Graves (San Francisco: Jossey-Bass, 1973), pp. 5-23.

Haire, M., E. E. Ghiselli, and L. W. Porter, *Managerial Thinking: An International Study* (New York: Wiley, 1966).

Hall, E. T., *Beyond Culture* (New York: Doubleday, 1976).

______, *The Silent Language* (Greenwich, Conn.: Fawcett, 1959).

______, "The Silent Language in Overseas Business," *Harvard Business Review* (May-June 1960), pp. 87-95.

Harbison, F., and C. A. Myers, *Management in the Industrial World: An International Study* (New York: McGraw-Hill, 1959).

Harris, P. R., and D. L. Harris, "Training for Cultural Understanding," *Training and Development Journal* (May 1972), pp. 8-10.

Harris, P. R., and R. T. Moran, *Managing Cultural Differences* (Houston: Gulf Publishing, 1979).

Hayes, R. D., C. M. Korrth, and M. Roudiani, *International Business: An Introduction to the World of the Multinational Firm* (Englewood Cliffs, N.J.: Prentice-Hall, 1972).

Heenan, D. A., "The Corporate Expatriate: Assignment to Ambiguity," *Columbia Journal of World Business* (May-June 1970), pp. 49-53.

Heenan, D. A., and W. J. Keegan, "The Rise of Third World Multinationals,"

Harvard Business Review (January-February 1979), pp. 101-9.

Heenan, D. A., and H. V. Perlmutter, *Multinational Organization Development* (Reading, Mass.: Addison-Wesley, 1979).

Heller, F. A., and B. Wilperet, "Managerial Decision Making: An International Comparison," in *Organizational Functioning in a Cross Cultural Perspective*, ed. G. W. England, A. R. Negandhi, and B. Wilpert (Kent, Ohio: Kent State University Press, 1979).

Hodges, M., *Multinational Corporations and National Government. A Case Study of the U.K.'s Experience 1964-1970* (Lexington, Mass.: Saxon House/ Lexington Books, Heath, 1974).

Hofstede, Geert, "The Color of Collars," *Columbia Journal of World Business* (September-October 1972), pp. 72-80.

______, *Culture's Consequences: International Differences in Work Related Values* (Beverly Hills: Sage, 1980).

______, "Nationality and Espoused Values of Managers," *Journal of Applied Psychology* 61, no. 2 (1976), pp. 148-55.

Hoijer, H., "The Sapir-Whorf Hypothesis," in *Intercultural Communication: A Reader*, ed. L. A. Samovar and R. E. Porter (Belmont, Calif.: Wadsworth, 1976), pp. 150-58.

______, ed., *Language in Culture* (Chicago: University of Chicago Press, 1954).

Holsti, J. J., "Change in the International System: Interdependence, Integration and Fragmentation," in *Change in the International System*, ed. R. Holsti, R. M. Siverson, and A. L. George (Boulder, Colo.: Westview Press, 1980), pp. 23-53.

Howard, C. G., "The Expatriate Manager and the Role of the MNC," *Personnel Journal* (October 1980), pp. 840-44.

Howell, I., "Theoretical Directions for Intercultural Communication," in *Handbook of Intercultural Communication*, ed. M. K. Asanti, E. T. Newmark, and C. E. Blake (Beverly Hills: Sage, 1979).

Hughes, C. L., and V. S. Flowers, "Shaping Personnel Strategies to Disparate Value Systems," *Personnel* (March-April 1973), pp. 8-23.

Jaggi, B., "The Impact of the Cultural Environment on Financial Disclosure," *International Journal of Accounting Education and Research* (January 1975), pp. 75-84.

______, "Job Satisfaction and Leadership Style in Developing Countries: The Case of India," *International Journal of Contemporary Sociology* (July-October 1977), pp. 230-36.

Jain, T. H., "Alternative Methods of Accounting and Decision Making: A Psycholinguistic Analysis," *Accounting Review* (January 1973), pp. 95-104.

Kanungo, R. N., and R. Wright, "A Cross-Cultural Comparative Study of Managerial Job Attitudes," *Journal of International Business Studies* (Fall 1983), pp. 115-29.

Kelley, L., and R. Worthley, "The Role of Culture in Comparative Management: A Cross-Cultural Perspective," *Academy of Management Journal* 24, no. 1 (1981), pp. 164-73.

Kluckhohn, F. R., and F. Strodtbeck, *Variations in Value Orientations* (Westport, Conn.: Greenwood Press, 1961).

Kobrin, S. J., "When Does Political Instability Result in Increased Investment Risk?" *Columbia Journal of World Business* (Fall 1978), pp. 113-22.

Kornadt, H. J., L. H. Eckensberger, and W. B. Emminghaus, "Cross Cultural Research on Motivation and Its Contribution to a General Theory of Motivation," in *Handbook of Cross-Cultural Psychology*, vol. 3, *Basic Processes*, ed. H. C. Triandis and W. Lonner (Boston: Allyn & Bacon, 1980).

Kroeber, Alfred L., and Clyde Kluckhohn, *Culture: A Critical Review of Concepts and Definitions*, Papers of the Peabody Museum of American Archeology and Ethnology (Cambridge, Mass.: Harvard University Press, 1952).

Landis, D., and R. W. Brislin, *Handbook of Intercultural Training*, vols. 1-3, (Elmsford, N.Y.: Pergamon, 1983).

La Palombara, J., and S. Blank, *Multinational Corporations in Comparative Perspective*, Report No. 725, (New York: Conference Board, 1977).

McMillan, C., C. Hinnings, D. Hickson, and R. Schneck, "The Structure of Work Organizations across Societies," *Academy of Management Journal* (1973), pp. 555-69.

Miller, S. W., and J. L. Simonetti, "Culture and Management: Some Conceptual Considerations," *Management International Review* (1974), pp. 87-100.

Mitchell, R. E., "Survey Materials Collected in Developing Countries: Sampling, Measurement and Interviewing Obstacles to Intra and International Comparisons," in *Comparative Management and Marketing*, ed. J. Boddewyn (Glenview, Ill.: Scott Foresman, 1969), pp. 232-52.

Murdock, G. P., "Common Denominator of Cultures," in *The Science of Man in the World Crises*, ed. R. Linton (New York: Columbia University Press, 1945), pp. 12-142.

Naroll, R., "Galton's Problem," in *A Handbook of Method in Cultural Anthropology in Social Research*, ed. H. M. Blalock and A. B. Blalock (New York: McGraw-Hill, 1968), pp. 236-77.

Negandhi, A. R., "Convergence in Developing Countries," in *Organizations Alike and Unlike*, ed. C. J. Lammers and D. J. Hickson (London: Routledge & Kegan Paul, 1979), ch. 17.

______, *Functioning of the Multinational Corporation: A Global Comparative Study* (Elmsford, N.Y.: Pergamon, 1980).

Negandhi, A. R., and B. R. Baliga, *Quest for Survival and Growth: A Comparative Study of American, European, and Japanese Multinationals* (New York: Praeger, 1979).

______, *Tables Are Turning: German and Japanese Multinational Companies in the United States* (Cambridge, Mass.: Odgeschlages, Quin and Hani, 1981).

Negandhi, A. R., and S. B. Prasad, *Comparative Management* (New York: Appleton-Century-Crofts, 1971).

Nord, W. R., "Culture and Organizational Behavior," in *Concepts and Controversy in Organizational Behavior*, 2d ed., ed. W. R. Nord (Santa Monica, Calif.: Goodyear, 1976), pp. 197-211.

Pahlman, R. A., J. S. Ang., and S. I. Ali, "Policies of Multinational Firms: A Survey," *Business Horizons* 19 (December 1976).

Perlmutter, Howard V., "The Tortuous Evolution of the Multinational Corporation," *Columbia Journal of World Business* (January-February 1969), pp. 9-18.

Perlmutter, H. V., and D. A. Heenan, *Multinational Organization Development: A Social Architectural Perspective* (Reading, Mass.: Addison-Wesley, 1979).

Phatak, A. V., *International Dimensions of Management* (Belmont, Calif.: Wadsworth, 1983).

Poortinga, Y. H., ed. *Basic Problems in Cross Cultural Psychology* (Lisse, Netherlands: Swets and Zeitlinger, 1977).

Prasad, S. B., and Y. K. Krishna Shetty, *An Introduction to Multinational Management* (Englewood Cliffs, N.J.: Prentice-Hall, 1976).

Robinson, R. D., *International Business Management: A Guide to Decision Making*, 2d ed. (Hinsdale, Ill.: Dryden, 1978).

———, *International Business Policy* (New York: Holt, Rinehart and Winston, 1964).

———, *Internationalization of Business: An Introduction* (New York: Dryden, 1984).

Ronen, Simcha, *Flexible Working Hours: An Innovation in the Quality of Work Life* (New York: McGraw-Hill, 1981).

Ronen, Simcha, and A. I. Kraut, "Similarities among Countries Based on Employee Work Values and Attitudes," *Columbia Journal of World Business* 12, no. 2 (1977), pp. 89-96.

Ronen, Simcha, and O. Shenkar, "Clustering Countries on Attitudinal Dimensions: A Review and Synthesis," *Academy of Management Review* 10, no. 3 (1985), pp. 435-54.

Rowthorn, R., *International Big Business 1957-1967* (London: Cambridge University Press, 1971).

Ruhly, D., *Orientation to Intercultural Communication* (Chicago: Science Research Associates, 1976).

Ryterband, E. C., and G. V. Barrett, "Manager's Values and Their Relationship to the Management of Tasks: A Cross-Cultural Comparison," in *Managing for Accomplishment*, ed. B. M. Bass, R. Cooper, and J. A. Hass (Lexington, Mass.: Heath, 1970), pp. 226-60.

Samovar, L. A., R. E. Porter, and N. C. Jain, *Understanding Intercultural Communication* (Belmont, Calif.: Wadsworth, 1981).

Schöllhammer, H., "Strategies in Comparative Management Theorizing," in *Comparative Management Teaching, Training and Research*, ed. J. Boddewyn (New York: New York University Comparative Management Workshop, 1970), pp. 13-44.

Sechrest, L., "On the Dearth of Theory in Cross Cultural Psychology: There is Madness in Our Method," in *Basic Problems in Cross Cultural Psychology*, ed. Y. H. Poortinga (Amsterdam: Swets and Zeitlinger, 1977), pp. 73-82.

Segall, M. H., *Cross Cultural Psychology: Human Behavior in Global Perspective* (Belmont, Calif.: Wadsworth, 1979).

Segall, M. H., D. T. Campbell, and M. J. Herskovitz, *The Influence of Culture on Visual Perception* (Indianapolis: Bobbs-Merrill, 1966).

Sekaran, U., "Methodological and Analytic Considerations in Cross-National Research," *Journal of International Business Studies* (Fall 1983), pp. 61-73.

Servan-Schreiber, J. J., *The American Challenge*, trans. R. Steel (New York: Atheneum, 1968).

Sirota, D., and J. M. Greenwood, "Understand Your Overseas Work Force," *Harvard*

Business Review 49, no. 1 (1971), pp. 53-60.

Sitaram, K. S., and R. T. Cogdell, *Foundations of Intercultural Communication* (Columbus, Ohio: Merrill, 1976).

Sitaram, K. S., and L. W. Haapanen, "The Role of Values in Intercultural Commuication," in *Handbook of Intercultural Communication*, ed. M. K. Asante, E. Newmark, and C. A. Blake (Beverly Hills: Sage, 1979).

Smith, E. C., and L. Fiber, *Towards Internationalism: Readings in Cross Cultural Communication* (Rowley, Mass.: Newbury House, 1979).

Stopford, J. M., and L. T. Wells, Jr., *Managing in the Multinational Enterprise* (New York: Basic Books, 1972).

Swartz, M. J., and D. K. Jordan, *Culture, The Anthropological Perspective* (New York: Wiley, 1980).

Tajfel, H., "Social and Cultural Factors in Perception," in *The Handbook of Social Psychology*, ed. G. Lindsay and E. Aronson (Reading, Mass.: Addison-Wesley, 1969).

Terpstra, V., *The Cultural Environment of International Business* (Cincinnati: South-western, 1978).

Tichy, N. M., "Organizational Innovations in Sweden," *Columbia Journal of World Business* (Summer 1974), pp. 18-27.

Toyne, B., "Host Country Managers of Multinational Firms: An Evaluation of Variables Affecting Their Managerial Thinking Patterns," *Journal of International Business Studies* (Spring 1976), pp. 39-55.

Triandis, H. C., "Subjective Culture and Interpersonal Behavior," in *Applied Cross-Cultural Psychology*, ed. J. W. Berry and W. J. Lonner (Amsterdam: Swets and Zeitlinger, 1975).

Triandis, H. C., and V. A. Vassiliou, "A Comparative Analysis of Subjective Cultures," in *The Analysis of Subjective Culture*, ed. H. C. Triandis et al. (New York: Wiley, 1972), pp. 299-335.

Triandis, H. C., V. Vassiliou, G. Vassiliou, Y. Tonaka, and A. V. Shanmugam, eds., *The Analysis of Subjective Culture* (New York: Wiley, 1972).

Tsurumi, Y., *Multinational Management: Business Strategy and Government Policy* (Cambridge, Mass.: Ballinger, 1984).

Vernon, R., "International Investment and International Trade in the Product Cycle," *Quarterly Journal of Economics* (May 1966), pp. 190-207.

Wallin, T. O., "The International Executive Baggage: Cultural Values of American Frontier," *MSU Business Topics* (Spring 1972), pp. 49-58.

Weinshall, T. D., *Culture and Management* (Middlesex, England: Penguin, 1977).

Welge, M. K., "A Comparison of Managerial Structures in German Subsidiaries in France, India and the United States," *Management International Review* (1981), pp. 5-21.

White, L., *The Science of Culture* (New York: Grove Press), 1949.

Yoshino, M. Y., "Emerging Japanese Multinational Enterprise," in *Managing and Organizing the Multinational Corporation*, ed. S. M. Davis (New York: Pergamon, 1979), pp. 474-94.

Zeira, Y., and E. Harari, "Managing Third Country Nationals in Multinational Corporations," *Business Horizons* (October 1977), pp. 83-88.

5

SEGMENTAL REPORTING

The growth of conglomerate multinational corporations, international accounting, and/or international trade has led to a need for segmental reporting. Rather than being limited to a reporting of the financial position, performance, and conduct of the whole firm, segmental reporting would add specific reporting on the activities of identifiable and reportable segments of the firm. There was, in addition, an international call for such reporting as firms expanded beyond their domestic activities to generate revenues and perform operations outside the borders of their parents' countries. Therefore, diversification, added to internationalization of firms, presented an opportunity for a change in the framework of accountability and disclosure toward a combination of aggregate and less aggregate forms of reporting. Like all reporting issues, segmental reporting generated a debate about its implementation, the nature of accounting standards, its impact on users and the market, and its potential predictive ability. This chapter elaborates on the various aspects of this debate and its international and managerial ramifications.

NATURE OF SEGMENTAL REPORTING

Firms have been reacting to their environment by adopting new organizational structures based on decentralization and the development or acquisition of domestic or foreign segments. What results is a more diversified company. Robert K. Mautz offers the following definition of a diversified company:

a company which is either so managerially decentralized, so lacks operational integration, or has such diversified markets that it may experience rates of

profitability, degrees of risk, and opportunities for growth which vary within the company to such extent that an investor requires information about these variations in order to make informed decisions.[1]

What appears from this definition is that first the phenomenon of diversification emanates from management decentralization, a lack of operational integration, or activity in diversified markets, and second, that the differences in the financial profits of the segments call for segmental reporting deemed useful to investors.

Segmental reporting consists, therefore, in providing relevant information about segments. It can be rationalized within the "Fineness Theorem" of the information economics literature.[2] It implies that the information system η_1 is said to be "as fine as" the information system η_0 if η_1 is a "subpartition" of η_0; that is if each data set of η_1 provides a partitioning of the states of nature which is at least as detailed (or as "fine") as that present in the data sets of η_0. Applied to segmental reporting it implies that the information system obtained by segmental reporting and consolidated data together is "finer" than the disclosure of consolidated data alone. The fineness argument does not, however, consider the incremental costs required by the additional disclosure. Rosanne M. Mohr elaborates as follows:

It must be noted, however, that the costs of the "finer" disclosures could impair the theoretical result. Although the gathering and reporting costs associated with segmental disclosure may be small (due to the use of similar data in managerial decision contexts), externalities and practical data limitations would still impose greater cost. For example, competitive reactions or managerial reluctance to adopt "risky" projects may affect the expected payoff to the decision maker. Furthermore, uncertainty about data reliability and comparability would inhibit the use of the more detailed disclosures. This latter assertion is particularly applicable to the incremental disclosure of segment earnings data, wherein differences in cost determination methods and in common cost allocation schemes can influence the reported amounts.[3]

EVALUATION OF SEGMENTAL REPORTING

Use of Segmental Reporting

The use of segmental reporting has been on the increase even before the international standard setters made some calls for it. Attitudinal studies of preparers and users in the United States showed at the time an expressed interest in the dissemination of segmental reporting. These studies include one on financial analysts and commercial bankers by Morton Backer and Walter B. McFarland,[4] and one on financial analysts and corporate executives by Mautz.[5] Another attitudinal study by J. Cramer reported

some of the perceived problems of segmental reporting experienced by corporate controllers, namely, in defining the segments, the restrictions on data comparability that might result from the use of different cost allocation and transfer pricing techniques, and finally, the externality costs associated with the development of auditing standards, the increased legal exposure of managers and auditors, and the reactions of competitors.[6]

S. J. Gray and Lee H. Radebaugh examined the extent of geographical information provided in practice in the United States and the United Kingdom, and the significant differences in the nature and content of disclosures between countries both in terms of voluntary disclosures and those required by accounting standards.[7] Given the greater flexibility in the applications of regulations governing segment disclosures in the United States as well as reduced scope in terms of the amount of information to be disclosed, it is not surprising that their findings indicate that U.S. firms disclose more segment information, especially with respect to intraenterprise sales, profits, and assets. In the case of employees, however, the increased emphasis on employee reporting in the United Kingdom may explain the greater disclosure of employee information in the United Kingdom. An interesting result was that U.S. firms disclosed fewer geographic segments than did U.K. firms, and a higher level of aggregation. The following explanation is provided:

> One final note relates to the demand of investors for information. U.K. segment disclosure practices are determined by the London Stock Exchange and, therefore, its investors. This has resulted in more segments than for U.S. firms, as summarized above, but certainly not in more information per segment. Large MNEs [multinational enterprises], such as those in this study, actively use the international markets to raise debt as well as equity capital, so they effectively compete with each other for capital. In spite of this, the more extensive information required of U.S. MNEs has not resulted in U.K. firms trying to match U.S. firms in terms of disclosure. It is evident that the capital market has not insisted on this information from U.K. firms, leading one to question the necessity of the fuller range of U.S. disclosure.[8]

Gray also examined the European experience with segmental reporting and found that U.K.-based companies exhibited greater disclosure of business analyses of profits and geographical analyses of sales and profits.[9] Factors explaining the differences included managerial (corporate strategy, organizational structure, and cost and competitive aspects), legal and political, professional, and stock market and investment environments. Two variables were singled out as more important: the structure of the company with respect to the extent of its economic integration and managerial coordination, and the differential stimulus to disclosure provided by the regulatory environment of legal, professional, and stock market requirements. According to Gray,

The impact of the former variable is difficult to assess from company reports, and further research into this aspect would seem useful to determine the feasibility of disclosure. With regards to the impact of the latter variable, there is little doubt about the unsatisfactory nature of existing disclosure requirements, such as they are. The critical problem is that of defining appropriate criteria for the identification of reportable segments. This is a difficulty which is currently thwarting the developing of segment reporting in the EEC, given that a case for providing such information is perceived to exist by some of the rule-making bodies concerned.[10]

Evaluation of Segmental Reporting

Various arguments have been made with regard to segmental reporting since business concerns began to grow and acquire a multisegmental characteristic.

The usefulness of segmental reporting was linked generally to (a) the informational content of the information in terms of the profitability, risk, and growth of the different segments of a firm, and (b) the relevance to users in their assessment of the earnings potential and the risk of the company as a whole, to governments in their development of public policy positions on multinational and/or large companies, and to management encouraging a corporate strategy. This last point is raised as follows:

> Managerial efficiency may be promoted by the attention to corporate strategy that the publication of segmented reporting will encourage. Management may also be concerned to evaluate their internal management control system. The provision of segmental reports will necessitate managerial evaluation of cost allocation procedures and the bases on which transfer prices between segments are calculated. Perhaps the most important spur to efficiency could be the increased competition that may result from segmental disclosures with consequent benefits to the economy as a whole. The effect of this may be exaggerated, however, as all companies will be similarly placed. But it may at least redress to some extent the competitive disadvantage experienced by the unitary company, with no business or geographical diversification, as compared to the multibusiness-multinational company whose operations have become progressively complex and whose financial statements have become correspondingly opaque.[11]

Naturally, as in all accounting issues, not all arguments are in favor of segmental reporting. Not only is the usefulness of segmental reporting questioned when compared to the role of consolidated data, but also the costs of disclosure are raised as a subject of concern. The question is whether the costs of segmental disclosure could serve to offset the theoretical benefits of "finer" information system. There is undoubtedly limited evidence with regard to the cost aspects of segmental disclosure, in addition to the lack of evidence on information-processing issues, data-reliability considerations, and externality costs. There is also the problem of the lack of comparability when "(i) apparently similar segments in different

firms may be identified differently, (ii) the treatment of inter-segment transfers may differ, and (iii) common costs may be allocated over different bases."[12]

THE U.S. POSITION ON SEGMENTAL REPORTING

Official Pronouncements

The U.S. position on reporting financial information by segment is mainly expressed in FASB Statement No. 14, *Financial Reporting for Segments of a Business Enterprise.* Other applicable authoritative statements include Statements 18, 21, 24, 30, and 69, and technical bulletins 79-4, 79-5, and 79-8. FASB Statement No. 14 requires public companies whose securities are publicly traded or which are required to file financial statements with the SEC to include disaggregated information about operations in various industries, foreign operations, export sales, and sales to major customers. FASB Statement No. 21, *Suspension of the Reporting of Earnings Per Share and Segment Information by Nonpublic Enterprises,* exempts nonpublic firms from the provisions of FASB Statement No. 14. Similarly, FASB Statement No. 24, *Reporting Segment Information in Financial Statements That Are Presented in Another Enterprise's Financial Report,* exempts the reporting entity whose consolidated financial statements contain separable financial statements in the following circumstances:

1. The separable financial statements are also consolidated or combined in a complete set of financial statements and both sets of financial statements are included in the same financial reports;
2. The separable financial statements are those of a foreign investee (not a subsidiary) of the primary reporting unit, and the separable financial statements do not follow the provisions of SFAS No. 14; or
3. The separable financial statements are those of an investee accounted for using the cost or equity method.

Therefore, SFAS No. 21 and No 24 affect the applicability of SFAS No. 14, by putting forth limitations.

Because SFAS No. 14 differentiates between domestic and foreign operations, the following presentation will make the same differentiation.

Domestic Operations

In SFAS No. 14 an industry segment is defined as a component of an enterprise, engaged in providing a product or service, or a group of related products and services, primarily to unaffiliated customers for a profit. The

first requirement of SFAS No. 14 is the determination of the industry segments that need to be reported separately. The three-step procedure goes as follows.

First: The company should identify sources of revenue (by product or service rendered) on a worldwide basis for the entity.

Second: The company should group related products and services into industry segments. Three factors from paragraph 100 of SFAS No. 14 are to be considered in determining industry segment as follows:

1. *The nature of the product.* Related products have similar purposes or end uses. Thus, they may be expected to have similar rates of profitability, similar degrees of risk, and similar opportunities for growth.
2. *The nature of the production process.* Sharing of common or interchangeable production or sales facilities, equipment, labor force, or service group or use of the same or similar basic raw materials may suggest that products or services are related. Likewise, similar degrees of labor intensiveness or similar degrees of capital intensiveness may indicate a relationship among products or services.
3. *Markets and marketing methods.* Similarity of geographic marketing areas, types of customers, or marketing methods may indicate a relationship among products or services. The sensitivity of the market to price changes and to changes in general economic conditions may indicate whether products and services are related or unrelated.

Third: The company should determine the reporting segments. Six tests are suggested to facilitate the decision, namely the *revenue test*, the *profitability test*, the *asset test*, the *comparability test*, the *dominance test*, and the *explanation test*. These tests are applied as follows:

The *revenue test* requires that the segment revenue be 10% or more of the combined revenue (sales to unaffiliated customers and intersegment sales or transfers) of all the enterprise's industry segments. Segment revenue is calculated as follows:

$$SR = S + IS + INTO + INTR$$

where SR = segment revenue,
S = sales to unaffiliated customers,
IS = intersegment sales and transfers,
$INTO$ = interest income from sources outside the firm,
$INTR$ = interest income from intersegment notes receivable.

The *profitability test* requires that the absolute of the segments operating profit or loss be 10% or more of the greater, in absolute amount, of (a) the combined operating profits of all industry segments that did not incur an operating loss or (b) the combined operating losses of all industry segments which did incur an operating loss. The operating profit or loss is segment revenue less operating expenses except the following items:

1. Any revenues earned at the corporate level and not related to any segment
2. General corporate expenses
3. Interest expense, except if segment operations are primarily of a financial nature
4. Domestic and foreign income taxes
5. Equity in earnings of unconsolidated subsidiaries or investees
6. Extraordinary items
7. Gains or losses on discontinued operations
8. Minority interest
9. Cumulative effect of changes in accounting principles

The *asset test* requires, if the segment fails both preceding tests, that the identifiable assets of the segments be ten percent or more of the combined segment identifiable assets. Identifiable assets include tangible and intangible assets net of valuation allowances used by the industry segment and the allocated portions of the assets used by two or more segments. Assets that are intended for general corporate purposes are excluded.

The *comparability test* requires that the segment be reported separately if management feels such a treatment is needed to achieve interperiod comparability.

The *test of dominance* requires that the segment not be reported separately if it can be classified as dominant. A dominant segment should represent 90% or more of the combined revenues, operating profits or losses, and identifiable assets, and no other segment meets any of the 10% tests.

The *explanation test* determines whether a substantial portion of an enterprise's operations is explained by its segment information. The combined total of the revenue from reportable segments must be 75% or more of all revenue from sales to unaffiliated customers. If combined revenues do not meet this test, additional segments must be added until the test is met.

The following example illustrates the application of operational tests.

Segment	Unaffiliated Revenue	Intersegment Revenue	Total Revenue	Operating Profit (Loss)	Identifiable Assets
U	50	50	100	10	50
V	100		100	10	40
W	150	100	250	(20)	100
X	200		200	10	150
Y	250	50	300	(100)	100
Z	300		300	100	80
	$1,050		$1,250	$ 10	$520

Revenue Test: (10%)($1,250) = $125

Reportable segments: *W*, *X*, *Y*, *Z*

Operating Profit or Loss Test: (10%)($130) = $13

Reportable segments: *W*, *Y*, *Z*

Because total operation profit ($130) is greater than the operating loss ($120), total operating profit is used as the base.

Identifiable Assets Test: (10%)($520) = $52

Reportable segments: *W*, *X*, *Y*, *Z*

Explanation Test: (75%)($1,050) = $787.50

Segments *W*, *X*, *Y*, and *Z* have total unaffiliated revenues of $900, which is greater than $787.50. Therefore, the explanation test is met and no additional segments need to be reported.

In conclusion, given the above tests and given that the number of reportable segments does not exceed ten and that there is no dominant segment, the reportable segments are *W*, *X*, *Y*, and *Z*.

Following the choice of the reportable segments, SFAS No. 14 suggests specific disclosure requirements using one of three methods:

1. In the financial statements, with reference to related footnote disclosures
2. In the footnotes to the financial statements
3. In a supplementary schedule, which is not part of the four financial statements

The information to be reported in the reportable segments includes the following:

1. Revenue information including (a) sale to unaffiliated customers, (b) intersegment sales or transfers, along with the basis of accounting for such sales or transfers, and (c) a reconciliation of both sales to unaffiliated customers and intersegment sales or transfers on the consolidated income statement
2. Profitability information
3. Identifiable assets information
4. Other disclosures including the aggregate amount of depreciation, depletion and amortization; the amount of capital expenditures; equity in unconsolidated but vertically integrated subsidiaries and their geographic location; the effect of a change in accounting principle on segment income, the type of products and services produced by each segment, specific accounting policies, the basis used to price intersegment transfers, the method used to allocate common costs, and the nature and amount of any unusual or infrequent items added to or deducted from segment profit

Foreign Operations

SFAS No. 14 requires separate disclosure of domestic and foreign activities. Foreign operations are those revenue-generating activities that

are located outside the enterprise's home country and are generating revenue either from sales to unaffiliated customers or from intraenterprise sales or transfer between geographic areas.

Two tests may be used to determine if foreign operations are to be reported separately: (a) revenue from sales to unaffiliated customers is 10% or more of consolidated revenue as reported in the firm's income statement and (b) identifiable assets of the firm's foreign operations are 10% or more of consolidated total assets as reported in the firm's balance sheet. After a foreign operation has been determined to be reportable, it must be added to foreign operations in the same geographic area. Geographic areas are defined as individual countries or groups of countries as may be determined to be appropriate in a firm's circumstances. The following factors are to be considered in grouping foreign operations: proximity, economic affinity, similarities in business environment, and nature, scale and degree of interrelationship of the firm's operations in the various countries.

The disclosure requirements for foreign operations are similar to those for domestic operations.

Export Sales and Sales to Major Customers

Export sales are those sales made by a domestic segment to unaffiliated customers in foreign countries. If export sales amount to 10% or more of the total sales to unaffiliated customers, they should be separately disclosed in the aggregate and by such geographic areas considered appropriate.

Similarly, if 10% or more of the revenue of a firm is derived from a single customer, a separate disclosure is required along with the segments making the sale. SFAS No. 30, "Disclosure of Information About Major Customers," identifies the following entities as being a single customer to comply with the 10% test: a group of entities under common control, the federal government, a state government, a local government, or a foreign government.

INTERNATIONAL POSITIONS

In the United Kingdom the 1981 Companies Act requires segmental reporting in the financial statements, stating specifically:

If in the course of the financial year, the company has carried out a business of two or more classes that, in the opinion of the directors, differ substantially from each other, there shall be stated in respect of each class (describing it):

(a) the amount of the turnover attributable to that class, and

(b) the amount of the profit or loss of the company before taxation which is in the opinion of the directors attributable to that class.

In addition, the act calls for a disclosure of turnover by geographic areas when the firm has been supplying different markets. The disclosure is generally made in the directors' reports.

The Canadian position is more comprehensive. It is expressed in Section 1700 of the Canadian Institute of Chartered Accountants (CICA) handbook. The requirements of the section are, in general, similar to the provision of SFAS No. 14. The only exception relates to the required disclosure of information about major customers of the firm. While the exposure draft preceding Section 1700 called for this information, it was later deleted from the final version.

The international position in segment reporting was reported in August 1981 by the release of IAS No. 14, *Reporting Financial Information by Segments,* by the International Accounting Standards Committee. It basically suggests the following disclosures for each reported industry and geographic segment: (a) sales or other operating revenues, distinguishing between revenue derived from customers outside the firm and revenue derived from other segments, (b) segment results, (c) segment assets employed, expressed either in monetary amounts or as percentages of the consolidated totals, and (d) the basis of intersegment pricing. The reportable segments are referred to as economically significant entities, defined as those subsidiaries whose levels of revenues, profits, assets, or employment are significant in the countries in which their major operations are conducted.

With regard to the European Economic Community, one of the provisions of the Fourth Directive requires turnover only to be analyzed by activity and geographic segment.

In Australia there is no requirement to disclose segment information except disclosure of the extent to which each corporation in a group contributes to consolidated profit or loss.

Segmental reporting is also recommended in the OECD guidelines for multinational corporations [13] and in the U.N. proposals for accounting and reporting by multinational corporations.[14]

PREDICTIVE ABILITY OF SEGMENTAL REPORTING

The predictive ability of segmental information has been examined in several studies. In the first study William R. Kinney, Jr., tested the relative predictive power of subentity earnings data for a sample of firms which have voluntarily reported sales and earnings data by subentity. He found that the predictions based on segment sales and earnings data and industry predictions were on the average more accurate than predictions based on models using consolidated performance data alone.[15]

In the second study Daniel W. Collins extended and updated the preliminary work of Kinney using data disclosed under the line-of-business report-

ing requirements initiated by the SEC.[16] The SEC had required, beginning December 31, 1970, that all registrants engaged in various segments report sales and profits before taxes and extraordinary items by product line in their annual 10-K report. The models used are shown in Exhibit 5.1. Collins's findings corroborated Kinney's earlier findings, suggesting that "SEC product line revenue and profit disclosures together with industry sales projections published in various government sources provide significantly more accurate estimates of future total-entity sales and earnings than the procedures that rely totally on consolidated data."[17]

The third study focused on the predictive ability of U.K. segment reports. C. R. Emmanuel and R. H. Pick confirmed in a U.K. setting the earlier findings that segmental disclosure of sales and profits data is useful in providing more accurate predictions of corporate earnings.[18] They also suggested more research with the predictive ability paradigm.

Future studies may prove rewarding in not only determining whether disclosure is worthwhile, but also what form it should take if the predictions are to become more accurate. Two contenders in this respect are segment reports presented in terms of an industrial/geographical segment matrix and the measurement of segment earnings in terms of contribution instead of profit before tax. This would allow national industrial growth forecasts to be accommodated in the segment-based models while the use of contribution would avoid the possibly significant distorting effects of transfer pricing and common cost allocations. Given the availability of data, the predictive ability criterion may prove more useful in gauging the most appropriate form which segmental disclosure should follow.[19]

Finally, P. Silhan provided no evidence that consistently supported the predictive superiority of either the "consolidated" or the "segmental" earnings data.[20] His study differed from the earlier research in two important aspects: (a) the earnings forecast models are based on the use of Box Jenkins time series analysis and (b) the use of a simulation approach permitting an examination of the effect of the number of segments on predictive accuracy.

Related studies examined the accuracy of published earnings forecasts in conjunction with segmental reporting. Both R. M. Barefield and E. Comiskey[21] and B. Baldwin[22] were able to show a relationship between the forecast accuracy and the presence of segmental reporting indicating that the availability of segmental data could improve the accuracy of analysts' earnings projections.

A positive evaluation of these results was stated as follows:

In summary, the studies addressing the accuracy of analysts' forecasts have utilized a variety of research techniques and have provided evidence that improved earnings predictions can accompany the disclosure of segmental data. Within the context of segmental reporting, improved accuracy of forecasts may be viewed as one of the

Exhibit 5.1
Mechanical Prediction Models

The mechanical prediction models examined by Collins [1976] are listed below. The four models which had been utilized in the earlier work of Kinney [1971] are marked with an asterisk (*).

Consolidated-Based Models

Model C_1: $E(X_{it}) = a_i + b_i X_{mt}$

(linear regression model)

Model C_2: $E(X_{it}) = X_{i,t-1}$

(strict martingale)

Model C_3: $E(X_{it}) = X_{i,t-1} + \frac{1}{n} \sum_{j=1}^{n} (X_{i,t-j} - X_{i,t-j-1})$

(submartingale)

Model C_4: $E(X_{it}) = \frac{1}{n} \sum_{j=1}^{n} X_{i,t-j}$

(pure mean reversion--no drift)

Model C_5: $E(X_{it}) = X_{i,t-1} - \frac{1}{n} \sum_{j=1}^{n} (X_{i,t-j} - X_{i,t-j-1})$

(moving average of a pure mean reverting process)

*Model C_6: $E(X_{it}) = \alpha X_{i,t-1} + (1-\alpha)\overline{X}_{i,t-2} + (\overline{X}_{i,t-1} - \overline{\overline{X}}_{i,t-1})$

(double exponential smoothing model)

*Model C_7: $E(X_{it}) = (1 + \Delta \hat{GNP}) \cdot X_{i,t-1}$

(GNP model)

where

$E(X_{it})$ = predicted (expected) value of the sales or earnings variable of firm i in period t.

X_{it} = actual value of the sales or earnings variable of firm i in period t.

X_{mt} = value of a market-wide index of the sales or earnings variable in period t.

Exhibit 5.1 *(continued)*

a_i, b_i = intercept and slope of the linear relationship betwen X_{it} and X_{mt} (estimated by a least-squares, time-series regression).

$\overline{X}_{i,t-j}$ = first-order exponentially smoothed average of the sales or earnings variable (smoothed through period t-j).

$\overline{\overline{X}}_{i,t-j}$ = second-order smoothed average of the sales or earnings variable (smoothed through period t-j). This number is determined by a smoothing of first-order averages.

α = smoothing constant ($0 < \alpha < 1$).

$\Delta \hat{GNP}$ = predicted change in GNP from period t-1 to period t.

<u>Segment-Based Models</u>

*Model S_1: $E(X_{it}) = \sum_k((1 + \hat{IS}_{kt}) \cdot s_{ik,t-1}) \cdot \hat{P}_{it}$

(segmental sales and consolidated profit margins)

*Model S_2: $E(X_{it}) = \sum_k((1 + \Delta\hat{IS}_{kt} \cdot s_{ik,t-1}) \cdot \hat{P}_{ikt})$

(segmental sales and segmental profit margins)

where

$E(X_{it})$ = predicted (expected) value of the sales or earnings variable of firm i in period t (as defined previously).

$\Delta\hat{IS}_{kt}$ = predicted percentage change in the sales of industry k from period t-1 to period t.

$s_{ik,t-1}$ = actual sales during period t-1 for the segment of firm i involved in industry k.

$\hat{P}_{it}$ = predicted consolidated profit margin of firm i in period t (derived from consolidated earnings data).

$\hat{P}_{ikt}$ = predicted profit margin during period t for the segment of firm i involved in industry k (derived from segmental earnings data).

Source: Rosanne M. Mohr, "The Segmental Reporting Issue: A Review of Empirical Research," *Journal of Accounting Literature* (Spring 1983), pp. 50-51. Reprinted with permission.

"benefits" implicit in the theoretical "fitness" result. But the earnings forecast studies have also provided some evidence with regard to another "fineness" comparison. Specifically, no predictive improvements beyond those associated with the availability of segmental sales were obtained when segmental earning amounts were added to the data set. Such a finding directs attention toward the desirability of testing for the decision effects of segmental earnings data in other contexts and assessing the costs of this added disclosure.[23]

USERS' PERCEPTIONS OF SEGMENTAL REPORTING

The early research investigated the "real world" perceptions of segment reporting and provided evidence showing users' and preparers' interest in the production and dissemination of segment sales and earnings data. Those studies relying mostly on survey data include Backer and McFarland,[24] Mautz,[25] and Cramer.[26] The other studies used controlled experiments to evaluate the impact of segmental disclosure on individual decision making. The first study was by J. C. Stallman.[27]

The second study was by Richard F. Ortman.[28] He asked financial analysts to assign a per share offering price to each diversified firm, one that included segmental data and one that did not. The firms were expected to go public in the immediate future. The results showed that with segmental data the value of each firm's stock was in accordance with the present value of its expected return as reflected by industry average P/E ratios, and without segmental data the reverse was experienced. He concluded as follows:

> The decrease in the variance with regard to the distributions of the per-share values of the diversified firms' stocks in this study may mean that segmental disclosure by all such firms could result in greater stability in the movement of the prices of these firms' stocks. The results of this study strongly suggest that diversified firms should include segmental data in their financial reports.[29]

This result could not, however, be taken as conclusive evidence of the impact of segmental reporting on users. As stated by Mohr:

> Ortman's selected industries (auto parts and office/computer equipment), and the radical changes in industry involvement that were revealed only in the segmental data, could have driven the observed results.[30]

MARKET PERCEPTIONS OF SEGMENTAL REPORTING

Various market-based studies examined the association between segmental reporting and mean returns on stocks. Twombly found no evidence of statistically significant differences between the mean return vector of the experimental portfolios (partitioned by segmental disclosure level and industry concentration) with the mean return vector of the control

portfolios (partitioned by industry concentration only).[31] He concluded that "the event of a firm's disclosure of both segment revenues and profits provided no unanticipated information to the capital market, whether the disclosures were conditional upon the market concentration or not."[32]

Because Twombly's study was limited to an examination of mean returns on stock of firms engaged in voluntary segmental reporting, Ajinka decided to conduct a comprehensive empirical evaluation of the proposition that "the SEC's LOB [line-of-business] earnings disclosure requirement . . . enabled market participants to reassess the risk-return characteristics of conglomeratge firms."[33] His results were, however, consistent with those reported by Twombly. A similar attempt by Horwitz and Kolodny provided similar evidence.[34] This evidence was, however, based on a portfolio, and the individual effects may be largely neutralized at the portfolio level. Other strategies were also tried. For example, Foster examined the association between residual returns and the good and bad "news" aspects of segmental disclosure in the insurance industry.[35] His findings indicated that return-assessments effects could be associated with the disclosure of a segmental data set. Similarly, R. F. Kochanek examined whether the predictive aspects of good versus poor quality segmental disclosure could influence the timing of market return assessments.[36] This evidence supported a relationship between return assessment, earnings prediction, and the disclosure of a segmental data set incorporating (at a minimum) segmental sales amounts.

Finally, Bimal K. Prodhan examined the impact of segmental geographic disclosure on the systematic risk profile of British multinational firms, showing an association between the two variables and finding that the onset of a geographic segmental disclosure is more likely to be abrupt than gradual.[37] Prodhan argued that his findings would provide some more evidential input to the debate on segmentation of the international capital market, known as the Grubel-Agmon controversy.[38] He makes the point as follows: "Since geographical information is associated with beta changes it can be said that the international capital markets are likely to be segmented, since an integrated international capital market share is unlikely to be a benefit from diversification across countries."[39]

Collins, however, tested the efficiency of the securities market and provided somewhat mixed evidence with respect to the assessment of segmental data on security returns.[40]

PUSH-DOWN ACCOUNTING

Nature of Push-Down Accounting

Push-down accounting has been defined as "the establishment of a new accounting and reporting basis for an entity in its separate financial

statements, based on a purchase transaction in the voting stock of the entity that results in a substantial change of ownership of the outstanding voting stock of the entity."[41]

The definition requires that the cost to the acquiring entity in a business combination accounted for by the purchase method be computed to the acquired entity. In other words, the valuation of the acquired entity's assets, liabilities, and stockholders' equity should be derived from the purchase transaction. The value paid for the stock by the investor is "pushed down" as the new basis for the net assets of the acquired firm.

Push-down accounting is certainly an ideal subject for definite pronouncements from the international standard-setting bodies. APB Opinion No. 16 does not address push-down accounting in the separate financial statements of acquired entities. It provides principles for the acquiring entity to assign values to the assets and liabilities of the acquired entity but does not address whether those new values should be reflected in the separate statements of the acquired entity. An authoritative book on auditing discusses the concept of the push-down theory as follows:

> The principle of recording asset values and goodwill in the accounts of the company to reflect the purchase of its stock by another entity or group of stockholders has been called the "push-down" theory. At present, the question of how far it should be carried is unanswered. . . . Until all of the ramifications of the push-down theory are fully explored, we would prefer to see its implementation limited to 100 percent (or nearly 100 percent—the pooling theory's 90 percent would be a good precedent) transactions.[42]

Some of the standard setters have attempted to provide some guidance for the implementation of push-down accounting. The SEC in Staff Accounting Bulletin (SAB) No. 54 expressed its views on push-down accounting, stating that push-down accounting should be required when the subsidiary is "substantially" wholly owned, with no publicly held debt or preferred stock, should be encouraged when the subsidiary has public debt or preferred stock that was outstanding when it became substantially wholly owned, and should not be required when there is an already existing large minority in the subsidiary. Another regulator, the Federal Home Loan Bank Board (FHLBB), which charters and supervises federal savings and loan associations and is empowered to establish policies and issue regulations for them relating to dividend rates, lending, and other aspects of operations, in its January 17, 1983, Memorandum R55, made push-down accounting acceptable provided at least 90% of the stock is acquired and is found in accordance with GAAP (generally accepted accounting principles) by the auditor.

The situation is not better in other countries. In Canada, for example, the CICA handbook does not provide definite guidance. Paragraph 3060.01

refers to the carrying value of fixed assets stating in part: "The writing up of fixed assets values should not occur in ordinary circumstances. It is recognized, however, that there may be instances where it is appropriate to reflect fixed assets at values that are different from historical costs, e.g., at appraised values assigned in a reorganization."

The decision of the Canadian preparer rests on whether a specific purchase can be defined as "ordinary circumstances"; otherwise a reevaluation of assets and liabilities is called for.

Historical Cost versus Push-Down Accounting

The differences between historical cost and push-down accounting can best be illustrated by a simple example. Let's suppose that an investor buys a firm in a leveraged buyout transaction, one in which a firm is acquired largely with borrowed funds. To secure the transaction the investor paid $5,000 and borrowed $10,000 to acquire 100% of the firm's outstanding stock. The estimated fair market value of the firm's property and equipment, found to be $8,000 by the appriaisers, was to be reduced to $7,000 for GAAP purposes to reflect the differences between market values and the tax basis.

Exhibit 5.2 shows the financial statements under both the historical cost and the push-down approach. Under the historical cost approach the balance sheet after acquisition presents a bleak financial position with a $7,000 deficit in the stockholders' equity account. However, under the push-down approach the balance sheet appears relatively stronger with a positive stockholders' equity account and a much stronger debt/equity ratio. In addition, the fixed assets under push-down accounting reflect the fair values paid for by the purchase of the stock.

Evaluation of Push-Down Accounting

The rationale for push-down accounting is that a new basis of accounting for the acquired firm would provide information that is more relevant to financial statement users. The substance of the transaction resulting from a total change of ownership is equivalent to the purchase of the net assets of the business and, therefore, the fair value paid for the purchase of the stock should be reflected in the balance sheet. In addition, symmetry in presentation is deemed necessary. First, separate financial statements of subsidiary companies should be based on the purchase price of the entity because that is the basis required in consolidated financial statements. Second, SFAS No. 14 requires that separate segmental information reflect the parent's cost basis for each segment. Although not every subsidiary is a segment, the symmetry condition calls for a similar presentation in the separate financial statement. "Issuing separate financial statements on a

Exhibit 5.2
Historical Cost versus Push-Down Accounting

	Historical Cost		Push-Down	
	Before Purchase	After Purchase	Push Down Entities	Purchase Taxes
Current Assets	$ 2,000	$ 2,000	--	$ 2,000
Fixed Assets	5,000	5,000	$ 2,000[1]	7,000
Goodwill			10,000[2]	10,000
Total Assets	$ 7,000	$ 7,000		$19,000
Current Debt	$ 1,500	$ 1,500	--	$ 1,500
Long-Term Debt	2,500	12,500	10,000[3]	12,500
Total Debt	$ 4,000	$ 14,000	10,000	$14,000
Common Stock	$ 2,000	$ 7,000	(2,000),[4] $5,000[5]	$ 5,000
Retained Earnings	1,000	1,000	(1,000)	--
	$ 3,000	$ 8,000	$ 2,000	$ 5,000
Treasury Stock	--	$(15,000)	--	--
Stockholders' Equity (Deficit)	$ 3,000	$ (7,000)	2,000	$ 5,000
Total	$ 7,000	$ 7,000		$19,000

[1]To adjust to tax basis value.
[2]Purchase accounting adjustments per APB Opinion No. 16 = ($15,000−$5,000).
[3]To increase the long-term debt by the amount of borrowing.
[4]To record purchase of outstanding shares.
[5]To record equity financing for acquisition.

basis other than push-down could result in the distribution of some conflicting financial information for the same segment or subsidiary."[43]

Opponents of the method would agree that push-down accounting is a current valuation method which violates the historical cost basis of accounting. It disregards the separate entity assumption, affects comparability, and may lead to violations of debt agreements. In addition,

there is no logical method of determining which stockholder transactions would qualify for a push down. In other words, what percentage of ownership is required for legitimizing a push down? Published examples seem to follow 100% change in ownership. The SEC staff bulletin requires push-down accounting when a subsidiary is "substantially" wholly owned. The SEC staff has interpreted "substantially" to mean 90% or more. The FHLBB memorandum called for at least a 90% change in ownership. Finally, the AICPA's task force members unanimously agreed on 51% change in ownership as being inappropriate. In fact, the AICPA's task force identified some strong arguments against push-down accounting:

- Transactions of an entity's stockholders are not transactions of the entity and should not affect the entity's accounting.
- A new basis of accounting would be detrimental to interests of holders of existing debt and nonvoting capital stock who depend on comparable financial statements for information about their investments and do not have access to other financial information. Push-down accounting would affect the ability of the entity to comply with debt covenants required by outstanding debt and would materially alter the relationships in the entity's financial statements. When minority owners and other investors are entitled to financial statements, those financial statements should be prepared based on transactions of that entity and not transactions of stockholders.
- FASB Statement No. 14 deals with reporting information on segments of a business and is irrelevant to push-down accounting.
- There is no logical way to establish limits for determining which owner's transactions should qualify for push-down accounting.[44]

The AICPA task force also raised pertinent questions about the desirability of push-down accounting in case of split-offs or spin-offs and concluded it was not desirable. There was, however, an agreement that if a new basis is established in a series of step transactions, it should be consistent with the parent's basis determined under the rules for the purchase method of accounting.

Other issues of importance were not raised by the task force. Examples include the following:

- If a company proposes to sell a number of subsidiaries (or a division), is it appropriate to use push-down accounting basis for presenting divisional statements that will be the subject of sale negotiations? Can this be considered in accordance with GAAP or an acceptable alternative disclosed basis of accounting?
- Where the purchase price on a corporation's acquisition is determined by future results, when is the appropriate time to establish the entity's fair market value—at the moment of acquisition or on determining the ultimate purchase price? Should historical values be used until the final purchase price is known?[45]

CARVE-OUT ACCOUNTING

Many multinational companies eager to raise huge amounts of cash have tended to sell off portions of subsidiaries, which became known as "carving out" subsidiaries. By doing so, they began tapping an uncommon source of financing—their equity in wholly owned subsidiaries. As stated by Schiff:

> The lure is particularly strong when the subsidiary is operating in one of the popular industries on Wall Street or is experiencing impressive growth. In such cases, the parent can command a significant premium per share over its investment, and therefore an attractive return. When deciding which subsidiary to sell, the natural choice is one operating in an industry whose stock is selling at high price-earnings ratios.[46]

To make the offerings attractive, some of these companies do not show the true cost of the unit. The true cost of the business is likely to be hidden because companies put subsidiary expenses on the books of the parent company. The bottom line for the parent is the same because its profits and losses include those of the subsidiaries. However, the subsidiaries' profits look better than they really are, which allows the parent company to sell the subsidiaries' stock at a much higher price than it is really worth. To stop this process and let the public know the true costs (and profits) of the subsidiaries, the SEC in 1983 issued Staff Accounting Bulletin (SAB) No. 55, "Allocation of Expenses to Subsidiaries, Divisions, and Lesser Business Components." The clear position was that the historical income statements of the subsidiary should reflect all of its costs of doing business, including those incurred by their parent company on their behalf. Examples of such expenses are

1. Officer and employer salaries
2. Rent or depreciation
3. Advertising
4. Accounting and legal services
5. Other selling, general, and administrative expenses
6. Interest and income tax expenses

In addition, SAB No. 55 requires that in those situations where expenses applicable to a subsidiary cannot be identified they must be allocated on some reasonable basis, with appropriate footnote disclosure of the allocation method and management's assertion that such method is reasonable. How effective was SAB No. 55? Schiff states:

> SAB 55 has resulted in more information disclosures of the relationship between a parent and its subsidiaries when they are issuing stock. The required disclosures put the subsidiary on a standalone basis and help the SEC carry out its mission to seek

full and fair disclosure. If the practice of carving out subsidiaries persists as a financing technique, the reporting requirements will also evolve and become more uniform. Negotiated agreements will probably increase in popularity as a "basis" for allocating costs because of their certainty and simplicity in resolving the issue of parent-provided services.[47]

NOTES

1. Robert K. Mautz, *Financial Reporting by Diversified Firms* (New York: Financial Executives Research Foundation, 1968).

2. J. Marschak and R. Radner, *Economic Theory of Teams* (New Haven, Conn.: Yale University Press, 1971), pp. 53-59.

3. Rosanne M. Mohr, "The Segmental Reporting Issue: A Review of Empirical Research," *Journal of Accounting Literature* (Spring 1983), pp. 41-42.

4. Morton Backer and Walter B. McFarland, *External Reporting for Segments of a Business* (New York: National Association of Accountants, 1968).

5. Mautz, *Financial Reporting by Diversified Firms.*

6. J. Cramer, "Income Reporting by Conglomerates," *Abacus* (August 1968), pp. 17-26.

7. S. J. Gray and Lee H. Radebaugh, "International Segment Disclosures by U.S. and U.K. Multinational Enterprises: A Descriptive Study," *Journal of Accounting Research* (Spring 1984), pp. 351-60.

8. Ibid., pp. 359-60.

9. S. J. Gray, "Segment Reporting and the EEC Multinationals," *Journal of Accounting Research* (Autumn 1978), pp. 242-53.

10. Ibid., pp. 252-53.

11. Sidney J. Gray, "Segmental or Disaggregated Financial Statements," in *Developments in Financial Reporting,* ed. Thomas A. Lee (London: Philip Allan, 1981), pp. 31-32.

12. Ibid., p. 33.

13. Organization for Economic Cooperation and Development, *International Investment and Multinational Enterprises* (Paris: OECD, 1979).

14. United Nations, *International Standards of Accounting and Reporting for Transnational Corporations* (New York: United Nations, 1977).

15. William R. Kinney, Jr., "Predicting Earnings: Entity vs. Subentity Data," *Journal of Accounting Research* 9 (Spring 1971), pp. 127-36.

16. Daniel W. Collins, "Predicting Earnings with Sub-Entity Data: Some Further Evidence," *Journal of Accounting Research* (Spring 1976), pp. 163-77.

17. Ibid., p. 175.

18. C. R. Emmanuel and R. H. Pick, "The Predictive Ability of UK Segment Reports," *Journal of Business Finance and Accounting* (Summer 1980), pp. 201-18.

19. Ibid., p. 216.

20. P. Silhan, "Simulated Mergers of Existent Autonomous Firms: A New Approach to Segmentation Research," *Journal of Accounting Research* 20 (Spring 1982), pp. 255-62.

21. R. M. Barefield and E. Comiskey, "Segmental Financial Disclosure by Diversified Firms and Security Prices: A Comment," *Accounting Review* 50 (October 1975), pp. 818-21.

22. B. Baldwin, "Line-of-Business Disclosure Requirements and Security Analyst Forecast Accuracy," D.B.A. diss., Arizona State University, 1979.

23. Mohr, "The Segmental Reporting Issue," pp. 31-52.

24. Backer and McFarland, *External Reporting for Segments of a Business.*

25. Mautz, *Financial Reporting by Diversified Companies.*

26. Cramer, "Income Reporting by Conglomerates," pp. 17-26.

27. J. C. Stallman, "Toward Experimental Criteria for Judging Disclosure Improvement," *Empirical Research in Accounting: Selected Studies, 1969,* supplement to *Journal of Accounting Research* 7 (1969), pp. 29-43.

28. Richard F. Ortman, "The Effects on Investment Analysis of Alternative Reporting Procedure for Diversified Firms," *Accounting Review* 50 (April 1975), pp. 298-304.

29. Ibid., p. 304.

30. Mohr, "The Segmental Reporting Issue."

31. J. Twombly, "An Empirical Analysis of the Information Content of Segment Data in Annual Reports from an FTC Perspective," in *Disclosure Criteria and Segment Reporting,* ed. R. Barefield and G. Holstrum (Gainesville: University Press of Florida, 1979), pp. 56-96.

32. Ibid., p. 77.

33. B. Ajinkya, "An Empirical Evaluation of Line-of-Business Reporting," *Journal of Accounting Research* 18 (Autumn 1980), pp. 343-61.

34. B. Horwitz and R. Kolodony, "Line of Business Reporting and Security Prices: An Analysis of an SEC Disclosure Rule," *Bell Journal of Economics* 8 (Spring 1977), pp. 234-49.

35. G. Foster, "Security Price Revaluation Implications of Sub-Earnings Disclosure," *Journal of Accounting Research* 13 (Autumn 1975), pp. 283-92.

36. R. F. Kochanek, "Segmental Financial Disclosure by Diversified Firms and Security Prices," *Accounting Review* 49 (April 1974), pp. 245-58.

37. Bimal K. Prodhan, "Geographical Segment Disclosure and Multinational Risk Profile," *Journal of Business Finance and Accounting* (Spring 1986), pp. 15-37.

38. J. Grubel, "Internationally Diversified Portfolios: Welfare Gains and Capital Flows," *American Economic Review* (1968), pp. 1299-1314; T. Agmon, "The Relationship among Equity Markets," *Journal of Finance* (May 1972), pp. 839-55.

39. Prodhan, "Geographical Segment Disclosure," p. 31.

40. D. Collins, "SEC Product-Line Reporting and Market Efficiency," *Journal of Financial Economics* (June 1975), pp. 125-64.

41. American Institute of Certified Public Accountants (AICPA), "Push-Down Accounting," Issues Paper by the Task Force on Consolidation Problems, Accounting Standards Division, New York, October 30, 1979.

42. P. L. Defliese, H. R. Jaenicke, J. D. Sullivan, and R. A. Gnospelius, *Montgomery's Auditing* (New York: John Wiley & Sons, 1984), p. 692.

43. AICPA, "Push-Down Accounting," p. 14.

44. Ibid., pp. 16-17.

45. James M. Sylph, "Push-Down Accounting: Is the U.S. Lead Worth Following?" *Canadian Chartered Accountant Magazine* (October 1985), p. 55.

46. Jonathan B. Schiff, "Carving Out Subsidiaries: Uncommon Financing and New Disclosure Requirements," *Corporate Accounting* (Spring 1986), p. 73.

47. Ibid., p. 75.

SELECTED BIBLIOGRAPHY

Ajinkya, B., "An Empirical Evaluation of Line-of-Business Reporting," *Journal of Accounting Research* 18 (Autumn 1980), pp. 343-61.

Arnold, J., W. W. Holder, and M. H. Mann, "International Reporting Aspects of Segment Disclosure," *International Journal of Accounting Education and Research* (Fall 1980), pp. 125-35.

Barefield, R., and E. Comiskey, "Segmental Financial Disclosure by Diversified Firms and Security Prices: A Comment," *Accounting Review* 50 (October 1975), pp. 818-21.

Bavishi, V. B., and H. E. Wyman, "Foreign Operations Disclosures by U.S.-Based Multinational Corporations: Are They Adequate?" *International Journal of Accounting Education and Research* (Fall 1980), pp. 153-68.

Collins, Daniel W., "Predicting Earnings with Sub-Entity Data: Some Further Evidence," *Journal of Accounting Research* (Spring 1976), pp. 163-77.

______, "SEC Product-Line Reporting and Market Efficiency," *Journal of Financial Economics* (June 1975), pp. 125-64.

Collins, D., and R. Simonds, "SEC Line-of-Business Disclosure and Market Risk Adjustments," *Journal of Accounting Research* 17 (Autumn 1979), pp. 352-83.

Cunningham, Michael E., "Push Down Accounting: Pros and Cons," *Journal of Accountancy* (June 1984), pp. 72-77.

Dascher, P., and R. Copeland, "Some Further Evidence on 'Criteria for Judging Disclosure Improvement,'" *Journal of Accounting Research* 9 (Spring 1971), pp. 32-39.

Emmanuel, C. R., and S. J. Gray, "Corporate Diversification and Segmental Disclosure Requirements in the USA," *Journal of Business Finance and Accounting* (Winter 1977), pp. 407-18.

Foster, G., "Security Price Revaluation Implications of Sub-Earnings Disclosure," *Journal of Accounting Research* 13 (Autumn 1975), pp. 283-92.

Gray, S. J., "Segment Reporting and the EEC Multinationals," *Journal of Accounting Research* (Autumn 1978), pp. 242-53.

Gray, S. J., and Lee H. Radebaugh, "International Segment Disclosures by U.S. and U.K. Multinational Enterprises: A Descriptive Study," *Journal of Accounting Research* (Spring 1984), pp. 351-60.

Holley, Charles L., Edward C. Spede, and Michael C. Chester, Jr., "The Push-Down Accounting Controversy," *Management Accounting* (January 1987), pp. 39-42.

Horwitz, B., and R. Kolodny, "Line of Business Reporting and Security Prices: An Analysis of an SEC Disclosure Rule," *Bell Journal of Economics* 8 (Spring 1977), pp. 234-49.

Kinney, William R., Jr., "Covariability of Segment Earnings and Multisegment Company Returns," *Accounting Review* 47 (April 1972), pp. 339-45.

______, "Predicting Earnings: Entity vs. Subentity Data," *Journal of Accounting Research* 9 (Spring 1971), pp. 127-36.

Kochanek, R. F., "Segmental Financial Disclosure by Diversified Firms and Security Prices," *Accounting Review* 49 (April 1974), pp. 245-58.

Ortman, Richard F., "The Effects of Investment Analysis of Alternative Reporting

Procedures for Diversified Firms," *Accounting Review* 50 (April 1975), pp. 298-304.

Prodhan, Bimal K., "Georgraphical Segment Disclosure and Multinational Risk Profile," *Journal of Business Finance and Accounting* (Spring 1986), pp. 15-37.

Ronen, J., and J. Linat, "Incentives for Segment Reporting," *Journal of Accounting Research* 19, no. 2 (Autumn 1981), pp. 459-81.

Schiff, Jonathan B., "Carving Out Subsidiaries: Uncommon Financing and New Disclosure Requirements," *Corporate Accounting* (Spring 1986), pp. 73-75.

Silhan, P., "Simulated Mergers of Existent Autonomous Firms: A New Approach to Segmentation Research," *Journal of Accounting Research* 20 (Spring 1982), pp. 255-62.

Stallman, J. C., "Toward Experimental Criteria for Judging Disclosure Improvement," *Empirical Research in Accounting: Selected Studies, 1969,* supplement to *Journal of Accounting Research* 7 (1969), pp. 29-43.

Sylph, James M., "Push-Down Accounting: Is the U.S. Lead Worth Following?" *Canadian Chartered Accountant Magazine* (October 1985), pp. 52-55.

Appendix 5.A

Segmental Reporting: Amoco Corporation, *Annual Report 1985*

Supplemental Information

Quarterly Results and Stock Market Data

	1985				1984			
millions of dollars, except per-share amounts	Fourth Quarter	Third Quarter	Second Quarter	First Quarter	Fourth Quarter	Third Quarter	Second Quarter	First Quarter
Revenues	**$7,395**	**$7,177**	**$7,292**	**$7,009**	$6,985	$7,071	$7,426	$7,526
Net income	**$ 390**	**$ 490**	**$ 600**	**$ 473**	$ 465	$ 600	$ 524	$ 594
Net income per share	**$ 1.51**	**$ 1.87**	**$ 2.28**	**$ 1.76**	$ 1.72	$ 2.14	$ 1.81	$ 2.03
Cash dividends per share	**$ .825**	**$ .825**	**$ .825**	**$ .825**	$ .75	$ .75	$ .75	$ .75
Common stock price range*								
High	**$ 70¼**	**$ 66⅝**	**$ 68¾**	**$ 63¾**	$ 60⅜	$ 60⅝	$ 59½	$ 56
Low	**$ 59½**	**$ 61⅞**	**$ 58¾**	**$ 50¼**	$ 51¼	$ 53¼	$ 53½	$ 48⅛

**The common stock price range is that on the New York Stock Exchange. Amoco's common stock is also traded on the Midwest, Pacific, Toronto, and four Swiss stock exchanges.*

From Amoco Corporation, *Annual Report 1985* (1986), pp. 44-51. Reprinted with permission.

Supplemental Information *(continued)*

Oil and Gas Exploration and Production Activities

The supplemental information about oil and gas exploration and production activities is reported in compliance with FASB Statement No. 69, Disclosures about Oil and Gas Producing Activities.

Results of Operations for Oil and Gas Producing Activities

millions of dollars	1985 United States	1985 Canada	1985 Europe	1985 Other Foreign	1985 World-wide	1984 United States	1984 Canada	1984 Europe	1984 Other Foreign	1984 World-wide	1983 United States	1983 Canada	1983 Europe	1983 Other Foreign	1983 World-wide
Oil and gas production revenues															
From consolidated subsidiaries	**$2,505**	**$284**	**$123**	**$2,658**	**$ 5,570**	$2,407	$ 54	$250	$2,791	$ 5,502	$2,315	$ 55	$203	$2,388	$4,961
From unaffiliated entities	**2,930**	**376**	**446**	**377**	**4,129**	3,536	625	306	424	4,891	3,343	590	201	358	4,492
Other revenues	**298**	**77**	**6**	**111**	**492**	179	48	23	134	384	236	74	17	104	431
Total revenues	**5,733**	**737**	**575**	**3,146**	**10,191**	6,122	727	579	3,349	10,777	5,894	719	421	2,850	9,884
Production costs															
Taxes other than income	**862**	**88**	**(17)**	**605**	**1,538**	1,005	102	82	801	1,990	1,195	95	48	725	2,063
Other production costs	**1,110**	**122**	**145**	**342**	**1,719**	1,100	110	61	378	1,649	1,085	103	70	358	1,616
Exploration expenses	**875**	**72**	**90**	**388**	**1,425**	842	62	76	306	1,286	800	62	92	202	1,156
Depreciation, depletion, and amortization expense	**964**	**52**	**123**	**330**	**1,469**	927	112	114	338	1,491	805	61	73	250	1,189
Other related costs	**292**	**21**	**54**	**200**	**567**	244	21	(7)	232	490	254	24	5	188	471
Total costs	**4,103**	**355**	**395**	**1,865**	**6,718**	4,118	407	326	2,055	6,906	4,139	345	288	1,723	6,495
Operating profit	**1,630**	**382**	**180**	**1,281**	**3,473**	2,004	320	253	1,294	3,871	1,755	374	133	1,127	3,389
Income tax expense	**716**	**235**	**93**	**732**	**1,776**	857	216	59	665	1,797	737	229	59	541	1,566
Results of operations	**$ 914**	**$147**	**$ 87**	**$ 549**	**$ 1,697**	$1,147	$104	$194	$ 629	$ 2,074	$1,018	$145	$ 74	$ 586	$1,823

Oil and gas production revenues reflect the market prices of net production sold or transferred, with appropriate adjustments for royalties, net profits interest, and other contractual provisions. Taxes other than income include the U.S. crude oil excise tax, production and severance taxes, and property taxes. Other production costs are lifting costs incurred to operate and maintain productive wells and related equipment, including such costs as operating labor, repairs and maintenance, materials, supplies, and fuel consumed. Also included are purchases of natural gas and other operating costs of natural gas liquids plants since the corporation includes the operations of these plants in the exploration and production segment. Production costs include administrative expenses and depreciation applicable to support equipment associated with production activities.

Exploration expenses include the costs of geological and geophysical activity, carrying and retaining undeveloped properties, and drilling exploratory wells determined to be non-productive. Depreciation, depletion, and amortization expense relates to capitalized costs incurred in acquisition, exploration, and development activities and does not include depreciation applicable to support equipment. Income taxes are generally assigned to the operations that give rise to the tax effects. Results of operations do not include interest expense and general corporate amounts nor their associated tax effects; accordingly, the amounts differ from net income reported for the exploration and production segment on page 36.

Average Sales Prices and Production Costs Per Unit of Oil and Gas Produced

	1985	1984	1983	1982	1981
Product revenues					
Crude oil and natural gas liquids (dollars per barrel)					
United States—crude oil-gross	**$26.49**	$28.31	$28.60	$31.37	$35.81
-net of excise tax	**$22.85**	$23.64	$22.09	$22.65	$23.45
—natural gas liquids	**$15.58**	$16.89	$19.38	$19.28	$20.27
Canada —crude oil	**$26.37**	$26.46	$26.45	$21.07	$15.76
—natural gas liquids	**$15.94**	$16.07	$19.53	$14.88	$14.10
Europe	**$27.28**	$29.26	$29.16	$31.67	$35.07
Other Foreign	**$22.84**	$24.22	$23.69	$25.31	$27.70
Natural gas (dollars per mcf)					
United States	**$ 2.76**	$ 2.93	$ 2.67	$ 2.60	$ 2.15
Canada	**$ 2.04**	$ 2.36	$ 2.36	$ 2.32	$ 2.23
Europe	**$ 1.50**	$ 1.47	$ 1.31	$ 1.29	$ 1.22
Other Foreign	**$ .72**	$ .80	$ .65	$ .69	$ .67
Production costs					
(dollars per equivalent barrel) (1)					
United States (2)	**$ 7.48**	$ 7.81	$ 8.79	$ 9.34	$10.27
Canada	**$ 5.76**	$ 5.99	$ 5.95	$ 6.25	$ 5.02
Europe	**$ 3.74**	$ 4.54	$ 4.24	$ 2.90	$ 3.18
Other Foreign	**$ 6.14**	$ 7.82	$ 8.22	$ 8.94	$10.35

(1) Production costs are shown on a dollar-per-barrel basis after converting natural gas into equivalent barrel units. Natural gas was converted on the basis of approximate relative energy content.

(2) Includes the crude oil excise tax which on an equivalent barrel basis averaged $1.70 in 1985, $2.19 in 1984, $3.11 in 1983, $4.05 in 1982, and $5.49 in 1981.

Supplemental Information *(continued)*

Oil and Gas Exploration and Production Activities *(continued)*

Capitalized Costs

The following table summarizes capitalized costs for oil and gas exploration and production activities, and the related accumulated depreciation, depletion, and amortization.

millions of dollars	United States	Canada	Europe	Other Foreign	World-wide
December 31, 1985					
Unproved properties					
Gross assets	**$ 2,215**	**$ 124**	**$ 96**	**$ 94**	**$ 2,529**
Accumulated amortization	**570**	**41**	**–**	**–**	**611**
Net assets	**$ 1,645**	**$ 83**	**$ 96**	**$ 94**	**$ 1,918**
Proved properties					
Gross assets	**$12,961**	**$1,290**	**$1,353**	**$3,775**	**$19,379**
Accumulated depreciation, depletion, etc.	**5,881**	**492**	**427**	**2,166**	**8,966**
Net assets	**$ 7,080**	**$ 798**	**$ 926**	**$1,609**	**$10,413**
Support equipment and facilities					
Gross assets	**$ 417**	**$ 34**	**$ 81**	**$ 299**	**$ 831**
Accumulated depreciation	**129**	**14**	**25**	**105**	**273**
Net assets	**$ 288**	**$ 20**	**$ 56**	**$ 194**	**$ 558**
December 31, 1984					
Unproved properties					
Gross assets	$ 2,141	$ 119	$ 76	$ 89	$ 2,425
Accumulated amortization	399	55	–	–	454
Net assets	$ 1,742	$ 64	$ 76	$ 89	$ 1,971
Proved properties					
Gross assets	$ 11,193	$ 1,249	$ 1,271	$ 3,305	$ 17,018
Accumulated depreciation, depletion, etc.	5,420	471	325	1,851	8,067
Net assets	$ 5,773	$ 778	$ 946	$ 1,454	$ 8,951
Support equipment and facilities					
Gross assets	$ 476	$ 33	$ 71	$ 248	$ 828
Accumulated depreciation	148	13	16	87	264
Net assets	$ 328	$ 20	$ 55	$ 161	$ 564

Standardized Measure of Discounted Future Net Cash Flows Relating to Proved Oil and Gas Reserves

The standardized measure of discounted future net cash flows relating to proved oil and gas reserves is prescribed by FASB Statement No. 69. The statement requires measurement of future net cash flows through assignment of a monetary value to proved reserve quantities and changes therein using a standardized formula. The amounts shown are based on prices, costs, and tax rates at the end of each period and a 10 percent annual discount factor. Because the calculation assumes static economic and political conditions and requires extensive judgment in estimating the timing of production, the resultant future net cash flows are not necessarily indicative of the fair market value of estimated proved reserves, but provide a reference point that may assist the user in projecting future cash flows. It should also be noted that subsequent to December 31, 1985, there has been a marked decrease in worldwide crude oil prices. As a result, currently effective crude prices are substantially lower than the year-end 1985 prices inherent in the 1985 data reported in the following schedules. Average crude oil prices used in calculating future cash inflows were $26.52 for the United States, $26.56 for Canada, $25.93 for Europe, and $23.66 for Other Foreign.

Summarized below is the standardized measure of discounted future net cash flows relating to proved oil and gas reserves at December 31, 1985 and 1984.

millions of dollars	United States	Canada	Europe	Other Foreign	World-wide
December 31, 1985					
Future cash inflows	**$71,837**	**$10,648**	**$6,289**	**$15,727**	**$104,501**
Future development and production costs	**24,568**	**2,698**	**3,005**	**6,678**	**36,949**
Future income taxes	**20,425**	**3,961**	**1,590**	**3,492**	**29,468**
Future net cash flows	**26,844**	**3,989**	**1,694**	**5,557**	**38,084**
Ten percent annual discount	**14,744**	**2,086**	**494**	**1,657**	**18,981**
Discounted net cash flows	**$12,100**	**$ 1,903**	**$1,200**	**$ 3,900**	**$ 19,103**
December 31, 1984					
Future cash inflows	$ 73,670	$ 11,087	$ 6,932	$ 14,359	$ 106,048
Future development and production costs	25,645	4,518	3,500	6,328	39,991
Future income taxes	20,934	4,288	1,638	3,178	30,038
Future net cash flows	27,091	2,281	1,794	4,853	36,019
Ten percent annual discount	14,815	1,210	532	1,375	17,932
Discounted net cash flows	$ 12,276	$ 1,071	$ 1,262	$ 3,478	$ 18,087

Future cash inflows are computed by applying the year-end prices of oil and gas to proved reserve quantities as reported in the table on page 47. Future price changes are considered only to the extent provided by contractual arrangements. Future development and production costs are estimated expenditures to develop and produce the proved reserves based on year-end costs and assuming continuation of existing economic conditions. Future income taxes are calculated by applying year-end statutory tax rates to future pre-tax net cash flows from proved oil and gas reserves less recovery of the tax basis of proved properties, and adjustments for permanent differences.

Statement of Changes in Standardized Measure of Discounted Future Net Cash Flows

The following table details the changes in the standardized measure of discounted future net cash flows for the three years ended December 31, 1985.

millions of dollars	1985	1984	1983
Balance at January 1	**$18,087**	$17,830	$18,665
Changes resulting from:			
Sales and transfers of oil and gas produced, net of production costs	**(6,442)**	(6,754)	(5,774)
Net changes in prices, and development and production costs	**(1,252)**	(414)	(3,240)
Current year expenditures for development	**1,815**	1,314	1,106
Extensions, discoveries, and improved recovery, less related costs	**1,961**	1,856	1,158
Purchases/(sales) of reserves in place	**504**	43	(74)
Revisions of previous quantity estimates	**2,189**	601	2,075
Accretion of discount	**2,877**	2,905	3,011
Net change in income taxes	**137**	(319)	1,096
Other	**(773)**	1,025	(193)
Balance at December 31	**$19,103**	$18,087	$17,830

Estimated Proved Reserves

Net proved reserves of crude oil (including condensate), natural gas liquids (NGL), and natural gas at the beginning and end of 1983, 1984, and 1985, with the detail of changes during those years, are presented below. Reported quantities include reserves in which the corporation holds an economic interest under production-sharing and other types of operating agreements with foreign governments. The estimates were prepared by corporation engineers and are based on current technology and economic conditions. The corporation considers such estimates to be reasonable and consistent with current knowledge of the characteristics and extent of proved production. The estimates include only those amounts considered to be proved reserves and do not include additional amounts that may result from extensions of currently proved areas, or amounts that may result from new discoveries in the future, or from application of secondary or tertiary recovery processes not yet determined to be commercial. Proved developed reserves are those reserves that are expected to be recovered through existing wells with existing equipment and operating methods.

Crude Oil and NGL in millions of barrels; Gas in billions of cubic feet	United States			Canada			Europe			Other Foreign		Worldwide		
	Crude Oil	NGL	Gas	Crude Oil	NGL	Gas	Crude Oil	NGL	Gas	Crude Oil and NGL	Gas	Crude Oil	NGL	Gas
Proved reserves														
December 31,1982	1,425	235	9,009	167	36	2,333	182	22	1,452	573	2,264	2,344	296	15,058
Revisions of previous estimates	91	15	687	2	—	1	(1)	—	68	73	(44)	165	15	712
Improved recovery applications	56	12	23	1	—	1	—	—	—	1	—	58	12	24
Extensions, discoveries, and other additions	21	1	360	6	1	20	1	—	16	2	—	30	2	396
Sales of reserves in place	(1)	—	(51)	(1)	—	(4)	—	—	—	—	—	(2)	—	(55)
Production	(127)	(22)	(637)	(13)	(4)	(89)	(9)	—	(110)	(113)	(109)	(261)	(27)	(945)
December 31,1983	1,465	241	9,391	162	33	2,262	173	22	1,426	536	2,111	2,334	298	15,190
Revisions of previous estimates	45	13	599	5	3	(90)	(18)	(2)	109	87	(54)	111	22	564
Improved recovery applications	72	1	20	3	—	2	—	—	—	3	—	77	2	22
Extensions, discoveries, and other additions	36	4	363	16	1	61	4	—	—	15	17	71	5	441
Purchases of reserves in place	12	—	41	—	—	—	—	—	—	—	—	12	—	41
Sales of reserves in place	(3)	—	(36)	(1)	—	(1)	—	—	—	—	—	(4)	—	(37)
Production	(126)	(23)	(694)	(16)	(4)	(89)	(13)	(1)	(101)	(127)	(135)	(282)	(28)	(1,019)
December 31,1984	1,501	236	9,684	169	33	2,145	146	19	1,434	514	1,939	2,319	299	15,202
Revisions of previous estimates	**56**	**8**	**566**	**3**	—	**(14)**	**3**	—	**30**	**166**	**(95)**	**223**	**13**	**487**
Improved recovery applications	**39**	**5**	**16**	**15**	**1**	**3**	—	—	—	**14**	—	**68**	**6**	**19**
Extensions, discoveries, and other additions	**25**	**(1)**	**259**	**21**	—	**148**	**4**	—	—	**42**	—	**92**	**(1)**	**407**
Purchases of reserves in place	**54**	**5**	**68**	—	—	—	—	—	—	—	—	**54**	**5**	**68**
Sales of reserves in place	**(2)**	—	**(17)**	—	—	—	—	—	—	—	—	**(2)**	—	**(17)**
Production	**(122)**	**(22)**	**(674)**	**(15)**	**(4)**	**(97)**	**(14)**	**(1)**	**(108)**	**(129)**	**(150)**	**(280)**	**(27)**	**(1,029)**
December 31,1985	**1,551**	**231**	**9,902**	**193**	**30**	**2,185**	**139**	**18**	**1,356**	**607**	**1,694**	**2,474**	**295**	**15,137**
Proved developed reserves														
December 31,1982	1,316	205	8,148	150	32	1,972	29	3	1,137	439	1,087	1,931	243	12,344
December 31,1983	1,361	216	8,788	144	29	1,902	59	8	1,273	446	1,279	2,007	256	13,242
December 31,1984	1,431	215	9,228	159	30	1,808	70	10	1,312	423	1,380	2,079	259	13,728
December 31,1985	**1,482**	**208**	**9,077**	**163**	**27**	**1,881**	**99**	**15**	**1,280**	**512**	**1,330**	**2,253**	**253**	**13,568**

Costs Incurred

Property acquisition costs include costs incurred to purchase, lease or otherwise acquire oil and gas properties. Exploration costs include the costs of geological and geophysical activity, carrying and retaining undeveloped properties, and drilling and equipping exploratory wells. Development costs include the costs of drilling and equipping development wells, CO_2 and certain other injected materials for enhanced recovery projects, and facilities to extract, treat, and gather and store oil and gas. Exploration and development costs include administrative expenses and depreciation applicable to support equipment associated with these activities. Costs incurred summarized in the table to the right include both amounts expensed and capitalized.

millions of dollars	United States	Canada	Europe	Other Foreign	Worldwide
Year 1985					
Property acquisition*	**$ 928**	**$ 26**	**$ 37**	**$ 26**	**$1,017**
Exploration	**1,359**	**90**	**124**	**460**	**2,033**
Development	**1,120**	**125**	**96**	**474**	**1,815**
	$3,407	**$241**	**$257**	**$960**	**$4,865**
Year 1984					
Property acquisition	$ 718	$ 14	$ —	$ 5	$ 737
Exploration	1,299	76	73	557	2,005
Development	810	99	123	282	1,314
	$ 2,827	$ 189	$ 196	$ 844	$ 4,056
Year 1983					
Property acquisition	$ 781	$ 8	$ —	$ —	$ 789
Exploration	1,047	70	143	346	1,606
Development	644	80	92	290	1,106
	$ 2,472	$ 158	$ 235	$ 636	$ 3,501

**Includes $746 million of producing property acquisitions, principally in the United States.*

Supplemental Information *(continued)*

Impact of Inflation

The financial statements and related data presented on pages 33 to 35 reflect the corporation's financial position and results of operations in terms of historical cost accounting. The amounts reported are based on actual dollars received or spent without regard to changes over time in purchasing power of the dollar. Continued inflation over a period of years has led to a growing concern that conventional historical cost based financial statements do not adequately measure the impact of inflation on a company's operations. FASB Statement No. 33, as amended by FASB Statement No. 82, prescribes the reporting of historical cost financial statements adjusted for the effects of specific changes in prices of individual types of assets (current costs).

The following statement of net income adjusted for changing prices compares operating results as reported in the historical cost financial statements with operating results measured under the current cost method. Net income in 1985 declined to $1,455 million or $5.53 per share, when measured on a current cost basis. Substantially all of the impact arises from the higher depreciation, depletion, and amortization expense that would be incurred had the investment in property, plant, and equipment been stated in current cost dollars.

In determining net income under the current cost method, only the cost of products sold and depreciation, depletion, and amortization expense are adjusted to reflect changes in specific prices. Revenues and other costs and expenses are considered to reflect the average price level for the period and, consequently, are not adjusted. The current costs of inventory and property, plant, and equipment are based on estimates derived generally from appropriate external indices.

Also shown in the statement of net income adjusted for changing prices is the effect of general inflation on the corporation's net holding of monetary assets and liabilities. Since monetary liabilities exceeded monetary assets in 1985, the corporation experienced a gain in purchasing power.

In reviewing the data presented herein, it should be kept in mind that development of inflation-adjusted information involves the use of many assumptions and estimates. Therefore, the information presented should be viewed in that context and not as a precise indication of the effects of inflation on the corporation.

The five-year table shown below presents a comparison of selected historical cost financial data with the same data adjusted for the effects of general inflation or specific price increases (current costs) stated in average 1985 dollars.

Statement of Net Income Adjusted for Changing Prices Average 1985 Dollars

millions of dollars	For Year Ended December 31, 1985 As Reported (Historical Cost)	As Adjusted for Changing Prices (Current Costs)
Total revenues	**$28,873**	**$28,873**
Purchases and operating expenses	**16,308**	**16,340**
Exploration expenses	**1,425**	**1,425**
Selling and administrative expenses	**1,390**	**1,390**
Taxes other than income taxes	**3,448**	**3,448**
Depreciation, depletion, and amortization	**2,059**	**2,525**
Interest expense	**432**	**432**
Total costs and expenses	**25,062**	**25,560**
Income before income taxes	**3,811**	**3,313**
Income taxes	**1,858**	**1,858**
Net income	**$ 1,953**	**$ 1,455**
Unrealized gain from decline in purchasing power of net amounts owed		**$ 302**
Increase in specific prices (current cost) of inventories and property, plant, and equipment held during the year*		**$ 7**
Increase due to general inflation		**949**
Difference between increase in specific prices and the increase due to general inflation		**$ (942)**

**At December 31, 1985, current cost of inventory was $3,250 and current cost of property, plant, and equipment (net) was $23,172.*

Five-Year Comparison of Selected Financial Information Adjusted for Effects of Changing Prices Stated in Average 1985 Dollars

millions of dollars, except as noted	1985	1984	1983	1982	1981
Total revenues					
—as reported	**$28,873**	$29,008	$29,494	$29,783	$31,729
—adjusted for general inflation	**$28,873**	$30,043	$31,846	$33,193	$37,530
Net income from operations					
—as reported	**$ 1,953**	$ 2,183	$ 1,868	$ 1,826	$ 1,922
—current costs	**$ 1,455**	$ 1,672	$ 1,261	$ 1,096	$ 1,129
Net income from operations per share					
—as reported	**$ 7.42**	$ 7.70	$ 6.39	$ 6.25	$ 6.56
—current costs	**$ 5.53**	$ 5.90	$ 4.31	$ 3.75	$ 3.86
Cash dividends per share					
—as reported	**$ 3.30**	$ 3.00	$ 2.80	$ 2.80	$ 2.60
—adjusted for general inflation	**$ 3.30**	$ 3.11	$ 3.02	$ 3.12	$ 3.08
Net assets at year-end					
—as reported	**$11,588**	$12,524	$12,440	$11,426	$10,665
—current costs	**$18,648**	$21,049	$22,777	$23,532	$25,222
Difference between increase in specific prices and the increase due to general inflation	**$ (942)**	$ (1,075)	$ (848)	$ (912)	$ 89
Unrealized gain from decline in purchasing power of net amounts owed	**$ 302**	$ 276	$ 274	$ 288	$ 587
Percentage of net income to average shareholders' equity					
—as reported	**16.2%**	17.5%	15.7%	16.5%	19.2%
—current costs	**7.5%**	7.6%	5.4%	4.5%	4.5%
Market price per share at year-end					
—as reported	**$ 61⅞**	$ 52⅞	$ 50⅝	$ 39¾	$ 52
—adjusted for general inflation	**$ 61⅞**	$ 54¾	$ 54⅝	$ 44¼	$ 61½
Average Consumer Price Index (1967 = 100)	**322.2**	311.1	298.4	289.1	272.4

Five-Year Operating Summary

Amoco Corporation and Subsidiaries

	1985	1984	1983	1982	1981
Exploration and Production Operations					
Oil and Gas					
Net production of crude oil and natural gas liquids (thousands of barrels per day)					
United States —crude oil	**338**	345	342	348	368
—natural gas liquids	**63**	64	61	61	69
Canada —crude oil	**42**	41	38	38	37
—natural gas liquids	**10**	12	11	10	11
Europe	**42**	39	24	11	11
Other Foreign	**352**	348	310	298	298
Total	**847**	849	786	766	794
Net production of natural gas (millions of cubic feet per day)					
United States	**1,869**	1,900	1,785	1,986	2,280
Canada	**279**	252	246	246	250
Europe	**299**	275	300	284	316
Other Foreign	**411**	370	299	273	250
Total	**2,858**	2,797	2,630	2,789	3,096
Net proved reserves at year-end					
Crude oil and natural gas liquids (millions of barrels)					
United States —crude oil	**1,551**	1,501	1,465	1,425	1,429
—natural gas liquids	**231**	236	241	235	245
Canada —crude oil	**193**	169	162	167	171
—natural gas liquids	**30**	33	33	36	38
Europe	**157**	165	195	204	222
Other Foreign	**607**	514	536	573	573
Total	**2,769**	2,618	2,632	2,640	2,678
Natural gas (billions of cubic feet)					
United States	**9,902**	9,684	9,391	9,009	8,857
Canada	**2,185**	2,145	2,262	2,333	2,244
Europe	**1,356**	1,434	1,426	1,452	1,557
Other Foreign	**1,694**	1,939	2,111	2,264	2,275
Total	**15,137**	15,202	15,190	15,058	14,933
Net wells drilled					
Exploratory					
Productive —United States	**282**	199	200	202	245
—Canada	**31**	26	17	30	39
—Europe	**1**	*	*	*	*
—Other Foreign	**3**	3	1	6	1
Dry —United States	**159**	153	111	131	188
—Canada	**40**	31	21	26	34
—Europe	**9**	2	6	3	4
—Other Foreign	**28**	24	11	17	12
Total	**553**	438	367	415	523
Development					
Productive —United States	**609**	514	495	411	467
—Canada	**95**	33	39	6	8
—Europe	**8**	8	4	2	—
—Other Foreign	**31**	34	20	44	67
Dry —United States	**28**	33	34	24	29
—Canada	**2**	3	2	1	—
—Other Foreign	**3**	—	1	1	4
Total	**776**	625	595	489	575
Total net wells drilled	**1,329**	1,063	962	904	1,098
Net wells owned at year-end					
Oil	**17,691**	17,483	17,513	17,578	17,502
Gas	**6,997**	6,732	6,668	6,583	6,444
Total	**24,688**	24,215	24,181	24,161	23,946

**The corporation's total proportionate interest in wells drilled during the year was less than one.*

Five-Year Operating Summary *(continued)*

	1985	1984	1983	1982	1981
Exploration and Production Operations *(continued)*					
Oil and Gas *(continued)*					
Net proved properties at year-end (thousands of acres)					
United States	**2,859**	2,803	2,806	2,972	2,890
Canada	**963**	939	987	1,142	1,152
Europe	**28**	29	29	36	28
Other Foreign	**119**	127	126	139	130
Total	**3,969**	3,898	3,948	4,289	4,200
Net unproved properties at year-end (thousands of acres)					
United States	**19,380**	21,524	23,325	23,561	26,425
Canada	**3,073**	3,323	4,070	7,057	7,303
Europe	**3,990**	3,636	3,094	2,618	2,697
Other Foreign	**124,209**	134,658	82,763	117,716	49,522
Subtotal	**150,652**	163,141	113,252	150,952	85,947
Acreage held under reservations, permits, and options	**16,060**	6,738	17,193	19,162	20,480
Total	**166,712**	169,879	130,445	170,114	106,427
Carbon Dioxide					
Net production (millions of cubic feet per day)	**171**	33	—	—	—
Net proved reserves at year-end (billions of cubic feet)	**3,146**	1,983	1,927	1,374	—
Net wells owned at year-end	**258**	238	198	160	144
Net properties at year-end (thousands of acres)	**817**	792	798	796	799
Sulfur					
Production (thousands of long tons)					
United States	**341**	298	274	129	112
Canada	**386**	459	462	437	487
Total production	**727**	757	736	566	599
Recovered from refinery operations (thousands of long tons)	**249**	199	179	156	124
Refining, Marketing, and Transportation Operations					
Refined products sold—trade (thousands of barrels per day)					
United States					
Gasoline	**510**	481	469	477	474
Distillates	**267**	239	244	231	217
Other products	**134**	140	147	144	140
Subtotal	**911**	860	860	852	831
United Kingdom	**61**	52	54	50	50
Other	**47**	61	99	122	133
Total	**1,019**	973	1,013	1,024	1,014
Average selling price (cents per gallon)					
United States					
Gasoline	**87.8**	87.0	92.5	100.7	109.3
Distillates	**78.0**	82.6	82.4	94.3	102.8
Other products	**54.7**	59.1	57.4	55.5	60.5
Total	**80.1**	81.3	83.6	91.3	99.4
United Kingdom	**75.3**	76.8	81.8	88.0	95.6
Average cost of crude input (cents per gallon)					
United States	**64.7**	70.2	70.9	78.1	89.5
United Kingdom	**65.2**	69.3	70.5	79.8	88.8

Amoco Corporation and Subsidiaries

	1985	1984	1983	1982	1981
Refining, Marketing, and Transportation Operations *(continued)*					
Refinery input to crude units (thousands of barrels per day)					
United States	**839**	828	820	796	818
Foreign	**60**	69	113	134	133
Operable refinery capacity at year-end (thousands of barrels per day)					
United States	**967**	1,011	1,011	1,011	1,134
Foreign	**71**	71	113	213	214
Percent of refinery capacity operated					
United States	**86.7**	81.9	81.1	74.4	69.5
Foreign	**84.6**	74.9	73.2	62.9	63.8
Pipeline mileage owned at year-end	**15,149**	15,283	15,020	15,308	15,428
Marine vessel capacity at year-end (thousands of deadweight tons)	**1,692**	1,936	2,016	2,560	2,540
Chemicals Operations					
Trade revenues (millions of dollars)					
Chemicals —fiber and film intermediates	**$ 846**	$ 759	$ 750	$ 621	$ 823
—industrial chemicals and other	**683**	692	685	709	788
Polymers	**356**	309	283	252	263
Plastics —synthetic fabrics	**696**	661	559	439	449
—other plastics	**261**	280	267	270	270
Other products	**—**	56	350	425	458
Total sales	**2,842**	2,757	2,894	2,716	3,051
Other revenues	**63**	77	12	70	37
Total	**$2,905**	$2,834	$2,906	$2,786	$3,088
Price and volume indices (1980 = 100)					
Chemicals —price	**81**	91	93	98	111
—volume	**130**	111	99	84	96
Polymers —price	**87**	103	96	101	108
—volume	**160**	121	117	88	91
Plastics —price	**98**	101	96	102	107
—volume	**126**	130	121	106	108
Joint-Venture Minerals Activities*					
Proved ore reserves at year-end					
Ok Tedi, Papua New Guinea (31.2 percent interest)					
Copper (millions of tons)	**129.1**	128.1	124.6	124.6	132.3
Average grade (percent)	**0.78**	0.72	0.72	0.72	0.67
Gold (millions of tons)	**10.4**	15.1	11.3	11.3	11.3
Average grade (ounces per ton)	**0.07**	0.08	0.08	0.08	0.08
Detour Lake, Ontario, Canada (50 percent interest)					
Gold (millions of tons)	**4.9**	5.6	17.1	15.9	15.5
Average grade (ounces per ton)	**0.12**	0.13	0.12	0.12	0.11
Net gold production (thousands of ounces)					
Ok Tedi	**165**	24	—	—	—
Detour Lake	**39**	39	9	—	—
Total	**204**	63	9	—	—
Average market price					
Gold (dollars per ounce)	**$320.06**	$357.90	$387.92	—	—

**Accounted for by the equity method. Data shown represents the corporation's proportionate interest.*

6

CASH-FLOW ACCOUNTING

There has been a continuous call for cash accounting from individuals and/or organizations all over the world. More recently there have been signs that their long struggle has been fruitful as more empirical research and more pronouncements on the subject have been made. Therefore, this chapter will introduce the reader to the various aspects of the debate on the desirability of cash-flow accounting for financial reporting and disclosure.

NATURE OF CASH-FLOW ACCOUNTING

The Problems with Accrual Accounting

The call for cash-flow accounting does not originate solely from the academic world. A good example is the following statement in 1982 by a commissioner of the Securities and Exchange Commission in the United States:

> Over time, the accounting equation requires, of course, that accrual earnings equal cash earnings, but in the short term timing variations between accruals and cash flows may be quite significant; they may even make the crucial difference between continuing operations and bankruptcy. In other words, although accrual accounting, with its matching of revenues and expenses, may be important to the analysis of long term profitability, cash flow is vital to survival.[1]

The most serious interest in cash-flow accounting was created by the limitations of accrual accounting. The advocates of cash-flow accounting questioned the importance and efficiency of accrual accounting and

identified a shift to the cash-flow approach in security analysis.[2] The efficacy of the accrual system was severely questioned in general as well. A. L. Thomas stated explicitly that all allocations, which are the basis of accrual accounting, are arbitrary and incorrigible.[3]

To be precise about allocation, Thomas defined it as follows:

1. The assignment of costs, revenues, income, cash flows, or funds flows to individual inputs or groups of inputs to the firm, including assignment to individual periods of time, divisions of the firm, etc.
2. The division of any total into parts.
3. The assignment of costs to revenues, called matching.[4]

Thomas claimed that many of the allocations used in conventional accounting are arbitrary and theoretically unjustified, in that they are unable to meet the following criteria:

1. Additivity: The whole should equal the parts; the allocation should exhaust the total, dividing up whatever is: no more and no less.
2. Unambiguity: Once the allocation method has been specified, it should be impossible to divide the total into more than one set of parts.
3. Defensibility: Any choice among allocation methods should have a conclusive argument backing it, defending the methods against all possible alternatives.[5]

Thomas then concluded that no legitimate purpose for financial accounting that has been advanced to date is furthered by making allocations, urging that financial accounting allocations should cease.[6]

Amounts reported on income statements are allocations of input cost to the expenses of individual years, and most of what appears in the nonmonetary portions of the balance sheet are the cumulative result of allocation. Three kinds of conventional allocations are distinguished: (1) annual contribution, (2) input contribution, and (3) annual profit (annual rate of return). The matching allocation of individual input costs to individual years (allocation methods 1 and 2) can result in the amount assigned to any specified year varying anywhere between zero and the total cost itself. It is also easy to prove that the annual profit allocation (method 3) is ambiguous, because any such allocation requires making an assumption about the input's book rate of return during each year.

All these problems arise because revenues are joint outputs of all inputs. Conventional matching attempts to associate joint revenue with cost. Actually, both joint revenue and all kinds of financial allocation have an identical form. In each case the fallacies of allocation are also identical.

Finally, Thomas concluded that we should forswear "matching fantasies," stop allocating, and prepare allocation-free financial statements. He recommended three possible kinds of such allocation-free statements:

1. Current Exit Value Reporting
2. Current Entry Value Reporting
3. Net Quick Asset Reporting or Cash-Flow Accounting

The principles Thomas proposed for the preparation of allocation-free "cash-flow" financial (funds) statements are as follows:

1. The category of funds should be net quick assets, i.e., total cash, receivables, and any other current monetary assets less current monetary liabilities.
2. A statement of current activities (a combination of conventional income and fund statements) should be prepared. It would begin with a detailed calculation of funds from operations and would make whatever distinction between ordinary and extraordinary items was appropriate. This would be followed by a report of purchases of nonmonetary assets, less proceeds from nonoperating sales of such assets, leading to a figure for funds from operations less funds consequences of transactions in nonmonetary assets. The latter figure corresponds to conventional net income. Comparative funds statements would be disclosed.
3. The subtotal for funds from operations less funds consequence of transactions in nonmonetary assets would be followed by the dividend and other data that customarily appear on a funds statement.
4. The conventional balance sheet would be replaced by (a) a statement of monetary assets and liabilities, and (b) a statement of unamortized magnitudes of all nonmonetary assets presently in service.
5. There would be minor departures from conventional income statement and balance sheet reporting, consistent with the use of funds statements. For example, tax allocation would cease.
6. Insofar as possible, a rigorous orientation of inflow and outflow of net quick assets would be preserved throughout the reports; they would not be attempts to match or otherwise allocate.
7. Introduction of the new-style reports should require a lengthy transition period during which the old (accrual) reports continued to be prepared.

The Meaning of Cash-Flow Accounting

Thomas's call was heard because the Study Group established by the American Institute of Certified Public Accountants stated in its report published in 1973: "An objective of financial statements is to provide information useful to investors and creditors for predicting, comparing, and evaluating potential cash flow to them in terms of amount, timing, and related uncertainty."[7] Thomas A. Lee also identified three common needs of the users of accounting information:

1. Each group is concerned with how well the company has survived in the past and how well it is likely to survive in the future.

2. Each group is concerned with making and monitoring decisions. Each of these decisions has financial consequences, and suitable information is needed to aid the decision makers.
3. There are common features to be found, the main one being that each group is concerned with the most basic resource in business—cash.[8]

These needs were to be met by cash-flow accounting. Although there are various definitions of cash-flow accounting, the best definition needs to differentiate it from other forms of accounting, namely, (a) the cash basis of accounting, (b) the accrual basis of accounting, and (c) the allocation basis of accounting. Barry E. Hicks provides a good definition of each as follows:

- The cash basis of accounting means reflecting only transactions involving actual cash receipts and disbursement occurring in *a given period* with no attempt to record unpaid bills (or amounts) owed to or by the entity.
- The accrual basis of accounting means keeping records so that in addition to recording transactions resulting from the receipt and disbursements of cash, the firm also records the amount it owes others and others owe it.
- The cash-flow basis of accounting means recording not only the cash receipts and disbursements of the period (the cash basis of accounting), but also the future cash flows owed to or by the firm as a result of selling and transferring title to certain goods.
- The allocation basis of accounting not only does all that the cash-flow basis of accounting does, but it goes beyond and subjects these cash flows to an allocation process. The allocation basis of accounting means: (a) taking the "real" cash flows and dividing them into parts until the parts no longer represent "real" cash flows, or (b) assigning the real cash flows or parts thereof to some period(s) other than the one in which they actually occur.[9]

CASH-FLOW ACCOUNTING SYSTEMS

Various cash-flow accounting proposals have been made, as evidenced by a survey of articles by Lee.[10] Most of these systems share to a certain extent the same components and the same general philosophy. These major elements include the following:

N = Net cash inflow or outflow from operations
R = Replacement investment
G = Growth investment
RG = $R + G$ = Total cash investment
T = Cash payments for taxation
D = Cash payments for dividends
I = Loan interest payments
E = New equity receipts
B = Borrowing

C = Residual change in cash resources of the period (usually cash and bank balances and deposits, but could include some near-cash items such as accounts receivable if these credit transactions are included with cash transactions).[11]

Using the above components the cash flow system proposed by G. H. Lawson[12] would appear along the lines of

$$N - R - G - T - I + E + B - C = D$$

The Lawson system focuses on the determination of the D, the disposable income or net surplus the firm can generate from its trading and productive (or service) activity. In addition, it makes a distinction between replacement and growth investment.

Using the same components, the cash-flow system proposed by Lee[13] would appear along the lines of:

$$N - [R + G] - T - I - D + E + B = C$$

which focuses on the cash residual, or

$$N - [R + G] - T - I - D = F$$

where $F = C - E - B$, which focuses on F, the residual financing charge during the period.[14] If the firm's transactions were financed internally, F would be positive; if it were financed out of cash balances and/or external sources, F would be negative.

Under both systems N could be expanded along these lines:

$$N = S - M - W = O$$

where S = Cash sales
M = Cash payments for goods or services for resale
W = Wage payments
O = Overhead cash payments

Another refinement would be to dichotmize T to distinguish foreign from nonforeign transactions.

Other variations on the above two proposals include approaches which would report both past and forecast cash flows.[15]

Yuji Ijiri makes the point for past and forecast cash-flow disclosure as follows:

Of course, if forecasted future cash flows can be obtained, they will certainly provide a useful supplement to a statement of past cash flows. The two should be

clearly separated so as not to mix hard figures and soft figures. The two statements on cash flows, one on past, the other on forecast, can provide a complete picture of what has happened and what is expected to happen in the future under the best estimate available now, all based on cash flows. Forecasts can then be checked with actual performance as time passes, as mentioned earlier. A reliability indicator may be prepared based on past discrepancy between forecast and actual. I think that this is a better approach than trying to capture the financial status of a company at one point in time in terms of a still picture of all of its assets and liabilities based on their current cost or current value. The latter covers all noncash assets, but static. The cash flow approach concentrates on cash flows only, but is dynamic in the sense that its focus extends over time and is most realistic since the statements are based on what has happened and what is expected to happen.[16]

Another proposal made would link *C* (the residual change in cash resources) to a statement of changes in net realizable value of resources, thereby transforming a simple cash-flow system to one including a profit figure. The combination of cash-flow and net-realizable-value accounting is the subject of the proposal. It would be accomplished by the mere segregation of net-realizable-value accounting data into realized cash flows as in cash-flow accounting, and unrealized cash flows as in net-realizable-value accounting.

REPORTING CASH FLOWS AND NET REALIZABLE VALUES

Lee argues that cash-flow accounting and net-realizable-value accounting are parts of a single system which concentrates on the importance and accessibility of cash in business enterprise activity.[17] The points of compatibility include the following:

1. Both are based on the importance of cash as a business response.
2. Both are allocation-free systems.
3. Both emphasize firm survival.
4. Both abandon the going-concern principle and focus on liquidity.
5. Both appear to be relevant given their focus on matters that appear to underlie most of the decision models, namely, cash, cash equivalents, and cash flows.[18]

Besides by limiting it to net-realizable-value accounting, cash-flow accounting would cease to be incomplete. The limiting is described as follows:

$$\Delta C + \Delta N = \Delta O$$

where ΔC = net realized change in the total cash resources of the firm for a defined period.

ΔN = total unrealized net cash flow representing the periodic change in the net realizable value of the non-cash assets of the firm.

ΔO = Total change in the various obligations of the firm.[19]

A description of the overall system, linking cash-flow accounting and net-realizable-value accounting, is presented in Exhibit 6.1, showing the opening and closing position statements, described as *Cash Resources Statement* rather than as conventional balance sheets. The cash resources statement represents an outline insufficient for financial reporting purposes, and therefore is complemented by a *Statement of Realized Cash Flows* (Exhibit 6.2); a *Statement of Total Cash-Flow Movements* (Exhibit 6.3); a *Statement of Net Cash and Cash Equivalent Resources* (Exhibit 6.4); and a *Statement of Retained Income* (Exhibit 6.5). As a result, the complete system will comprise a realized cash-flow statement, a cash-based funds

Exhibit 6.1
Cash Resources Statement

Opening Cash Resources Statement	£000	Total Cash Flow Statement	£000	Closing Cash Resources Statement	£000
Realized cash	5	Realized cash flow	39	Realized cash	44
Readily realizable assets	43	Increase in potential cash flow	17	Readily realizable assets	60
Not readily realizable assets	18	Increase in potential cash flow	12	Not readily realizable assets	30
Non-realizable assets	--	Increase in potential cash flow	--	Non-realizable assets	--
	66		68		134
Short-term obligations	32	Additional credit received	18	Short-term obligations	50
Long-term obligations	10	Additional borrowings received	8	Long-term obligations	18
Indefinite obligations	24	Additional funds accruing	42	Indefinite obligations	66
	66		68		134

Source: T. A. Lee, "Reporting Cash Flows and Net Realizable Values," *Accounting and Business Research* (Spring 1981), p. 165. Reprinted with permission.

Exhibit 6.2
Statement of Realized Cash Flows

	£000
Cash receipts from customers	187
Less: cash payments for materials, wages and overheads	124
Cash Operating Margin	63
Less: loan interest paid	2
Pre-tax Cash Flow	61
Less: taxation paid	13
Distributable Cash Flow	48
Less: dividends paid	10
Operating Cash Flow Available for Investment	38
Add: long-term loans received	8
Total Cash Flow Available for Investment	46
Less: cash payments for new buildings	7
Total Increase in Cash Resources	39

Source: T. A. Lee, "Reporting Cash Flows and Net Realizable Values," *Accounting and Business Research* (Spring 1981), p. 166. Reprinted with permission.

statements, a realizable income statement, and a net-realizable-value position statement. This system is assumed to have the following advantages:

1. The two cash flow statements clearly separate and identify the objectively measured realized cash flow data from the far more subjective potential cash flow data described by the unrealized movements in the enterprise's assets and liabilities.
2. Although it can be argued that there is no need to ensure the articulation of the "surplus" and "position" statements, the above scheme of reporting ensures a proper reconciliation of actual with potential cash flows.
3. The accounting practices used in the above statements are simple and straightforward.
4. The combined system ought to satisfy the advocates of both CFA and NRVA.[20]

Exhibit 6.3

Statement of Total Cash-Flow Movements (Period t_1 to t_2)

	£000	£000
Realized Cash Flows		
Net realized cash flow for the period (as per Statement of Realized Cash Flows)		39
Readily Realizable Cash Flows		
Potential cash flows represented by an increase (decrease) in the net realizable values of readily realizable assets:		
Amounts due by customers	7	
Stocks of finished goods	8	
Motor vehicles	(6)	
Land and buildings	8	17
		56
Not Readily Realizable Cash Flows		
Potential cash flows represented by an increase (decrease) in the net realizable values of not readily realizable assets:		
Work-in-process	15	
Plant and machinery	(3)	12
Total Potential Increase in Cash Resources		68
Change in Short-Term Obligations		
Potential cash outflows in the near future resulting from increases in:		
Amounts due to suppliers	9	
Taxation due to Inland Revenue	7	
Distribution due to owners	2	18
Change in Long-Term Obligations		
Potential cash outflows in the long-term resulting from increases in:		
Borrowings from merchant bank		8
Change in Indefinite Obligations		
Indeterminate future cash outflows resulting from increases in:		
Funds pertaining to owners (see Statement of Realizable Income)		42
Total Potential Increase in Obligations		68

Source: T. A. Lee, "Reporting Cash Flows and Net Realizable Values," *Accounting and Business Research* (Spring 1981), p. 167. Reprinted with permission.

Exhibit 6.4
Statement of Net Cash and Cash Equivalent Resources (as at t_1 and t_2)

	t_1 £000	t_2 £000
Resources		
Realized Cash Resources		
Bank, cash and deposit balances	5	44
Readily Realizable Non-Cash Resources		
Amounts due to customers	11	18
Stocks of finished goods	10	18
Motor vehicles	10	4
Land and buildings	12	20
	43	60
Not Readily Realizable Non-Cash Resources		
Work-in-progress	9	24
Non-specialist plant and machinery	9	6
	18	30
Non-realizable Non-Cash Resources		
Specialist plant and machinery	--	--
	66	134
Obligations		
Short-Term Obligations		
Amounts due to suppliers	9	18
Taxation due to Inland Revenue	13	20
Distributions due to owners	10	12
Long-Term Obligations	32	50
Borrowings from merchant bank	10	18
Indefinite Obligations		
Funds pertaining to owners (see Statement of Retained Income)	24	66
	66	134

Source: T. A. Lee, "Reporting Cash Flows and Net Realizable Values," *Accounting and Business Research* (Spring 1981), p. 168. Reprinted with permission.

Exhibit 6.5
Statement of Retained Income (Period t_1 to t_2)

	£000
Realized income	74
Less: taxation provided	20
Distributable Income	54
Less: dividends provided	12
Retained Income for Period	42
Add: retained income of previous periods	24
Total Retained Income (as per Statement of Net Cash and Cash Equivalent Resources)	66

Source: T. A. Lee, "Reporting Cash Flows and Net Realizable Values," *Accounting and Business Research* (Spring 1981), p. 168. Reprinted with permission.

RECOVERY RATE AND CASH-FLOW ACCOUNTING

Ijiri strongly suggested that the evaluation of a company's performance should be based on cash flow.[21] He noted that while in investment decisions the primary factor is cash flow with such cash flow based on indicators as payback period, internal discounted cash flow (DCF), rate of return, and present value, performance evaluation is evaluated mainly on earnings and related indicators such as return on investment. The choice is obviously for more symmetry where either investment decision should be based on earnings or performance evaluation should be based on cash flows. Because earnings is a residual mixture of cash items and noncash items, Ijiri suggests a cash-flow-based indicator, called the "recovery rate," which is the cash flow in a period divided by the gross investment. If, for example, a company made an initial investment of $50,000 and recovered each year $5,000, the recovery rate is 10%. Assuming a uniform cash flow, the recovery rate is the reciprocal of the payback period (10 years for the above example). In addition, "Assuming uniform cash flows, the recovery rate is equal to the DCF rate if the project has an infinite life, and is an excellent approximation of the DCF rate if the recovery rate is over 15 percent and the project life is over 15 years, which is perhaps the case in a majority of capital investment decisions."[22]

The recovery rate can be extended to a whole segment of a firm to become a corporate recovery rate, a useful indicator of corporate performance. In such case it will be computed as follows:

$$\text{Corporate Recovery Rate} = \frac{\text{Cash Recoveries}}{\text{Gross Assets}}$$

where Cash Recoveries = (Funds from Operations) + (Proceeds from Disposal of Long Term Assets) + (Decrease in Total Current Assets) + (Interest Expense)

Gross Assets = (Total Assets) + (Accumulated Depreciation), averaged between beginning and ending balances.[23]

Such a cash-flow-based indicator, the corporate recovery rate, is deemed superior to the more established rate of return on investment (ROI), since it is "more easily understandable, intuitively appealing, and less subject to ambiguities, arbitrariness, and potential mainpulations than ROI."[24] The concept of recovery rate if generalized to the entire field of accounting calls for some form of cash-flow accounting.

Following on the work of Ijiri, Gerald L. Salamon derived an estimate of the IRR (internal rate of return) from CRR (cash recovery rate) and other information about the firm.[25] Basically, he showed that the cash recovery rate in any year $n + j$, where $j \geq 0$, is a constant and a function of five parameters: n (useful life of firm's "representative composite project"), p' (the annual rate of change in all prices, $p' > -1$), g' (the annual rate of growth in real gross investment, $g' > -1$), r' (the real IRR of all firm projects, $r' > -1$), and b (project cash-flow pattern parameter). Letting $1 + g' = g$, $1 + p' = p$ and IRR + 1 = r, Salamon showed that

$$CRR = \left[\frac{(1 - pg)p^n g^n}{1 - p^n g^n}\right] \left[\frac{g^n - b^n}{g^n(g - b)}\right] \left[\frac{r^n(r - b)}{r^n - b^n}\right].$$

D_{n+j}, the cash flows, are assumed to grow indefinitely at a constant growth rate. That is,

$$D_{n+j} = p^j g^j D_n$$

where $j = 0, 1, 2, \ldots$

Therefore, the IRR may be derived by estimating, p, g, n, b, and CRR and solving equation 1 for r. While CRR, g, and n, may be estimated from historical accounting data, the cash-flow pattern, b, is a more difficult case. F. M. Fisher and J. J. McGowan maintained that the parameter, b, could be

estimated from a regression of cash recoveries on a distributed log of past investment.[26] If b is equal to 1 then the firm's CRR converges to the constant given in:

$$CRR = r/[1 - (1+r)^{-n}]$$

On the basis of these formulae Salamon developed conditional IRR estimates to demonstrate that the ARR (accounts rate of return computed as net income divided by the book value of assets) contains systematic—not random— measurement error in the context of studies of the relationship between firm profitability and firm size.[27] Two avenues of research were suggested:

> The first avenue concerns the determination of the nature of the measurement error in ARR in studies where explanatory variables other than firm size are the subject of analysis. Systematic measurement error is likely to be found in some of these studies because of the dependence of the ARR on the accounting methods adopted by firms and the documented systematic association between some economic variables and these accounting methods. . . . The second avenue for future research arises because the IRR estimates relied upon in this paper are conditional on assumed knowledge of the cash flow profiles of firm projects. A broad based study involving regression of cash recoveries on a distributed lag of past investment . . . would provide empirical evidence on the cash flow profiles of actual firms. This evidence would provide guidance to analytic work on the relationship between a firm's CRR and IRR so that future empirical research would be able to rely on more refined IRR estimates than those used in the current study.[28]

Not everybody shares the enthusiasm of Salamon; for example, R. P. Brief questions the external validity of the CRR as computed by Salamon's formulae.[29] He states:

> The problem of predicting future cash flows is not dealt with explicitly in the derivation of the CRR method. Instead, the prediction model is embedded in the assumptions underlying the method. These assumptions imply that after year n when the steady rate is reached, a firm's cash flow will grow indefinitely at a constant annual growth rate of *pg*. . . . Since the CRR method was devised as a general method of estimating a firm's IRR, its usefulness depends on whether or not the environment reflects the assumptions thereby giving the prediction model . . . external validity.[30]

To add to the controversy, Andrew W. Stark showed that the cash recovery rate, as defined by the mathematical model-building exercises of Ijiri and Salamon, is unobservable directly from published financial statement data if the firm has current asset balances (as is clearly the case).[31] The debate continues.

IS CASH-FLOW ACCOUNTING ALLOCATION-FREE?

B. A. Rutherford made a distinction between two types of allocations; *distributional allocation*, which takes place at the discretion of the party or parties concerned, and *metrical allocation*, which is the apportionment of a measure of an individual phenonenon over more than one locus.[32] It is the metrical allocation which has been characterized by others as arbitrary and incorrigible, invalidates any financial reporting scheme, and justifies the adoption of cash-flow accounting. Because in the absence of economic interaction, the allocation or decomposition may be given quasi-empirical meaning by "viewing the allocations as measures of the potentially real events that would have occurred had the loci over which the allocation is being performed experienced separate phenomena such that the overall effect was the same as the actual effect of the shared experience."[33] However, in the presence of economic interaction, metrical allocation loses that meaning and becomes simply arbitrary and incorrigible. Rutherford extends the analysis to cash-flow accounting to argue that economic interaction affects cash flows as well as costs and revenues. Basically, he argues that *cash flow is not allocation-free* and provides examples including segmented reports (entity allocation), capital/revenue, recurrent/nonrecurrent and operating/financing (classificatory allocation), cash-flow cutoffs (time-period or classificatory allocation), and noncash transactions (classificatory allocation). Rutherford argues that cash-flow accounting includes time-period allocations, sometimes for smoothing purposes, and classificatory allocations for disclosure purposes, and that may be detrimental to cash-flow accounting. He concludes as follows:

> Much of this paper may appear to adopt a rather unfriendly attitude towards cash flow statements. It is not, however, the intention of the author to undermine the development of cash flow reporting; the construction of measures which have empirical referents would represent a substantial advance in the development of financial accounting. We must be extremely careful, though, not to bring a system of cash flow accounting rapidly and wastefully into disrepute by imposing on its measurements interpretations which they cannot bear.[34]

As expected, Lee reacted to the argument by claiming that most allocations can be avoided in cash-flow accounting.[35] He basically argued that time-period allocations are excluded in cash-flow accounting, cash-flow manipulations are not strictly an accounting problem, entity allocations are unnecessary if entities are viewed as autonomous, and classificatory allocations are mere labeling to be avoided if the users are left to judge fully explained and disclosed data of a material nature.[36]

EVALUATION OF CASH-FLOW ACCOUNTING

Like any accounting system, cash-flow accounting has its supporters and detractors. It has generated a debate in the profession and in research which has finally resulted in some of the standard setters paying attention to the concept.

The advantages attributed to cash-flow accounting are numerous. They include the following:

1. Cash-flow accounting would rely on the price/discounted flow ratio as a more reliable investment indicator than the present price/earnings ratio, because of the arbitrary allocations used to compute the present accrual earnings per share figure and the international differences in the computation of earnings per share.
2. As stated earlier, cash-flow accounting may be allocation-free.
3. Cash-flow accounting retains money as the unit of measurement which is familiar and not confusing to people.
4. Cash-flow accounting when expanded to include projected cash flows may help the investor to assess the ability of the firm to pay its way in the future and also its planned financial policy.
5. If the investor's interest is in the survival of the firm together with the ability to provide a stream of dividends, then cash-flow accounting will be more useful by providing accounting information about the current and anticipated cash positions of the firm. Liquidity assessment is a critical aspect of performance evaluation in the sense that cash flow and net profit are the end result of a firm's activities.[37]
6. Cash flow does not require price level adjustments because cash transactions reflect prices of the period in which they occur. It is, however, appropriate to note that some general price level adjustment is needed for cash plans occurring in different periods.
7. Cash-flow information fits as an important variable in the decision models of various users because of the concerns associated with the firm's ability to pay dividends to investors, interest and capital to lenders and bankers, amounts due to suppliers, wages and other benefits to employees, rectification and maintenance services for customers, and transaction to governments.[38]
8. Cash-flow information is argued to be more objective and relevant than accrual-based information. According to Lee,

> First, in its historic form, it is perhaps the most objective information possible, avoiding most of the subjectiveness which enters into the technical adjustments involved in the traditional accrual accounting; it is the most relevant information for purposes of comparison with forecast information should this be measured on a cash basis. Second, forecast cash flows, although involving a great deal of uncertainty (however, no more so than budgeted profits on the accrual basis), clearly avoid the necessary subjectiveness of accrual judgments and opinions. Therefore, they appear to be far less subjective in a *total* sense than profit forecasts.[39]

9. There is the suspicion that the popularity of the all-embarrassing measures of performance such as profit may well have caused firms to underestimate the importance of performance measures such as market domination, productivity, and quality of products and services.[40]
10. Cash-flow accounting is the ideal system to correct the gaps in practice between the way in which an investment is made (generally based on cash flows) and the ways the results are evaluated (generally based on earnings).

Naturally, those opposed to cash-flow accounting question each of the above advantages which leaves the debate at the hand of the researchers. Accordingly, in what follows the empirical research on the desirability of cash-flow accounting is reviewed.

REPORTING CASH FLOWS IN THE UNITED STATES

Interest in OCBOA

There is definitely an interest in the United States to alternatives to GAAP, basically in financial statements prepared with other comprehensive bases of accounting (OCBOA). The motivations to switch to OCBOA came from the changes in the tax laws made by the Economic Recovery Act of 1981 and the increasing separation of tax accounting from GAAP accounting, the increase in the number of partnerships, the subchapter S corporations and other entities which prefer to present tax or cash basis financial statements, and finally, the tentative conclusions of the AICPA accounting standards overload special committee in favor of OCBOA.[41] Guidance to practitioners faced with OCBOA statements is provided in the 1976 AICPA statement on Auditing Standards No. 14 *Special Reports.*[42] Of the four types of reports identified, one is based on OCBOA. To be classified as an OCBOA, a basis must meet one of four criteria:

1. A basis of accounting necessary to meet regulatory requirements. It is basically a *GAAP for regulated companies.*
2. A basis of accounting which may be used for income tax returns. It is basically the *tax basis of accounting.*
3. A basis of accounting based on cash receipts and disbursements with or without some accrual support. It is basically the *cash basis* or the *modified cash basis of accounting* (MCBOA).
4. A basis of accounting resulting from the application of a definite set of criteria. *Current value statements* or *price level adjusted financial statements* are good examples.

As one of the criteria indicates, the cash basis, or the MCBOA, is classified as acceptable OCBOA. It is, however, admitted that the pure cash basis is

rarely used. The MCBOA is favored if it has *substantial support*. The AICPA provides the following classification:

Modifications of the cash basis of accounting to record depreciation and equipment and to accrue income taxes were recognized in SAS No. 14. Ordinarily, a modification would have "substantial support" if the method is equivalent to the accrual basis of accounting (such as recording revenue on the accrual basis and recording purchases and other costs on the cash basis). If modifications to the cash basis of accounting do not have substantial support, the auditor should include an explanatory paragraph and modify the recommended language.[43]

The MCBOA has not been well defined. In fact, modifications arose through common usage in practice. Wayne Alderman, Dan Guy, and Dennis Meals give the following examples of modifications recognized in practice as having substantial support:

- Property, plant and equipment purchased for cash.
- Material amounts of inventory purchased for cash.
- Liabilities arising from the receipt of borrowed cash.
- Employee Federal Insurance Contributions Act and withholding taxes not deposited with the Internal Revenue Service.
- Federal income taxes accrued on current year's cash income.[44]

However, the use of MCBOA, or any other OCBOA, by a small business is not without its problems.

First, according to SAS No. 14, the auditor's report should contain a second explanatory paragraph that

1. States, or preferably refers to the note to the financial statements that states, the basis of presentation of the financial statements on which the auditor is reporting.
2. Refers to the note to the financial statements that describes how the basis of presentation differs from [GAAP]. (The monetary effect of such differences need not be stated.)
3. States that the financial statements are not intended to be presented in conformity with [GAAP].[45]

Second, SAS No. 14 requires a third paragraph that expresses the auditor's opinion (or disclaims an opinion) on whether the financial statements are presented fairly in conformity with the basis of accounting described and whether the basis of accounting used has been applied in a manner consistent with that of the preceding period.

Third, SAS No. 14 recommends that the financial statements not be captioned or otherwise referred to as "balance sheet" or "income statement" without appropriate modification.

Fourth, an auditing interpretation, "Adequacy of Disclosure in Financial Statements Prepared on a Comprehensive Basis of Accounting other than Generally Accepted Accounting Principles," offers general guidances on OCBOA disclosures. It states the following:

> The criteria the auditor should apply are essentially the same as those applicable to financial statements prepared in conformity with generally accepted accounting principles. The criteria are discussed in SAS No. 5, "The Meaning of 'Present Fairly in Conformity with Generally Accepted Accounting Principles'" in the Independent Auditor's report, paragraph 4. The auditor's opinion should be based on his judgment regarding whether the financial statement, including the related notes, are informative of matters that may effect [*sic*] their use, understanding and interpretation.[46]

Interest in Cash Flows

In 1963 the Accounting Principles Board (APB) issued Opinion No. 3, *The Statement of Sources and Applications of Funds,* in which it recommended the presentation of the funds statements in the annual report. After the SEC in 1961 began requiring funds statements in annual filings, the APB issued in 1971 Opinion No. 19, *Reporting Changes in Financial Position,* requiring the presentation of a fund statement which summarizes changes in financial position and is based on a broad concept of funds. The interest in cash flow rather than funds increased with the publication of the Trueblood Report and the advent of the conceptual framework. For example, FASB Concepts Statement No. 1, *Objectives of Financial Reporting by Business Enterprises,* states in Paragraph 37 that:

> Financial reporting should provide information to help present and potential investors and creditors and other users in assessing the amounts, timing, and uncertainty of prospective cash receipts from dividends or interest and the proceeds from the sale, redemption, or maturity of securities or loans. The prospects for those cash receipts are affected by an enterprise's ability to generate enough cash to meet its obligations when due and its other cash operating needs, to reinvest in operations and to pay cash dividends.

After the issuance of a Discussion Memorandum on the subject,[47] the FASB followed in October 31, 1980, by an exposure draft entitled *Statement of Cash Flows.* The proposed statement was expected to supersede APB Opinion No. 19 and requires a statement of cash flows instead of a statement of changes in financial position. It was expected to help investors, creditors, and others to assess (a) the entity's ability to generate positive future net cash flows, (b) the entity's ability to meet its obligations and pay dividends, and its needs for external financing, (c) the reasons for the

differences between income and associated cash receipts and payments, and (d) both the cash and noncash aspects of the entity's investing and financing transactions during the period.

This statement would classify cash receipts and cash payments by investing, financing, and operating activities and would also provide information about investing and financing activities not involving cash receipts or cash payments in the period so that information is provided about all investing and financing activities.

The cash flow from operating activities may be presented using the *direct method* as the difference between cash receipts and cash payments or *the indirect method* as net income plus appropriate adjustments by removing from net income the effects of all deferrals of past cash receipts and payments and all accruals of expected future cash receipts and payments. Three presentations were considered:

1. Cash flow from operating activities is reported directly. Noncash transactions are reported in a separate schedule.
2. Cash flow from operating activities is presented indirectly and reported in a separate schedule. Noncash transactions are reported in a separate schedule.
3. Cash flow from operating activities is reported indirectly. Noncash transactions are reported in the body of the statement with reconciliation to cash within categories.

The following example about the activities of the X Corporation for the year ending December 31, 19x7, will be used to illustrate the three presentations:

1. Company X acquired new property, plant, and equipment for $20,000. It also sold some of it with a book value of $9,500 for $12,500.
2. Company X entered into a capital lease for the use of new equipment resulting in a lease obligation of $3,750.
3. Company X acquired all the common stock of Company Y for $4,500 in cash. It thereby acquired Company Y's working capital other than cash (a net current liability of $500) and its property, plant, and equipment valued at $15,000, while assuming Company Y's long-term debt of $10,000.
4. Cash borrowed by Company X for the year consisted of short-term debt of $375 and long-term debt of $6,250.
5. Company X paid $1,500 on its short-term debt and $625 on capital lease obligations during the year.
6. Company X issued $3,750 in common stock during the year, $1,250 of which was to settle long-term debt and $2,500 of which was issued in cash.
7. Company X paid $2,250 as dividends to its stockholders during the year.

8. Company X's financial service activities during the year includes purchases and sales of investment securities amounting to $23,500 and $25,000, respectively. Lending activities produced new loans of $37,500 and collections of loans of $29,000. Customer deposits in its banking subsidiary total $5,500.
9. Company X's operations for the year resulted in

Net income	$15,000
Depreciation and amortization	7,500
Deferred taxes	750
Changes in operating working capital items other than cash:	
Increase in inventory	20,000
Decrease in accounts receivable	10,000
Increase in accounts payable	5,750
Changes in interest accruals:	
Increase in interest earned but not received	1,750
Increase in interest accrued but not paid	500
Cash received from customers for sales of goods	50,000
Cash dividends received	3,500
Cash paid to suppliers and employees	30,000
Cash paid for interest and taxes	8.750

10. The effect of cash and cash equivalents of changes in the exchange rate for the year was $500. Cash equivalents are short-term highly liquid investments.

The results according to the various methods suggested by the FASB are shown in Exhibits 6.6, 6.7, and 6.8.

RESEARCH AND CASH-FLOW ACCOUNTING

Users' Reactions to Cash-Flow Accounting

Survey results show a general fixation of users with accrual-based information and an ignorance of cash-flow-based information, considered to be secondary information.[48]

The results of experiments are mixed. R. G. Walker examined accountants' and students' reactions to the addition of the funds statements in a financial information package used to form judgments about the financial performance, position, and prospects of a firm.[49] His findings show a rather limited usefulness of the funds statements with regard to the improvements of accuracy of judgments, the confidence of the respondents and the time taken to complete the experimental task. A. Rashad Abdel-Khalik and Thomas F. Keller presented their subjects with reported earnings numbers and cash flows as impacted by the changes in the accounting method of valuing inventory.[50] They found results consistent with the hypothesis of

functional fixation in the sense that in spite of the changes in inventory valuation techniques and their impact on liquidity the subjects do not readily change the weights assigned to reported earnings informing expectations about the prospects of the firm. Using a content analysis of the Wall Street transcripts, containing the analyses of security analyst firms, Vijayaraghavan Govindarajan showed that security analysts emphasize earnings analysis more than cash-flow analysis.[51] Govindarajan, however, cautions about the possible discrepancy between "what security analysts do" and "what they publish," stating that

> The argument could be made that security analysts target their reports to "naive" investors and since naive investors probably have a better understanding of earnings rather than cash flows, the security analysts publish the earnings analysis rather than the cash flow analysis. There is some merit in this argument even though it is just as easy (in view of the dearth of empirical evidence) to put forth a counter argument that a naive person understands cash flows better than earnings.[52]

Finally, Ahmed Belkaoui conducted an experiment in which bank loan officers evaluated a loan application which was accompanied by financial statements based on either accrual accounting or modified cash basis of accounting.[53] The loan officers first decided whether to grant a loan and then determined one appropriate interest rate. Second, they evaluated the financial statements' information in these quality attributes: overall reliability, freedom from clerical errors, and freedom from the effects of fraud. A clear preference for accrual accounting was found.

Finally, the hypothesis made by income theorists like R. J. Chambers,[54] Kenneth MacNeal,[55] and P. R. Sterling[56] is that people have natural perceptions of assets, liabilities, and profits and are intuitively inclined to think in terms of current values rather than historical costs. The hypothesis made by cash-flow theorists like R. K. Jaedicke and R. T. Sprouse[57] and A. L. Thomas[58] is that cost allocation is alien to laymen who rely on cash-flow accounting in making calculations about their own private affairs. In two experiments D. P. Tweedie and Tom Lee[59] investigated the two hypotheses and showed that (a) persons with no prior knowledge of accounting rely on cash flow and/or net realizable values in the income statements, and net realizable values in the balance sheet, (b) persons with prior experience rely on historical costs in both statements. Basically, the learning process or acculturation caused the subject to abandon the intuitive cash-flow and net-realizable-value concepts and switch to historical cost accounting, which may put the whole question of the potential success of cash-flow accounting and net-realizable-value accounting back to what indoctrination takes place in the classroom. Lee states the following:

> The combination of cash flow and net realizable values had intuitive appeal to those students previously uninvolved in accounting. The teaching process, perhaps not

Exhibit 6.6

Cash Flow from Operating Activities Is Reported Directly—Noncash Transactions Are Reported in a Separate Schedule

Cash Flows from Operating Activities:		
Cash received from customers	$50,000	
Dividends received	3,500	
Cash provided by operating activities		$53,500
Cash paid to suppliers and employees	30,000	
Interest and taxes paid	8,750	
Cash disbursed for operating activities		38,750
Net cash flow from operating activities		14,750
Cash Flows from Investing Activities:		
Purchases of property, plant, equipment	(20,000)	
Proceeds from disposals of property, plant, equipment	12,500	
Acquisition of Company ABC	(4,500)	
Purchases of investment securities	(23,500)	
Proceeds from sales of investment securities	25,000	
Loans made	(37,500)	
Collections on loans	29,000	
Net cash used by investing activities		(19,000)
Cash Flows from Financing Activities:		
Net increase in customer deposits	5,500	
Proceeds of short-term debt	375	
Payments to settle short-term debt	(5,100)	
Proceeds of long-term debt	6,250	
Payments on capital lease obligations	(625)	
Proceeds from issuing common stock	2,500	
Dividends paid	(2,250)	

Exhibit 6.6 *(continued)*

Net cash provided by financing activities		10,250
Effect of exchange rate changes on cash		500
Net increase (decrease) in cash		$ 6,500
Schedule of noncash investing and financing activities:		
Capital lease obligations incurred for use of equipment	$3,750	
Acquisition of Company ABC:		
Working capital other than cash acquired	$ (500)	
Property, plant, and equipment acquired	15,000	
Long-term debt assumed	(10,000)	
Cash paid to acquire Company ABC	$4,500	
Common stock issued to settle long-term debt	$ 1,250	

Exhibit 6.7
Cash Flow from Operating Activities Is Presented Indirectly and Reported in a Separate Schedule—Noncash Transactions Are Reported in a Separate Schedule

Net cash flow from operating activities		$14,750
Cash Flows from Investing Activities:		
Purchases of property, plant, equipment	(20,000)	
Proceeds from disposals of property, plant, equipment	12,500	
Acquisition of Company ABC	4,500	
Purchase of investment securities	(23,500)	
Proceeds from sales of investment securities	25,000	
Loans made	37,500	
Collections on loans	29,000	
Net cash used by investing activities		19,000
Cash Flows from Financing Activities:		
Net increase in customer deposits	5,500	
Proceeds of short-term debt	375	
Payments to settle short-term debt	(1,500)	
Proceeds of long-term debt	6,250	
Payments on capital lease obligations	(625)	
Proceeds from issuing common stock	2,500	
Dividends paid	2,250	
Net cash provided by financing activities		10,250
Effect of exchange rate changes on cash		500
Net increase (decrease) in cash		$ 6,500

Exhibit 6.7 *(continued)*

Schedule Reconciling Earnings to Net Cash Flow from Operating Activities:		
Net income	$15,000	
Noncash expenses, revenues, losses, and gains included in income:		
Depreciation and amortization	7,500	
Deferred taxes	750	
Net increase in receivables, inventory, and payables	(4,250)	
Increase in interest earned but not received	(1,750)	
Increase in interest accrued but not paid	500	
Gain on sale of property	(3,000)	
Net cash flow from operating activities		14,750

Schedule of Noncash Investing and Financing Activities:	
Capital lease obligations incurred for use of equipment	$ 3,750
Acquisition of Company ABC:	
Working capital other than cash acquired	(500)
Property, plant, and equipment acquired	15,000
Long-term debt assumed	(10,000)
Cash paid to acquire Company ABC	$ 4,500
Common stock issued to settle long-term debt	$ 1,250

Exhibit 6.8

Cash Flow from Operating Activities Is Reported Indirectly—Noncash Transactions Are Reported in the Body of the Statement with Reconciliation to Cash within Categories

Net Cash Flow from Operating Activities:		
Net income	$15,000	
Noncash expenses, revenues, losses, and gains		
included in income:		
Depreciation and amortization	7,500	
Deferred taxes	750	
Net increase in receivables, inventory,		
and payables	(4,250)	
Increase in interest earned but not received	(1,750)	
Increase in interest accrued but not paid	500	
Gain on sale of property	(3,000)	
Net cash flow from operating activities		14,750
Cash Flows from Investing Activities:		
Acquisition of property, plant, equipment	(23,750)	
Less: Capital lease obligations incurred	3,750	
Cash outflows for property, plant, equipment	(20,000)	
Proceeds from disposals of property, plant, equipment	12,500	
Acquisition of Company ABC:		
Working capital other than cash acquired	500	
Property, plant, and equipment acquired	(15,000)	
Long-term debt assumed	10,000	
Cash outflow to acquire Company ABC	(45,000)	
Purchase of investment securities	(23,500)	
Proceeds from sales of investment securities	25,000	
Loans made	(37,500)	
Collection on loans	29,000	

Exhibit 6.8 *(continued)*

Net cash used by investing activities		(19,000)
Cash Flows from Financing Activities:		
Net increase in customer deposits	5,500	
Proceeds of short-term debt	375	
Payments to settle short-term debt	(1,500)	
Issuance of long-term debt	20,000	
Less: New capital lease obligations	(3,750)	
Long-term debt assumed in acquisition	(10,000)	
Cash proceeds of long-term debt	6,250	
Payments on capital lease obligations	625	
Issuance of common stock	3,750	
Less: Issuance to settle long-term debt	(1,250)	
Cash proceeds from issuing common stock	2,500	
Dividends paid	(2,250)	
Net cash provided by financing activities		10,250
Effect of exchange rate changes on cash		500
Net increase (decrease) in cash		6,500

surprisingly, was sufficiently persuasive to override these intuitions and replace them with what was being taught. Thus, it will be a considerable task to persuade those accounting policy-makers, report producers and accounting report users that alternatives to historical cost accounting are relevant and acceptable irrespective of their early intuitions.[60]

Predictive Ability of Cash-Flow Information

Various studies have examined the predictive ability of cash-flow information with regard to stock price changes, bankruptcy, or future cash-flow measures.

With regard to the predictive ability of cash-flow information about stock price changes the evidence is mixed. Ray Ball and Philip Brown's results indicated that residual cash flow was less successful than residual earnings changes in predicting the sign of residual price changes.[61] Similarly, W. H. Beaver and R. E. Dukes found that residual changes in security prices were more highly associated with residual changes in earnings than in cash flows.[62] Both studies used are inadequate cash-flow surrogates (i.e., earnings plus depreciation and amortization) instead of cash flow from operations. Based on a cash-flow variable measured as working capital from operations, J. Patell and Robert Kaplan would not reject the hypothesis that additional information content associated with cash-flow information exists.[63]

More recently, William Beaver, Paul Griffin, and Wayne Landsman, testing for the incremental information effects of cash flow and replacement cost data beyond those available from historical cost earnings data, found little support for the notion of incremental effects that were incremental to historical cost data.[64] Similarly, Belkaoui examined the relative merits of accounting indicators derived from accrual accounting and cash-flow accounting.[65] The hypothesis was that the number most favored by the market and/or reflected in the market price would show less variability and higher persistency than other numbers. The result was that the balance-sheet-oriented and accrual-accounting-based number showed a lower variability and a higher persistency that the cash-flow-accounting-based number and the income-statement-oriented and accrual-accounting-based number, indicating again that market prices for securities are more responsive to accrual-based numbers than to cash-flow-based numbers. Similarly, Thomas Schaeffer and Michael Kennelly presented results indicating that no improvement in association with risk-adjusted security returns is obtained by using the refined cash-flow definitions.[66]

With regard to the predictive ability of cash-flow information in the case of financial distress the evidence is also mixed. Beaver found funds flow (defined as net income plus depreciation, depletion, and amortization) to total debt and net income to total assets to have the most predictive power

in the year prior to failure in 87% of the cases.[67] In a first study Casey and Bartczak reported that accrual-based multivariate discriminant models forecast corporate bankruptcy more accurately than any single operating cash-flow ratio.[68] In a second study their focus was on the marginal predictive content of the operating cash-flow ratios, rather than their invariate predictive value.[69] Their results suggesting that operating cash flow does not provide incremental predictive power over accrual-based ratios are consistent with the results of J. A. Gentry, Paul Newbold, and D. T. Whitford[70] and M. J. Gombola, M. J. Gombola and J. E. Ketz,[71] neither of which found cash-flow information to improve classification accuracy significantly. Their results were, however, inconsistent with those of Raja, Nosworthy, and Gourlia, who found cash flow/total debt to be the most significant discrimination,[72] and J. A. Largay and C. P. Stickney,[73] who found that cash flow from operations provided a more accurate and timely signal of W. T. Grant's impending failure than the other measures.

With regard to the predictive ability of cash-flow information in the case of future cash flow, the evidence was negative. Robert R. Greenberg et al. provided empirical evidence supporting the FASB assertion that information about an enterprise's earnings based on accrual accounting generally provides a better indication of a company's ability to generate cash flows than information about cash flows themselves.[74] Similarly, Gombola and Ketz using factor analysis found that cash-flow ratios contain information that is separate and distinct from earnings-based information.[75]

CONCLUSIONS

As the above discussion indicates, cash-flow accounting is emerging internationally as a subject of research and interest to academicians, practitioners, and/or standard setters. Although its alleged benefits, its impact on users' reactions, and its predictive ability are in need of more empirical evidence, its implementation seems to be gaining favor with the standard setters, who express fervent interest in its implementation. Cash-flow accounting has always been with us. It lost credibility for a while to the advantage of accrual accounting. Now it is making an international return. The return of cash-flow accounting to its well-deserved place of importance is best stated by Lee as follows:

> Cash flow accounting and reporting has a long and honorable history in the development of business enterprises. It was superseded by the sophisticated statements of allocated data which are by now such a familiar part of financial reporting practice. Perhaps, with liquidity such a vital issue in business today, the wheel will turn full circle, and cash flow accounting will again be restored to its rightful place as a useful and relevant source of financial information about business enterprises for a variety of report users.[76]

NOTES

1. Barbara S. Thomas, "Reporting Cash Flow Information," *Journal of Accounting* (November 1982), p. 99.

2. D. Hawkins and W. Campbell, *Equity Valuation: Models, Analysis and Implications* (New York: Financial Executives Institute, 1978).

3. A. L. Thomas, *The Allocation Problem in Financial Accounting Theory*, Studies in Accounting Research No. 3 (Sarasota, Fla.: American Accounting Association, 1969); A. L. Thomas, *The Allocation Problem, Part Two*, Studies in Accounting Research No. 9 (Sarasota, Fla.: American Accounting Association, 1974).

4. Ibid., *The Allocation Problem in Financial Accounting Theory*, p. 25.

5. Ibid., p. 30.

6. Ibid., p. 42.

7. American Institute of Certified Public Accountants, Study Group on the Objectives of Financial Statements, *Objectives of Financial Statements* (New York: American Institute of Certified Public Accountants, 1973), p. 16.

8. T. A. Lee, "The Simplicity and Complexity of Accounting," in *Accounting for a Simplified Firm Owning Depreciable Assets*, ed. R. R. Sterling and A. L. Thomas (Lawrence, Kans.: Scholars Book Co., 1979), p. 4.

9. Barry E. Hicks, "The Cash Flow Basis of Accounting," in *Cash Flow Accounting*, ed. Barry E. Hicks and Pearson Hunt (Sudbury, Ontario: School of Commerce and Administration, 1981), p. 30.

10. Thomas A. Lee, "Cash Flow Accounting and Reporting," in *Essays in British Accounting Research*, ed. M. Bromwich and A. Hopwood (London: Pitman, 1981), pp. 63-78.

11. The potential inclusion of near cash items is raised in Thomas A. Lee, "Cash Flow Accounting and Reporting," in *Developments in Financial Reporting*, ed. Thomas A. Lee (London: Philip Allan, 1981), p. 150.

12. G. H. Lawson, "The Cash Flow Performance of UK Companies," in *Essays in British Accounting Research*, ed. M. Bromwich and A. Hopwood (London: Pitman, 1981), pp. 79-100.

13. T. A. Lee, "A Case for Cash Flow Reporting," *Journal of Business Finance* (Summer 1972), pp. 27-36.

14. T. A. Lee, "What Cash Flow Analysis Says about BL's Finances," *Financial Times* (October 23, 1981), p. 15.

15. R. J. Briston and R. A. Fawthrop, "Accounting Principles and Investor Protection," *Journal of Business Finance* (Summer 1971), pp. 9-10; C. J. Jones, "Accounting Standards: A Blind Alley?" *Accounting and Business Research* (Autumn 1975), pp. 273-79; T. A. Climo, "Cash Flow Statements for Investors," *Journal of Business Finance and Accounting* (Autumn 1976), pp. 3-14.

16. Yuji Ijiri, *Historical Cost Accounting and Its Rationality*, Research Monograph No. 1 (Vancouver, B.C.: Canadian Certified General Accountants' Research Foundation, 1981), p. 75.

17. R. A. Lee, "Reporting Cash Flows and Net Realizable Values," *Accounting and Business Research* (Spring 1981), pp. 163-70.

18. Ibid., pp. 163-64.

19. Ibid., p. 164.

20. Ibid., p. 169.

21. Yuji Ijiri, "Recovery Rate and Cash Flow Accounting," *Financial Executive* (March 1980), pp. 54-60.

22. Ibid., p. 55.

23. Ibid.

24. Ibid., p. 58.

25. Gerald L. Salamon, "Cash Recovery Rates and Measures of Firm Profitability," *Accounting Review* (April 1982), pp. 292-302.

26. F. M. Fisher and J. J. McGowan, "On the Misues of Accounting Rates of Return to Infer Monopoly Profits," *American Economic Review* (March 1983), pp. 82-97.

27. Gerald L. Salamon, "Accounting Rates of Return," *American Economic Review* (June 1985), pp. 495-504.

28. Ibid., p. 503.

29. R. P. Brief, "Limitations of Using the Cash Recovery Rate to Estimate the IRR: A Note," *Journal of Business Finance and Accounting* (Autumn 1985), pp. 473-75.

30. Ibid., p. 475.

31. Andrew W. Stark, "On the Observability of the Cash Recovery Rate," *Journal of Business Finance and Accounting* (Spring 1987), pp. 99-108.

32. B. A. Rutherford, "The Interpretation of Cash Flow Reports and the Other Allocation Problem," *Abacus* (June 1982), p. 40.

33. Ibid., p. 41.

34. Ibid., pp. 48-49.

35. T. A. Lee, "Cash Flow Accounting and the Allocation Problem," *Journal of Business Finance and Accounting* (Autumn 1982), pp. 342-52.

36. Ibid., p. 351.

37. T. A. Lee, "Cash Flow Accounting, Profit and Performance Measurement: A Response to a Challenge," *Accounting Business Research* (Spring 1985), p. 93.

38. Lee, "Cash Flow Accounting and Reporting," p. 152.

39. Lee, "A Case for Cash Flow Reporting," p. 31.

40. R. S. Kaplan, "Measuring Manufacturing Performance: A New Challenge for Managerial Accounting Research," *Accounting Review* (October 1982).

41. C. Wayne Alderman, Dan M. Guy, and Dennis R. Meals, "Other Comprehensive Bases of Accounting: Alternatives to GAAP?" *Journal of Accounting* (August 1982), pp. 52-63.

42. American Institute of Certified Public Accountants, Statement of Auditing Standards No. 14, *Special Reports* (New York: American Institute of Certified Public Accountants, 1976).

43. Ibid., Sect. 1500.05.

44. Alderman, Guy, and Meals, "Other Comprehensive Bases of Accounting," p. 53.

45. American Institute of Certified Public Accountants, *Professional Standards*, vol. 1 (Chicago: Commerce Clearing House, 1985), Sect. 621.05.

46. Ibid., Sect. 9621.34-39.

47. Financial Accounting Standards Board, *An Analysis of the Issues Related to Reporting Funds, Flows, Liquidity and Financial Flexibility* (Stamford, Conn.: FASB, December 13, 1980).

48. J. J. Benjamin and K. G. Stanza, "Differences in Disclosure Needs of Major

Users of Financial Statements," *Accounting and Business Research* (Summer 1977), pp. 187-92; R. H. Chenhall and R. Juchna, "Investor Information Needs: An Australian Study," *Accounting and Business Research* (Spring 1977), pp. 111-19; T. A. Lee and D. P. Tweedie, "Accounting Information: An Investigation of Shareholder Understanding," *Accounting and Business Research* (Winter 1975), pp. 3-17; T. A. Lee and D. P. Tweedie, "The Private Shareholder: His Source of Information and His Understanding of Reporting Practices," *Accounting and Business Research* (Autumn 1976), pp. 303-14; T. A. Lee and D. P. Tweedie, *The Private Shareholder and the Corporate Report* (London: Institute of Chartered Accountants in England and Wales, 1977); T. A. Lee and D. P. Tweedie, *The Institutional Investor and Financial Information* (London: Institute of Chartered Accountants in England and Wales, 1981); R. Anderson, "The Usefulness of Accounting and Other Information Disclosed in Corporate Annual Reports to Institutional Investors in Australia," *Accounting and Business Research* (Autumn 1981), pp. 259-65.

49. R. G. Walker, "Funds Statements and the Interpretation of Financial Data: An Empirical Investigation," *Working Paper Series 18* (Sydney: University of South Wales, 1981).

50. A. Rashad Abdel-Khalik and Thomas F. Keller, *Earnings on Cash Flows: An Experiment on Functional Fixation and the Valuation of the Firm,* Studies in Accounting Research No. 16 (Sarasota, Fla.: American Accounting Association, 1979).

51. Vijayaraghavan Govindarajan, "The Objectives of Financial Statements: An Empirical Study of the Use of Cash Flow and Earnings by Security Analysts," *Accounting, Organizations and Society* (December 1980), pp. 383-92.

52. Ibid., p. 391.

53. Ahmed Belkaoui, "Accrual Accounting, Modified Cash Basis of Accounting and the Loan Decision: An Experiment," Unpublished manuscript, University of Illinois at Chicago, 1987.

54. R. J. Chambers, *Accounting, Evaluation and Economic Behavior* (Englewood Cliffs, N.J.: Prentice-Hall, 1986), pp. 77-123.

55. Kenneth MacNeal, *Truth in Accounting* (Lawrence, Kans.: Scholars Book Co., 1970), pp. 1-19 and 323.

56. R. R. Sterling, *Theory of Measurement of Enterprise Income* (Lawrence: University of Kansas Press, 1970).

57. R. K. Jaedicke and R. T. Sprouse, *Accounting Flows: Income, Funds and Cash* (Englewood Cliffs, N.J.: Prentice-Hall, 1965), p. 37.

58. Thomas, *The Allocation Problem in Financial Accounting Theory.*

59. D. P. Tweedie, "Cash Flows and Realizable Values: The Intuitive Accounting Concepts? An Empirical Test," *Accounting and Business Research* (Winter 1977), pp. 2-13; Tom Lee, "Cash Flows and Net Realizable Values: Further Evidence of the Intuitive Concepts," *Abacus* (December 1984), pp. 125-37.

60. Lee, "Cash Flows and Net Realizable Values," p. 136.

61. Ray Ball and Philip Brown, "An Empirical Evaluation of Accounting Income Numbers," *Journal of Accounting Research* (Autumn 1968), pp. 159-78.

62. W. H. Beaver and R. E. Dukes, "Interperiod Tax Allocation, Earnings Expectations, and the Behavior of Security Prices," *Accounting Review* (April 1972), pp. 320-32.

63. J. Patell and Robert Kaplan, "The Informational Content of Cash Flow Data

Relative to Annual Earnings," Working Paper, Stanford University, 1977.

64. William Beaver, Paul Griffin, and Wayne Landsman, "The Incremental Information Content of Replacement Cost Earnings," *Journal of Accounting and Economics* (April 1982), pp. 15-39.

65. Ahmed Belkaoui, "Accrual Accounting and Cash Accounting: Relative Merits of Derived Accounting Indicator Numbers," *Journal of Business Finance and Accounting* (Summer 1983), pp. 299-312.

66. Thomas Schaeffer and Michael Kennelly, "Alternative Cash Flow Measures and Risk-Adjusted Returns," *Journal of Accounting, Auditing and Finance* (Fall 1986), pp. 278-87.

67. W. F. Beaver, "Financial Ratios and Predictors of Failure," *Empirical Research in Accounting: Selected Studies,* supplement to *Journal of Accounting Research* 4 (1966), pp. 71-111.

68. C. Casey and N. Bartczak, "Cash Flow: It's Not the Bottom Line," *Harvard Business Review* (July-August 1984), pp. 60-66.

69. C. Casey and N. Bartczak, "Using Operating Cash Flow Data to Predict Financial Distress: Some Extensions," *Journal of Accounting Research* (Spring 1985), pp. 384-401.

70. J. A. Gentry, Paul Newbold, and D. T. Whitford, "Classifying Bankrupt Firms with Funds Flow Components," *Journal of Accounting Research* (Spring 1985), pp. 146-60.

71. M. J. Gombola and J. E. Ketz, "Cash Flow as a Predictor of Failure," Working Paper, Pennsylvania State University, July 1983.

72. A. Raja, M. Nosworthy, and D. Gourlia, "Diagnosis of Financial Health by Cash Flow Analysis," Working Paper, London Business School, 1980.

73. J. A. Largay and C. P. Stickney, "Cash Flows, Ratio Analysis and the W. T. Grant Company Bankruptcy," *Financial Analysts Journal* (July-August 1980), pp. 51-54.

74. Robert R. Greenberg, Glen L. Johnson, and K. Ramesh, "Earnings versus Cash Flow as a Predictor of Future Cash Flow Measures," *Journal of Accounting, Auditing and Finance* (Fall 1986), pp. 278-87.

75. Michael Gombola and J. Edward Ketz, "A Note on Cash Flow and Classification Patterns of Financial Ratios," *Accounting Review* (January 1983), pp. 105-14.

76. Lee, "Cash Flow Accounting and Reporting," p. 169.

SELECTED BIBILOGRAPHY

Accounting Standards Committee, "Extraordinary Items and Prior Year Adjustments," *Statement of Standard Accounting Practice* 6 (1974), pp. 15-25.

Arnold, J., and A. Hope, "Reporting Business Performance," *Accounting and Business Research* (July 1975), pp. 96-105.

Barlev, B., and H. Levy, "On the Variability of Accounting Income Numbers," *Journal of Business Finance and Accounting* (Summer 1983), pp. 305-15.

Beaver, W. H., and R. E. Dukes, "Interperiod Tax Allocation, Earnings Expectations, and the Behavior of Security Prices," *Accounting Review* (April 1972), pp. 320-32.

Beaver, W. H., and D. Morse, "What Determines Price-Earnings Ratios?" *Financial Analysts Journal* (July-August 1978), pp. 65-76.

Belkaoui, Ahmed, *Accounting Theory* (New York: Harcourt Brace Jovanovich, 1981).

______, "Accrual Accounting and Cash Accounting: Relative Merits of Derived Accounting Indicator Numbers," *Journal of Business Finance and Accounting* (Summer 1983), pp. 299-312.

Bird, Peter, "Objectives and Methods of Financial Reporting: A Generalized Search Procedure," *Accounting and Business Research* (Fall 1975), pp. 162-67.

Bodenhorn, Diran, "Balance Sheet Items as the Present Value of Future Cash Flows," *Journal of Business Finance and Accounting* (Winter 1984), pp. 493-510.

______, "An Economic Approach to Balance Sheets and Income Statements," *Abacus* (June 1978), pp. 3-30.

Bromwich, Michael, "Standard Costing for Planning and Control," *Accountant* (April-May 1969), pp.

Canning, J., *The Economics of Accountancy* (New York: Ronald Press, 1929).

Chambers, R. J., *Accounting, Evaluation and Economic Behavior* (Englewood Cliffs, N.J.: Prentice-Hall, 1966).

______, "Continuously Contemporary Accounting: Additivity and Action," *Accounting Review* (October 1967), pp. 751-57.

______, "Income and Capital: Fisher's Legacy," *Journal of Accounting Research* (Spring 1971), pp. 137-49.

______, "Second Thoughts on Continuously Contemporary Accounting," *Abacus* (September 1970), pp. 39-55.

______, "Third Thoughts," *Abacus* (December 1974), pp. 129-37.

Climo, T. A., "Cash Flow Statements for Investors," *Journal of Business Finance and Accounting* (Autumn 1976), pp. 3-14.

Daily, R. A., "The Feasibility of Reporting Forecast Information," *Accounting Review* (October 1971), pp. 686-92.

Edey, H. C., "Accounting Principles and Business Reality," *Accountancy* (November 1963), pp. 998-1002.

Edwards, E. O., "The Fundamental Character of Excess Current Income," *Accounting and Business Research* (Autumn 1980), pp. 375-94.

Edwards, E. O. and P. Bell, *The Theory and Measurement of Business Income* (Berkeley: University of California Press, 1961).

Egginton, D. A., "Cash Flow, Profit and Performance Measures for External Reporting: A Rejoinder," *Accounting and Business Research* (Spring 1985), pp. 109-112.

______, "In Defense of Profit Measurement, Some Limitations of Cash Flow and Value Added as Performance Measures for External Reporting," *Accounting and Business Research* (Spring 1984), pp. 99-111.

Fama, E. F., and M. H. Miller, *The Theory of Finance* (New York: Holt, Rinehart and Winston, 1972).

Ferrara, W. L., "A Cash Flow Model for the Future," *Management Accounting* (June 1981), pp. 12-17.

Financial Accounting Standards Board, *Statement of Financial Accounting Concepts No. 1* (Stamford, Conn.: FASB, November 1978).

Glautier, M.W.E., and B. Underdown, *Accounting Theory Practice* (London: Pitman, 1976).

Gordon, M. J., "Postulates, Principles and Research in Accounting," *Accounting Review* (April 1964), pp. 221-63.

Grimlund, Richard A., and Robert Capettini, "Sign Tests for Actual Investments with Latter Period Net Cash Outflows," *Journal of Business Finance and Accounting* (Spring 1983), pp. 83-193.

Gross, M. J., Jr., *Financial and Accounting Guide for Nonprofit Organizations* (New York: Ronald Press, 1972).

Hawkins, D., and W. Campbell, *Equity Valuation: Models, Analysis and Implications* (New York: Financial Executives Institute, 1978).

Hendriksen, E. S., *Accounting Theory*, rev. ed. (Homewood, Ill.: Irwin, 1970).

Hicks, Barry E., *The Cash Flow Basis of Accounting* (Sudbury, Ontario: Laurentian University, 1980).

Ijiri, Y., "Cash-Flow Accounting and Its Structure," *Journal of Accounting, Auditing Finance* (May 1978), pp. 331-48.

______, "A Simple System of Cash-Flow Accounting," in *Accounting for a Simplified Firm Owning Depreciable Assets,* ed. Robert R. Sterling and A. L. Thomas (Houston: Scholars Book Company, 1979).

Lawson, G. H. "Accounting for Financial Management: Some Tentative Proposals for a New Blueprint," *Problems of Investment,* ed. R. Shone (London: Blackwell, 1971), pp. 36-64.

______, "Cash-Flow Accounting I and II," *Accountant* (October 28 and November 4, 1971), pp. 15-20.

______, "The Cash Flow Performance of UK Companies," in *Essays in British Accounting Research,* ed. M. Bromwich and A. Hopwood (London: Pitman, 1981), pp. 79-100.

______, "Initial Reactions to ED 18," *Certified Accountant* (December 1976), pp. 13-20.

______, "The Measurement of Corporate Performance on a Cash Flow Basis: A Reply to Mr. Egginton," *Accounting and Business Research* (Spring 1985), pp. 99-108.

______, "Measuring Divisional Performance," *Management Accountant* (May 1971), pp. 147-52.

______, "Memorandum Submitted to the Inflation Accounting Committee," *Working Paper No. 12* (Manchester: Manchester Business School, 1975).

______, "Profit Maximization Via Financial Management," *Management Decision* (Winter 1969), pp. 6-12.

______, "The Rationale of Cash, Flow Accounting," *Analyst* (December 1976), pp. 22-30.

Lee, T. A., "The Accounting Entity Concept, Accounting Standards and Inflation Accounting," *Accounting and Business Research* (Spring 1980), pp. 176-86.

______, "A Case for Cash Flow Reporting," *Journal of Business Finance* (Summer 1972), pp. 27-36.

______, *Cash Flow Accounting* (London: Van Nostrand Reinhold, 1984).

______, "Cash Flow Accounting and the Allocation Problems," *Journal of Business Finance and Accounting* (Autumn 1982), pp. 341-52.

______, "The Cash Flow Accounting Alternative for Corporate Financial Reporting," *Trends in Managerial and Financial Accounting,* vol. 1, ed. C. Van Dam (London: Martinus Nijhoff, 1978), pp. 63-84.

______, "Cash Flow Accounting and Corporate Financial Reporting," in *Essays in British Accounting Research,* ed. M. Bromwich and A. Hopwood (London: Pitman, 1981), pp. 63-78.

———. "Cash Flow Accounting, Profit and Performance Measurement: A Response to a Challenge," *Accounting and Business Research* (Spring 1985), pp. 93-97.

———, "Cash Flows and Net Realizable Values: Further Evidence of the Intuitive Concepts," *Abacus* (December 1984), pp. 125-37.

———, "The Contribution of Fisher to Cash Flow Accounting," *Journal of Business Finance and Accounting* (Autumn 1979), pp. 321-30.

———, "Goodwill: An Example of Will-o'-the-Wisp Accounting," *Accounting and Business Research* (Autumn 1971), pp. 318-28.

———, "Laker Airways: The Cash Flow Truth," *Accountancy* (June 1982), pp. 115-16.

———, "A Note on the Nature and Determination of Income," *Journal of Business Finance and Accounting* (Spring 1974), pp. 145-47.

———, "A Note on Users and Uses of Cash Flow Information," *Accounting and Business Research* (Spring 1983), pp. 103-6.

———, "Reporting Cash Flows and Net Realizable Values," *Accounting and Business Research* (Spring 1981), pp. 163-70.

———, "A Survey of Accountants' Opinions on Cash Flow Reporting," *Abacus* (December 1981), pp. 130-44.

———, "Towards a Practice of Cash Flow Analysis," *Discussion Paper* 13 (Edinburgh: University of Edinburgh, 1981).

———, "What Cash Flow Analysis Says About BL's Finances," *Financial Times* (October 23, 1981), p. 15.

Lee, T. A., and A. W. Stark, "A Cash Flow Disclosure of Government-Supported Enterprises' Results," *Journal of Business and Accounting* (Spring 1984), pp. 1-11.

Lee, T. A., and D. P. Tweedie, *Institutional Use and Understanding of Corporate Financial Information* (London: Institute of Chartered Accountants in England and Wales, 1981).

———, *The Private Shareholder and the Corporate Report* (London: Institute of Chartered Accountants in England and Wales, 1977).

Loscalzo, William, *Cash Flow Forecasting* (New York: McGraw-Hill, 1982).

Mason, Perry Empey, *Cash Flow Analysis and Funds Statement* (New York: American Institute of Certified Public Accountants, 1961).

Meyer, P. E., "The Accounting Entity," *Abacus* (December 1973), pp. 116-26.

Milling, Bryan E., *Cash Flow Problem Solver: Procedures and Rationals for the Independent Businessman* (Radnor, Pa.: Chilton, 1981).

Paton, W., *Accounting Theory* (Chicago: Accounting Studies Press, 1962).

Revsine, L., *Replacement Cost Accounting* (Englewood Cliffs, N.J.: Prentice-Hall, 1973).

Rutherford, B. A., "Cash Flow Reporting and Distributional Allocations: A Note," *Journal of Business Finance and Accounting* (Summer 1983), pp. 313-16.

———, "The Interpretation of Cash Flow Reports and the Other Allocation Problem," *Abacus* (June 1982), pp. 40-49.

Stamp, E., "Financial Reports on Entity: EX Uno Plures," *Accounting for a Simplified Firm Owing Depreciable Assets*, ed. R. R. Sterling and A. L. Thomas (Houston: Scholar Books, 1979), pp. 163-80.

———, "Useful Arbitrary Allocations," *Accounting Review* (July 1971), pp. 472-79.

Staubus, G. J., *Making Accounting Decisions* (Houston: Scholars, 1977).

______, "The Relevance of Cash Flows," *Asset Valuation*, ed. R. R. Sterling, (Houston: Scholars, 1971).

______, *A Theory of Accounting to Investors* (Berkeley: University of California Press, 1961).

Sterling, R. R., "In Defense of Accounting in the United States," *Abacus* (December 1966), pp. 180-83.

______. "Earnings Per Share Is a Poor Indicator of Performance," *Omega* (1974), pp. 11-32.

______, *Theory of the Measurement of Enterprise Income* (Lawrence: University of Kansas Press, 1970).

______, *Towards a Science of Accounting* (Houston: Scholars, 1979).

Thomas, A. L., *The Allocation Problem in Financial Accounting Theory*, Studies in Accounting Research No. 3 (Evanston, Ill.: American Accounting Association, 1969).

______, *The Allocation Problem: Part Two*, Studies in Accounting Research No. 9 (Sarasota, Fla.: American Accounting Association, 1974).

______, *A Behavioral Analysis of Joint-Cost Allocation and Transfer Pricing* (Houston: Stipes Publishing, 1970).

______, "Matching: Up From Our Black Hole," in *Accounting for a Simplified Firm Owning Depreciable Assets*, ed. R. R. Sterling and A. L. Thomas (Houston: Scholars, 1979).

Tweedie, D. P., "Cash Flows and Realizable Values: The Intuitive Accounting Concepts? An Empirical Test," *Accounting and Business Research* (Winter 1977), pp. 2-13.

Vatter, W. J., *The Fund Theory of Accounting and Its Implications for Financial Reports* (Chicago: University of Chicago Press, 1947).

Whittington, G., "Accounting and Economics," *Current Issues in Accounting*, ed. B. Carsberg and T. Hope (London: Philip Allan, 1977).

7

ACCOUNTING FOR THE DEVELOPING COUNTRIES

The developing countries face difficult problems in their attempts to achieve progress in their economic development programs. Their efforts led to the use of a new economic subdiscipline, namely, development economics, to address the various problems and policies affecting economic development. These problems and policies are either domestic (such as growth, poverty and income distribution, unemployment, population growth, education, agricultural transformation and rural development) or international (such as international trade and development, foreign investment aid, and a new international economic order).[1]

Accounting plays a crucial role in economic development too by providing the right information necessary to implement the above mentioned policies. This role is particularly important in development planning in general and project appraisal in particular. Accordingly, the role of accounting in economic development, development planning, and project appraisal is examined in this chapter. In addition, the theories of international accounting as they affect the Third World, the standard-setting strategies for the developing countries, and the actors involved in international standard setting are also explored.

THE STATE OF ACCOUNTING IN THE DEVELOPING COUNTRIES

History has shown that the rate of growth and the development of a nation's economy in both the private and public sector are tied to a certain extent to the adequacy of the accounting system and the accounting development process in that country. As the developing countries suffer

from relatively low growth rate, we may safely propose that action in the development accounting process is urgently needed in the developing countries. There are in effect serious challenges facing accounting in the developing coutries. George M. Scott feels that the accounting information in these nations is deficient, irrelevant, unreliable, and often lacking credibility.[2] He suggests that this rudimentary level of accounting is a result of some of the environmental factors of each particular nation. For example, the presence of a class elite controlling major domestic firms may have an adverse effect on accounting development because it inhibits the growth of private capital markets. As this elite has a strong prerogative on inside information, there is no tradition of providing adequate financial information to the public to facilitate decision making. Another phenomenon perceived as detrimental to the growth of an accounting tradition is the lack of identification with governmental policies. This leads to an attitude of noncooperation with and even hostility to the government, often reflected by the common practice of tax evasion.

It is appropriate, however, to note that the natural erosion of the elite class system and the consequent social mobility has created in some of these countries a new atmosphere more favorable to economic and accounting development.

The insignificant role played by accounting as a source of relevant information for decision making is described by R. Dominguez of the Inter-American Development Bank as follows:

Many sectors do not properly recognize the part that accounting has to play in enterprise management, and they have not made appropriate use of it. Among entrepreneurs and managers, including those from the public sector, there is insufficient awareness of the value of accounting and of the information it may provide as an instrument of administrative and financial control. Business ownership, even of large-scale enterprises, is often concentrated among a few individuals. There may be no capital market; if there is one, its field of action is quite limited. This system of broadly based ownership faces a variety of difficulties, and the climate of trust and confidence needed to make it viable is, for several reasons, nonexistent. Lacking broadly based investment by numerous minority shareholders, the need for the protection afforded by the regulation of enterprises of this kind has not been felt, and this extends even to the accounting aspects. Business affairs are frequently conducted in secrecy. Rather than relying on their clients' financial statement—in which they have little confidence—financial institutions emphasize other factors in their credit investigations, such as reputation and personal knowledge of the owners of the borrowing enterprises and substantial security pledged in the form of personal property.

Financial accounting is often limited to the deficient recording of transactions; it is rudimentary and not kept up to date. It is maintained solely for the purpose of satisfying the formalities required by law and the tax authorities. The information provided by such records is consequently of little value in assessing the performance of an enterprise. Accounting methods and practices are usually outdated, even

anachronistic, and there is no consistency in their application. In fact, accounting is not organized in such a way as to provide useful information. Most of the countries have not adopted—in some cases they have not even made efforts to adopt—a body of accounting standards to govern the recording of transactions and the presentation of financial statements. Accounting literature from the more developed countries has had considerable influence, but this in itself is a problem because the developed countries have different practices for recording the same transactions. Add to this variances introduced locally, which quite often have not been based on sound technical grounds, and the problem of standardization is compounded.[3]

THEORIES OF INTERNATIONAL ACCOUNTING AND THE THIRD WORLD

International accounting has tended to mean different things to different people, and that has colored the extant theories of international accounting. Various authors find themselves proposing various definitions of international accounting and henceforth of international accounting theories. I. L. Fantl suggests three concepts of international accounting: (a) a universal system, (b) a descriptive and informative approach including all the methods and standards of all countries, and (c) accounting practices of foreign subsidiaries and parent companies.[4] The same classification was used by Mahmoud Qureshi, and by Thomas R. Weirich, Clarence G. Avery, and Henry R. Anderson, for establishing a framework for viewing the different concepts of international accounting.[5] Weirich, Avery, and Anderson's classification included world accounting, international accounting, and accounting for parent company and foreign subsidiary.[6]

The concept of "universal" or "world accounting" is by far the largest in scope. It directs international accounting to the formulation and study of a universally accepted set of accounting principles. It aims for an internationally complete standardization of accounting principles. The definition of Weirich, Avery, and Anderson is:

World Accounting. In the framework of this concept, international accounting is considered to be a universal system that would be adopted in all countries. A worldwide set of generally accepted accounting principles (GAAP), such as the set maintained in the United States, would be established. Practices and principles would be developed which were applicable to all countries. This concept would be the ultimate goal of an international accounting system.[7]

While very commendable, this goal is unlikely to be reached in the near future and may be safely characterized as highly idealistic by some and even utopian by others. As will be seen in the rest of the book, pessimistic attitudes are based on the many obstacles to a complete standardization of accounting principles. Chapter 2 examines in detail some of the factors determining accounting differences internationally.

The concept of "*comparative*" or "*international accounting*" directs international accounting to a study and understanding of national differences in accounting. It involves awareness of the international diversity in corporate accounting and reporting practices, understanding of the accounting principles and practices of individual countries, and ability to assess the impact of diverse accounting practices on financial reporting. There is a general consensus in accounting literature that the term *international accounting* refers to "comparative accounting principles." Weirich, Avery, and Anderson define the term as follows:

> *International Accounting.* A second major concept of the term international accounting involves a descriptive and informative approach. Under this concept, international accounting includes all varieties of principles, methods and standards of accounting of *all* countries. This concept includes a set of generally accepted accounting principles established for each country, thereby requiring the accountant to be multiple principle conscious when studying international accounting. . . . No universal or perfect set of principles would be expected to be established. A collection of all principles, methods and standards would be considered as the international accounting system. These variations result because of differing geographic, social, economic, political and legal influences.[8]

The concept of "*parent-foreign subsidiary* accounting" or "accounting for foreign *subsidiaries*" is by far the oldest and narrowest in scope. It reduces international accounting to the process of consolidating the accounts of the parent company and its subsidiaries and translating foreign currency into local currency. Weirich, Avery, and Anderson provide the following definition:

> *Accounting for Foreign Subsidiaries.* The third major concept that may be applied to "international accounting" refers to the accounting practices of a parent company and a foreign subsidiary. A reference to a particular country or domicile is needed under the concept for effective internal financial reporting. The accountant is concerned mainly with the translation and adjustment of the subsidiary's financial statement. Different accounting problems arise and different accounting principles are to be followed depending upon which country is used as a reference for translation and adjustment purposes.[9]

The advent of new international accounting books on the market expanded the framework to include new notions of international accounting. As a result, an exhaustive list of the international accounting concepts and theories was provided by F. E. Amenkhienan to include the following:

1. Universal or world theory;
2. Multinational theory;
3. Comparative theory;
4. International transactions theory; and
5. Translation theory.[10]

These theories imply respectively

> (1) a universal concept being nurtured by the pragmatists who believe that the solutions to the problems raised in internal reporting lie in worldwide uniformity in accounting; (2) a multinational concept which suggests that international accounting includes all the varieties of principles, standards, and practices of all countries; (3) a comparative concept which suggests an analytical classification of national accounting systems as has been done in the other social sciences such as economics, politics and law; (4) an international concept built around accounting information needed in international trade and international investment decisions; and (5) a translational concept which is used to characterize accounting for parent companies and foreign subsidiaries.[11]

Each of these theories provides some grounds for the development of a conceptual framework for international accounting. While arguments can be made for the desirability of one theory over the others, the first three—universal, multinational, and comparative—have generated better following than the other two. The debate lies between those favoring uniformity leading to a universal theory, those favoring standardization leading to a multinational theory, and those favoring analysis of different national accounting systems leading to a comparative theory. The position of the Third World is divided along the three lines, with some countries taking an open approach to the North and favoring either uniformity or standardization, like Indonesia or Nigeria, and some favoring a separate, distinct system, like Algeria.

STANDARD-SETTING STRATEGIES FOR THE DEVELOPING COUNTRIES

The developing countries are characterized by relatively inadequate and unreliable accounting systems and generally new and untested standard-setting institutions. Theory development and academic and professional accounting research add to the economic, social, political, and institutional problems that may be acting as deterrents to an effective standard setting. In spite of these limitations the development of basic accounting systems and procedures and the process of standard setting has accelerated as evidenced by the increasing number of professional organizations, standard-setting books, and academic accounting associations as well as by the increasing membership of these groups in international standard-setting bodies.

The standard-setting process in the developing countries has not followed a unique strategy proper to these countries and their context. In fact, four strategies may be identified: (a) the evolutionary approach, (b) the development through transfer of accounting technology, (c) the adoption of international accounting standards, and (d) the development of accounting

standards based on analysis of accounting principles and practices in the advanced nations against the backdrop of their underlying investment.[12] These strategies are reviewed below.

The Evolutionary Approach

The evolutionary approach consists of an isolationist approach to standard setting whereby the developing country develops its own standard without any outside interferences or influences. The particular developing country defines its own specific accounting objectives and needs and proceeds to meet them by developing its own techniques, concepts, institutions, profession, and education in isolation. The particular country may feel its context to be unique enough to justify this drastic approach of standard setting. The learning process in this approach has to come from the local experiences rather than the international experiences. It assumes the foreign partners will adapt to its own idiosyncratic rules and may have to if they want to continue to trade with the country and/or maintain operations. Naturally, it may create an additional cost to the foreign partners who may feel the conditions onerous enough to justify complete cooperation. In addition, the absence of an adequate local accounting technology may hamper not only the local firms but also the foreign firms operating in the country.

The Transfer of Technology Approach

The development through transfer of accounting technology may result from either the operations and activities of international accounting firms, multinationals, and academicians practicing in the developing countries, or the various international treaties and cooperative arrangements calling for exchanges of information and technology. Adolf Enthoven, for example, describes the benefits of U.S. accounting assistance to the developing world as follows:

> U.S. accounting and accountants have already had a positive effect on accounting systems, procedures and training in many developing economies. For example, the affiliates of U.S. MNEs have developed sound financial management systems. Other U.S. companies have entered into joint ventures with foreign companies or have set up their own organizations in these countries for the production and sale of goods and services. Good financial and managerial accounting methods have accompanied these investments. Many U.S. CPA firms have either established corresponding relationships with foreign firms or set up branch offices abroad. Although much of value has been accomplished by U.S. accountants in CPA firms and in industry developing economies, such activities have generally been directed toward certain companies or to serve CPA firm clients. More might be done; however, I recognize that this task isn't the first priority of accountants in public practice and industry.[13]

Because most developing countries may not have given formal attention to the formation and implementation of a strategy which facilitates the transfer of accounting technology, or the development of an indigenous accounting profession, Belverd Needles, Jr., proposed a conceptual framework by which a country may formulate a strategy for the international transfer of accounting technology as part of its overall economic plan.[14] It is shown in Exhibit 7.1. Basically, national goals combine with the social, political, and economic environment and general resources and constraints to influence the overall economic plan. The economic plan itself contains as a subplan a strategy for the transfer of accounting technology, composed of (a) objectives for the accounting technology transfer, (b) strategy, (c) channels of transfer, and (d) levels of accounting technology. The three types of technology, individual, organizational, and independent professional, are defined as follows:

T_1 — level of technical accounting knowledge possessed by individuals;

T_2 — level of sophistication of accounting techniques used by government and business organizations; and

T_3 — level of advancement of an independent accounting profession.[15]

While the mere transfer of accounting technology may appear to be a direct benefit to the developing countries, there is the cost associated with (a) the transfer of the wrong or inapplicable technology, (b) the lack of appropriate infrastructure for the correct application of the technology, (c) the increased dependence on outside experts, (d) the lack of incentives for developing local standards, and (e) the horrible loss of pride by some culture groups. These costs ought to be compared with the benefits of technology transfer by each of the developing countries. It is a strategic decision which is an integral part of the overall economic plan as suggested earlier. The whole process of development ought to include not only economic growth strategies but accounting growth strategies, and therein lies the question of the desirability of accounting technology transfer by the developing countries.

The Adoption of International Accounting Standards

The strategy available to the developing countries consists of joining the International Accounting Standards Committee (IASC) or some of the other international standards bodies identified earlier and adopting "wholesale" their pronouncements. The rationale behind such strategy may be to (a) reduce the setup and production costs of accounting standards, (b) join the international harmonization drive, (c) facilitate the growth of foreign investment which may be needed, (d) enable its profession to

emulate well-established professional standards of behavior and conduct, and (e) legitimize its status as a full-fledged member of the international community. In fact, some of the developing countries give more credence to the IASC and other standards than do some of the developed countries that have a dominant influence in the preparation of such standards.

Exhibit 7.1
Framework for the International Transfer of Accounting Technology

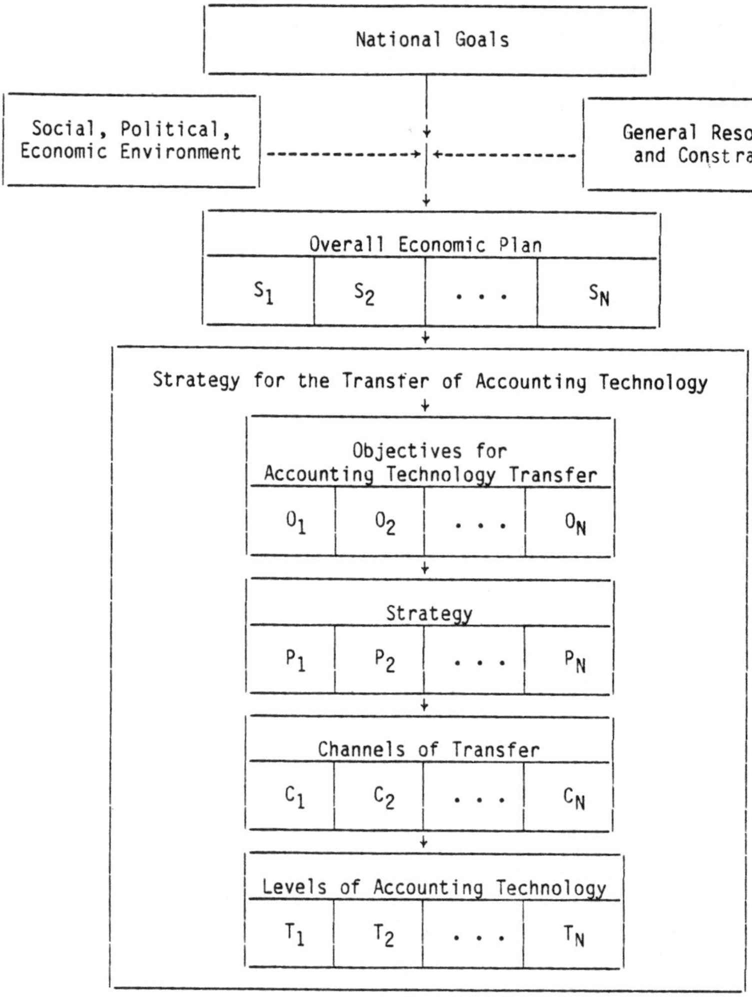

Source: B. E. Needles, Jr., "Implementing a Framework for the International Transfer of Accounting Technology," *International Journal of Accounting, Education and Research* (Fall 1976), p. 49. Reprinted with permission.

The question is whether the benefits described as accruing to the developing countries from the mere adoption of the international accounting standards may be outweighed by the misspecifying of costs. Indeed, the international standards for accounting for various transactions occurring in the advanced countries may be totally irrelevant to some of the developing countries as these transactions have little chance of occurring or may be occurring in a fashion more specific to the context of the developing countries. The particular situations occurring in the developing countries call for specific and local standard setting. In addition, the institutional and market factors of these countries are different enough in some contexts to justify a more "situationist" approach to standard setting. Amenkhienan makes the same point as follows:

> The case against the adoption of international standards by developing nations as an alternative to developing their own local standards is a conclusive one. Accounting in each country should develop in a manner relevant to the needs and objectives of that country. The situational variables should determine the patterns of development.[16]

This situationist strategy has also been labeled as the zero-based option, or what George Scott refers to as "fresh start" because its use established international standards as a basis toward a better fitting with the particular economic development context of the developing country. Scott elaborates as follows: "The major alternative is to effect a relatively clean break with accounting tradition in developing nations and to attempt to develop accounting with a 'fresh start' on the basis of the standards of accounting education, practices and professionalism that are embodied in economic evaluation accounting."[17]

The Situationist Strategy

The situationist strategy was also labeled as "the development of accounting standards based on an analysis of accounting principles and practices in the advanced nations against the backdrop of their underlying environments."[18] Basically, it calls for a consideration of the diagnostic factors which determine the development of accounting in the developing countries. A standard meeting the constraints imposed by these factors can be deemed relevant and useful to the developing countries. The total of these standards constitutes the system of reporting and disclosure of the developing country. The factors influencing it may be represented as being influenced by the cultural linguistics, political and civil rights, economic and demographic characteristics, and legal and tax environment of the country in question. In other words, based on cultural relativism, linguistic relativism, political and civil relativism, economic and demographic relativism, and legal and tax relativism, the accounting concepts and the reporting and disclosure systems in any given country rest on the varying aspects of that country.[19]

ACTORS INVOLVED IN THE HARMONIZATION DRIVE

Whatever strategy for standard setting is chosen by the developing countries, they can't escape the fact that there is an ongoing international harmonization drive. They could either learn from it or become a legitimate partner depending on the strategy they choose.

Accountants International Study Group (AISG)

The AISG was formed as a three-nation group to study accounting and auditing requirements and practices in the United States, the United Kingdom, and Canada. Its terms of reference were as follows: "To institute comparative studies as to accounting thought and practice in participating countries, to make reports from time to time, which, subject to the prior approval of the sponsoring Institutes, would be issued to members of those Institutes." Before being disbanded, the AISG issued 20 studies, which are listed in Exhibit 7.2. Most of the studies were comparative and were not binding on the sponsoring institutes.

Exhibit 7.2
Studies Produced by the Accountants International Study Group (AISG)

1. Accounting and Auditing Approaches to Inventories in Three Nations (1968)
2. The Independent Auditor's Reporting Standards in Three Nations (1969)
3. Using the Work and Report of Another Auditor (1970)
4. Accounting for Corporate Income Taxes (1971)
5. Reporting by Diversified Companies (1972)
6. Consolidated Financial Statements (1972)
7. The Funds Statement (1973)
8. Materiality in Accounting (1974)
9. Extraordinary Items, Prior Period Adjustments, and Changes in Accounting Principles (1974)
10. Published Profit Forecasts (1975)
11. Comparative Glossary of Accounting Terms in Canada, the United Kingdom and the United States (1975)
12. Accounting for Goodwill (1975)
13. Interim Financial Reporting (1975)
14. International Financial Reporting (1976)
15. Going Concern Problems (1976)
16. Audit Committees (1976)
17. Independence of Auditors (1977)
18. Accounting for Pension Costs (1977)
19. Related Party Transactions (1978)
20. Revenue Recognition (1978)

International Federation of Accounting Committee (IFAC)

Various international organizations preceded the creation of the IFAC. First, the International Congress of Accounts (ICA) was founded in 1904 with the general objective of increasing interaction and exchange of ideas between accountants of different countries. Second, in 1972 the ICA founded the International Coordination Committee for the Accounting Profession (ICCAP) with the objective to conduct specific studies of professional accounting ethics, education and training, and the structure of regional accounting organizations. Third, the ICCAP dissolved in 1976 to be reconstituted as the International Federation of Accounting Committee (IFAC). The goals of the IFAC are best expressed by the following 12-point program to guide its efforts:

1. Develop statements that would serve as guidelines for international auditing practices.
2. Establish a suggested minimum code of ethics to which it is hoped that member bodies would subscribe and which could be further refined as appropriate.
3. Determine the requirements and develop programs for the professional education and training of accountants.
4. Evaluate, develop, and report on financial management and other management accounting techniques and procedures.
5. Collect, analyze, research, and disseminate information on the management of public accounting practices to assist practitioners in conducting their practices more effectively.
6. Undertake other studies of value to accountants such as, possibly, a study of the legal liability of auditors.
7. Foster closer relations with users of financial statements, including preparers, trade unions, financial institutions, industry, government, and others.
8. Maintain close relations with regional bodies and explore the potential for establishing other regional bodies as well as for assisting in their organization and development, as appropriate. Assign appropriate projects to existing regional bodies.
9. Establish regular communication among the members of IFAC and with other interested organizations through the medium of a newsletter.
10. Organize and promote the exchange of technical information, educational materials, and professional publications and other literature emanating from other bodies.
11. Organize and conduct an International Congress of Accountants approximately every five years.
12. Seek to expand the membership of the IFAC.[20]

As of 1984, IFAC's membership reached 85 professional accountancy bodies from 63 countries. Its governing bodies consist of an assembly

comprising one representative designated as such by each member of the IFAC and a council comprising 15 representatives of member bodies from 15 countries. The agenda of the IFAC is set by the following seven standing committees: education, ethics, international auditing practices, international congresses, management accounting, planning, and regional organizations. The International Auditing Practices Committee (OAPC) of the IFAC is the most active and most important.

International Accounting Standards Committee (IASC)

The IASC was founded in 1973 with the following objectives contained in its constitution:

a. to formulate and publish in the public interest accounting standards to be observed in the presentation of financial statements and to promote their worldwide acceptance and observance;
b. to work generally for the improvement and harmonization of regulations, accounting standards and procedures relating to the presentation of financial statements.[21]

This translates into a goal of developing a common international approach to standards setting in accounting aimed at a worldwide harmonization and improvement of accounting principles used in the preparation of financial statements for the benefit of the public.

The IASC has an operating structure composed of the IASC board, the consultative group, and various steering committees. Its procedure of exposure and comment is as follows:

a. After discussion, the IASC Board selects a topic that is felt to need an International Accounting Standard, and assigns it to a Steering Committee. All IASC member bodies are invited to submit material for consideration.
b. The Steering Committee, assisted by the IASC Secretariat, considers the issues involved and presents a point outline on the subject to the Board.
c. The Steering Committee receives the comments of the Board and prepares a preliminary draft on the proposed standard.
d. Following review by the Board, the draft is circulated to all member bodies for their comments.
e. The Steering Committee prepares a revised draft, which, after approval by at least two-thirds of the Board, is published as an Exposure Draft. Comments are invited from all interested parties.
f. At each stage in the consideration of drafts, member bodies refer for guidance to the appropriate accounting research committees in their own organizations.
g. At the end of an exposure period (usually six months) comments are submitted to IASC and are considered by the Steering Committee responsible for the project.

h. The Steering Committee then submits a revised draft to the Board for approval as an International Accounting Standard.

i . The issue of a Standard requires approval by at least three-quarters of the Board, after which the approved text of the Standard is sent to all member bodies for translation and publication.[22]

As of 1984 the following fiscal standards have been produced.

IAS1 Disclosure of Accounting Policies (1975)

IAS2 Valuation and Presentation of Inventories in the Context of the Historical Cost System (1975)

IAS3 Consolidated Financial Statements (1976)

IAS4 Depreciation Accounting (1976)

IAS5 Information to Be Disclosed in Financial Statements (1976)

IAS6 Accounting Responses to Changing Prices

IAS7 Statement of Changes in Financial Postion (1977)

IAS8 Unusual and Prior Period Items and Changes in Accounting Policies (1978)

IAS9 Accounting for Research and Development Activities (1978)

IAS10 Contingencies and Events Occurring after the Balance Sheet Date (1978)

IAS11 Accounting for Construction Contracts (1979)

IAS12 Accounting for Income Taxes (1979)

IAS13 Presentation of Current Assests and Current Liabilities (1979)

IAS14 Preparing Financial Information by Segment (1981)

IAS15 Information Reflecting the Effects of Changing Prices (1981)

IAS16 Accounting for Property, Plant and Equipment (1982)

IAS17 Accounting for Leases (1982)

IAS18 Revenue Recognition (1983)

IAS19 Accounting for Retirement Benefits in Financial Statements of Employers (1983)

IAS20 Accounting for Government Grants and Disclosure of Government Assistance (1983)

IAS21 Accounting for the Effects of Changes in Foreign Exchange Rates (1983)

IAS22 Accounting for Business Combinations (1983)

IAS23 Capitalization of Borrowing Costs (1984)

IAS24 Disclosure of Related Party Transactions (1984)

IAS25 Accounting for Investments

IAS26 Accounting and Reporting by Retirement Benefit Plans (1987)

The success of the IASC's efforts naturally rests on acceptance of the standards by member countries and recognition and support international-

ly. Noncompliance with international standards has been attributed to the following reasons by Sir Henry Benson, the founder of IASC:

> Some countries take the view that they cannot require compliance locally until they are satisfied that the Standards are internationally acceptable. Some see local legislation as an obstacle to the introduction of international standards. Some accounting bodies do not have the power of discipline over their members, and cannot therefore impose compliance with either national or international standards. Some countries have not yet overcome stubborn local resistance from the business community.[23]

Besides these obstacles there is definite evidence that effort toward harmonization is not equally shared by all members of IASC. T. R. Douglas summarized the situation as follows:

> Some accountancy bodies have declared to their members that international accounting standards are to be accorded the same status as domestic accounting standards. Each IAS is accompanied by an explanation of the relationship between the international standard and any domestic standard dealing with the same subject.
>
> Other accountancy bodies have issued statements declaring support for the concept of international standards and strongly encouraging their members to accept them. Some of these bodies indicate the extent to which an international standard differs from the related domestic standard. They often offer to review, or encourage the relevant body to review, the basis of the domestic standard, with the objective of eliminating any differences.
>
> There are some member countries, however, that have not yet presented any format statement of the status of IAS's to the members of the accountancy profession.[24]

One piece of evidence, however, of increasing compliance and national support of IASC pronouncements is a letter written in November 1980 by member bodies in Canada to the 300 largest companies quoted on the Toronto Stock Exchange, urging them to include a reference such as: "The accompanying financial statements are prepared in accordance with accounting principles generally accepted in Canada and conform in all material respects to International Accounting Standards."[25] In fact, the IASC's success rests on the best efforts of local professional organizations to ensure that published financial statements in their countries comply with the International Accounting Standards in all material respects.

A second piece of evidence has been provided by the International Finance Corporation (IFC), which is an investment institution established by its member governments to further economic development by encouraging the growth of productive private enterprise in developing member countries. In effect, a recent publication of IFC "Financial Reporting Requirements (Manufacturing and Commercial Enterprises)" contains the following statement:

IFC recognizes that accounting policies vary from country to country. This could result in IFC receiving financial statements which are based on differing accounting policies. Hence, it is essential to include a summary of accounting policies applied as the first note to the financial statements as is adherence, in general, to generally accepted standards of reporting and disclosure. In deciding on accounting policies reference should be made, whenever applicable and practicable, to International Accounting Standards issued by the International Accounting Standards Committee (IASC). The IASC formulates and publishes basic standards to be observed in the presentation of audited accounts and financial statements.

United Nations

The United Nations (UN) became interested in accounting and the need for improved corporate reporting when the Group of Eminent Persons appointed to study the impact of multinational corporations advocated the formulation of an international, comparable system of standardization accounting and reporting. It also recommended the creation of a Group of Experts on International Standards of Accounting and Reporting. The group was created in 1976 with the following objectives:

a. To review the existing practice of reporting by transnational corporations and reporting requirements in different countries;
b. To identify gaps in information in existing corporate reporting and to examine the feasibility of various proposals for improved reporting;
c. To recommend a list of minimum items, together with their definition, that should be included in reports by transnational corporations and their affiliates, taking into account the recommendations of various groups concerned with the subject matter.[26]

As a result the group issued a report which included a 34-page list of recommended items to be disclosed by the "enterprise as a whole," that is, consolidated data, and by individual member companies, including the parent company. Following issuance of the report, an Intergovernmental Working Group of Experts on International Standards of Accounting and Reporting was formed with the objective of contributing to the harmonization of accounting standards. It does not function as a standards-setting body: its mandate is to review and discuss accounting and reporting standards. The group will consider, among other issues, whether the UN should promulgate accounting standards. Needless to say, this effort by the UN has created mixed international reaction. Most of the concerned institutions have expressed the feeling that accounting standards at the domestic or the international level are best set in the private sector. These same institutions are united in their support for the work of the IASC and national accountancy groups.

It is regrettable, however, that some nations do not agree with the UN effort. On May 20, 1966, the Permanent Representative of the United States to the UN informed the UN that the United States government had decided to resign from its position on the Intergovernmental Working Group. The reason for this withdrawal had been stated on February 26, 1986:

> The current work of the Working Group is of little usefulness to either the United States government or to the business community. Discussions of accounting and reporting practices and standards is covered adequately by international professional groups such as the International Accounting Standards Committee (IASC). Harmonization of standards, to the extent feasible, is best handled in more limited groupings such as the Organization of Economic Cooperation and Development (OECD).

While nobody is contesting the efforts of the IASC and OECD, it is still regrettable than the United States is withdrawing from an international effort to further accounting development. One would sincerely hope that this irrational act will be corrected with a more international and developing country-oriented administration in the White House.

Organization for Economic Cooperation and Development

The OECD is an organization whose members include 24 relatively industrialized noncommunist countries in Europe, Asia, North America, and Australia. A Declaration on International Investment and Multinational Enterprises was issued in 1976, including an annex titled "Guidelines for Multinational Enterprises," a section of which is subtitled "Disclosure of Information."[27] The major elements suggested to be disclosed are listed below:

> Enterprises should publish within reasonable time limits, on a regular basis, but at least annually, financial statements and other pertinent information relating to the enterprise as a whole comprising in particular:
>
> - the structure of the enterprise, showing the name and location of the parent company, its main affiliates, its percentage ownership, direct and indirect, in these affiliates, including shareholdings between them;
> - the geographical areas where operations are carried out and the principal activities carried on therein by the parent company and the main affiliates;
> - the operating results and sales by geographical area and the sales in the major lines of business for the enterprise as a whole;
> - significant new capital investment by geographical area and, as far as practicable, by major lines of business for the enterprise as a whole;
> - a statement of the sources and uses of funds by the enterprise as a whole;

- the average number of employees in each geographic area;
- research and development expenditure for the enterprise as a whole;
- the policies followed in respect of intra-group pricing; and
- the accounting policies, including those on consolidation, observed in compiling the published information.[28]

European Economic Community (EEC)

The EEC has also been active in achieving regional harmonization of accounting principles through a series of directives which, within the Treaty of Rome, are not as binding as regulations. The directive anticipates given results, but the mode and means of implementation are left to the member countries. The EEC is in fact the first supranational body to have important authority in financial reporting and disclosure. Its influence is so pervasive that its directives are perceived to have important effects on non-EEC-based multinationals operating in the community. Particularly relevant to international accounting are the fourth, fifth, and seventh directives.

The Fourth Directive

The fourth directive, formally adopted in 1978, deals with the annual financial statements of public and private companies, other than banks and insurance companies.[29] Its purposes have been summarized as follows:

1. Coordinating national laws for the protection of members and third parties relating to the publication, presentation, and content of annual accounts and reports of limited-liability companies, and the accounting principles used in their preparation.
2. Establishing in the EEC minimum equivalent legal requirements for disclosure of financial information to the public by companies which are in competition with one another.
3. Establishing the principle that annual accounts should give a true and fair view of a company's assets and liabilities, and of its financial position and profit or loss.
4. Providing the fullest possible information about limited companies to shareholders and third parties (with some relief to smaller companies).[30]

The major aspects relevant to international accounting were Articles 1 and 2 on types of companies covered by the directive and the general reporting requirements; Articles 3-27 on the format of annual reports; Articles 28-39 on the valuation rules; Articles 44-50 on publication requirements; and Articles 51-52 on the procedural, statutory changes in national laws required for compliance.

The Fifth Directive

The proposed fifth directive, revised in 1984, deals with the structure, management, and external audits of limited-liability corporations. In the

revised draft, the directive proposes to require a company that employs more than 1,000 workers in the EEC (or is part of a group of companies that employs more than 1,000 workers in the EEC) to allow the employees to participate in the company's decision-making structure. In addition, the proposal specifies certain rules concerning annual meetings of shareholders, the adoption of the company's annual financial statements, and the appointment, compensation, and duties of the company's auditors.

The Seventh Directive

The seventh directive, issued in June 1983, addresses the issue of consolidated financial statements and offers some guidelines for more standardization of accounting reporting. Companies in EEC member countries and non-EEC corporations with subsidiaries in a member country are required to file consolidated financial statements in the country. However, each of the ten EEC countries has five years to pass legislation to implement the directive, and annual reports do not have to conform until 1990.

Other Actors

The preceding sections identify the most important actors involved in the harmonization drive. Various other national, regional, and international groups are emerging as active in the same drive. They include basically the following.

1. ASEAN Federation of Accountants (AFA)
2. African Accounting Council (AAC)
3. Union Européene des Experts Comptables Économiques et Financiers (UEC)
4. Asociación Interamericana de Contabilidad (AIC)
5. Confederation of Asian and Pacific Accountants (CAPA)
6. Nordic Federation of Accountants (NFA)
7. Association of Accountancy Bodies in West Africa (ABWA)
8. American Accounting Association (AAA)
9. Canadian Association of Academic Accountants (CAAA)
10. European Accounting Association (EAA)
11. Japan Accounting Association (JAA)
12. Association of University Instructors in Accounting (AUIA)
13. Financial Analysts Federations (FAF)
14. Financial Executives Institute (FEI)
15. Arab Society of Certified Accountants (ASCA)

Given the proliferation of actors involved or willing to be involved in the harmonization drive, one would expect a lot on interrelationships among these bodies and cross-representation in an attempt to exercise some influence in the international accounting arena.

THE ROLE OF ACCOUNTING IN ECONOMIC DEVELOPMENT

The role of accounting in economic development rests on a clear understanding of what is required to efficiently achieve and implement economic and social policies. First, accounting has to be structured in developing countries to conform to the social, political, and economic systems and institutions. Accordingly, an examination of the development of accounting in the developing countries is the first objective of this section. Second, economic development rests on development planning in general and project appraisal in particular. Both concepts are also examined in this section. Third, the role of accounting in economic development rests in its usefulness and adaptability to the environment of development planning. Standardization of accounting is suggested as the solution. Finally, the importance of accounting education to economic development is examined.

The Development of Accounting in the Developing Countries

Accounting in the developing countries has for a long time been the result of the spread of Western accounting, which in turn resulted from colonialism, or powerful foreign investors, or through the influence of multinational companies, foreign aid, and education. Consider, for example, the following statement by T. L. Wilkinson:

> The accounting principles of one country have never been "sold" to another country on the basis of convincing arguments in support of those principles. Accounting principles of one country have moved to another country when two conditions have existed:
>
> 1. The second country had no organized body of accounting principles in the first place and
> 2. Large amounts of capital from the first country were invested in business in the second country, with the consequent ability on the part of those investors to impose their own accounting requirements on the businesses.[31]

Given this situation, the solution which seems the most obvious and acceptable to the developing countries is to accept these "foreign" techniques and accept the harmonization or internal legitimization and extension of currently dominant practices. Some developing countries have adopted this kind of strategy. Indonesia, for example, as a result of factors

such as multinationals, international firms of accountants, U.S. aid, and language, is adopting American techniques to the point where university courses are biased toward American texts and courses are structured with much more emphasis upon finance and management. The resulting situation is impractical, as described in the following statement:

> As a consequence of this evolution, the Indonesian profession is Dutch in its qualification structure, but the training (which is exclusively undertaken in universities) and philosophy are American. Neither, however, is the least relevant to the needs of Indonesia, a country with no companies act, no capital market, a massive public sector, and an economic and cultural environment totally dissimilar to that of the Netherlands or of the United States.[32]

The question is, then, to determine whether the developing countries should continue in their efforts to comply with the international harmonization efforts, which some may label as merely the internal legitimization and extension of Western dominant practices; or should they concentrate upon an assessment of their information needs in the private, public, and national accounting sectors and educate their accountants to produce and use that information?

Most of those familiar with the economic, cultural, political, and social conditions in the developing countries would argue that each developing country should create an accounting system appropriate to its own needs. Various arguments are used to support this position. A general argument used in support of a unique system for each developing country is that harmonization in international accounting can be achieved only when all countries have the same objectives from the accounting systems.

Second, international harmonization attempts as currently dominated by Anglo-American accounting principles and practices are merely legitimizing certain values worldwide and may be harmful to the developing countries. J. M. Samuels and J. C. Oliga argue the case as follows:

> The point is that most developing countries had little chance to evolve accounting systems which truly reflected the needs and circumstances of their own societies. Their existing systems are largely extensions of those in developed countries. In this light, the benefits of their being more deeply integrated into systems that predominantly suit developed countries become questionable. For the Third World, international harmonization may do more harm than good if it preempts the possibility of changing the old, inappropriate systems and evolving new ones which are better suited to their development needs. Furthermore, given that Anglo-American accounting principles and practices currently dominate the attempts at harmonization, the attempt becomes largely a one-sided exercise, and "international" standards essentially represent internationalization of domestic standards of dominant members of the standard-setting bodies.[33]

Third, international standards, which may result from the international harmonization of accounting, can only assist users to make decisions at an international level, which is far different from the needs of users from developing countries. Besides, the needs of users in the developing countries are not essentially restricted to financial costs and returns. These needs are more complex. As emphasized in the cost-benefit literature, the economic decisions in a developing country should be based on a knowledge of shadow prices and costs. That includes more information than that provided by accounts conforming to international standards. In most developing countries, the public sector is larger than the private sector and relies on different information requirements for economic decisions than those provided by accounting standards of the private sector. As a result, developing countries may have to supplement accounting standards for the private sector by assessing their information needs in the government and national accounting sectors and corresponding accounting standards.

The developing countries need an accounting system most uniform to their historical, political, economic, and social conditions. There are a lot of questions which need to be answered before the construction of such a system. Examples of such questions include the following:

> To what extent should current costs, replacement costs, social costs, benefits, and so on be taken into account? What use should be made of sensitivity analysis? Should a feasibility study be made subject to independent audit? If so, should this be carried by an internal auditor, a private external auditor, or a government auditor? At the max level, what are the objectives of the government and what information is necessary to devise plans for the attainment of those objectives? What rules are necessary to ensure that the private sector provides the necessary information in an easily accessible fashion? Does information need to be submitted to the government on foreign exchange transactions, investment plans, projected imports and exports, profits (if so, how defined), social costs and benefits, and such? Which accountancy system will permit this information to be collected in the most efficient and best-integrated fashion? How are the decisions of multinationals to be monitored? Should these be controlled through formal concession agreements? If so, what right of access is the government to be given to obtain information to ensure that the agreement is being adhered to? Should the government have the right to monitor investment plans and feasibility studies therefor?[34]

Development Planning and Accountancy

Development planning is generally accepted as essential to the economic development of the developing and even some of the developed countries. The need for planning in the developing countries is accentuated by the "failure" of the market in those countries to price factors of production correctly. This argument was forcefully made in a 1965 UN Conference on Planning as follows:

> It is an integrated task of planning to achieve the best possible use of scarce resources for economic development. . . . The need for using appropriate criteria for selecting projects arose because of the failure of the market mechanism to provide a proper guideline. In less-developed economies, market prices of such factors of production as labor, capital and foreign exchange deviated substantially from their social opportunity costs and were not, therefore, a correct measure of the relative scarcity or abundance of the factor in question.[35]

Besides the market-failure argument, development planning was justified for a better resource mobilization and allocation, a better development-oriented atmosphere, and as grounds for foreign aid.[36] Given this rationale for development planning, the questions become to effectively define and implement it.

Various definitions of development planning exist in the literature. Michael P. Todaro refer to "a deliberate governmental attempt to coordinate economic decision making over the long run to influence, direct, and in some cases even control the level and growth of a nation's principal economic variables (income, consumption, employment, investment, saving, exports, imports, etc.) in order to achieve a predetermined set of development objectives."[37] Enthoven speaks of "the preparatory evaluation and decision making process of a forward-looking character for an economy, in which alternatives have to be measured, weighed and outlined, and priorities for the use of resources established."[38] Both definitions point to the guidance of development by a deliberate attempt to quantify, measure, and control the level of crucial economic variables to reach an acceptable level of growth. Thus, development planning rests on a well-defined, comprehensive economic policy for reaching well-specified goals and targets and a deliberate governmental attempt to formulate and monitor the required development plans.

Three basic strategies are used for the implementation of development planning, namely, aggregate growth models based on a forecasting of macrovariables, multisector input-output models based on the interrelationships and flows among the various industries, and project appraisal through cost-benefit analysis. These three stages are also labeled the macrophase, middle phase, and microphases of development planning. They have been adequately described as follows:

> The macrophase has to show the most desirable development in macro-economic terms, without subdivision in regions or industries. In this phase, then, only such overall figures are used as the national product and capital, the total investments, imports and exports and state expenditure. In the middle phase, the picture resulting from the macrophase is made clearer by distinguishing a number of sectors of industries and a number of regions. Finally, in the microphase, an even clearer and more detailed picture is obtained by dealing with separate projects and even smaller geographical regions, perhaps even separate rural and urban districts.[39]

Because the accounting-oriented data are most needed for the project appraisal or microphase, the next section deals only with that phase.[40]

Project Appraisal in Development Planning

Project appraisal in development planning rests to a large extent on the use of cost-benefit analysis. It is a method used to assess the desirability of projects, when it is necessary to take both a long and a wide view of the impact of a proposed project on the general welfare of a society.[41] It calls, first, for enumerating and evaluating all the relevant costs and benefits the project may generate and, second, for choosing the alternatives that maximize the present value of all benefits less costs, subject to specified constraints and given specified objectives. Cost-benefit analysis is useful when all the economic impacts of a project, side effects as well as direct effects, have to be considered. It is a favorite method of analysis by governmental agencies for assessing the desirability of particular program expenditures or policy changes. In fact, it has been formally adopted into U.S. government budgetary procedures under the Planning-Programming-Budgeting System (PPBS).[42] It acts as a structure of a general theory for government resource allocation. Above all, it is a decision technique whose aims are, first, to take all effects into consideration and, second, to maximize tthe present value of all benefits less that of all costs, subject to specified constraints. This brings into focus the major principles of cost-benefit analysis:

1. What are the objectives and constraints to be considered?
2. Which costs and benefits are to be included?
3. How are the costs and benefits to be valued?
4. What are the investment criteria to be used?
5. Which discount rate should be used?

Objectives and Relevant Constraints of Cost-Benefit Analysis

The main objective of cost-benefit analysis is to determine whether a particular expenditure is economincally and socially justifiable. The basic criterion used is an efficiency criterion. One such criterion is that of Pareto optimality. A program is said to be Pareto-efficient if at least one person is made better off and no one is made worse off. The criterion is too impractical for cost-benefit analysis given that few programs are likely to leave some individuals better off and no one worse off. A weaker notion of efficiency, known as the Kaldor-Hikes criterion, is generally used for cost-benefit analysis. Under this criterion, also known as the "potential" Pareto improvement criterion, a program is acceptable if it is Pareto-optimal or if it could redistribute the net benefits to everyone in the community so that

everyone is at least as well off as he or she was before initiation of the program.[43] Basically, a program is efficient and should be undertaken if its total discounted societal benefits exceed the total discounted costs.

Besides the objectives of cost-benefit analysis which are basically to maximize society's wealth, it is important to recognize some of the constraints. Otto Eckstein provided a helpful classification of constraints.[44] These include the following:

1. *Physical constraints*: The program alternatives considered may be constrained by the state of technology and more generally by the production function, which relates the physical inputs and outputs of a project.
2. *Legal constraints:* The program alternatives considered must be done within the framework of the law. Examples of legal constraints include property rights, time needed for public inquiries, regulated pricing, the right for public inquiries, regulated pricing, the right of eminent domain, limits to the activities of public agencies, and so on.
3. *Administrative constraints*: Each of the alternative programs requires the availability and hiring of individuals with the right administrative skills.
4. *Distributional constraints*: Any program is bound to generate gainers and losers. The unfavorable effects on income distribution may be alleviated by expressing the objective of cost-benefit analysis as either maximizing the excess of total benefits less costs of particular groups, or maximizing the net gain (or minimizing the net loss) to a particular group subject to a constraint relating to total benefits and costs.
5. *Political constraints*: Political considerations may act as constraints, shifting the decision from what is *best* to what is *possible*. Regional differences and the presence of various competing interest groups are examples of actors bound to create political constraints on the choice of the best program.
6. *Budgetary constraints*: Capital rationing and evaluating may act as constraints, shifting the objective function from maximizing to suboptimizing of net benefit given a target budget.
7. *Social and religious constraints*: Social and religious taboos are bound to act as constraints, shifting the decision from what is *best* to what is *acceptable*.

Enumeration of Costs and Benefits

Enumeration of costs and benefits is important because it deals with the question of determining which of the costs and benefits of a particular project should be included in a cost-benefit analysis. Benefits of a project are either direct or indirect. Direct (primary) benefits of a project are those benefits which "accrue directly to the users of the service provided by the project." They consist of "the value of goods or services that result from conditions with the project as compared to conditions without the project."[45] Indirect (secondary) benefits are those benefits accruing to entities other than the users of the service provided by the project. They are

of two types: real (technological) benefits or pecuniary benefits.[46] Real benefits are those benefits resulting from changes in total production possibilities and consumption opportunities. For example, if a dam causes a reduction of flooding and more pleasant scenery, these benefits are real benefits. Pecuniary benefits are those benefits which alter the distribution of total income without changing its volume. They generally take the form of lower input costs, increased volumes of business, or changes in the land values. Only direct real benefits should be included; pecuniary benefits should be excluded from the enumeration of benefits of a project. Other benefits, of an intangible nature and difficult to specify, should also be considered. Costs of a project are also either direct or indirect. Direct costs are those which are incurred directly by the users of the service provided by the project. They include the capital costs, operating and maintenance costs, and personnel expenses required by the project. They may also be either real or pecuniary. Again, only the real secondary costs should be counted in the cost-benefit analysis.

Briefly, in enumerating the costs and benefits of a project, the analyst must be careful to distinguish their allocative effects from their pecuniary or distributional effects. In fact, the confusion of pecuniary and allocative effects constitutes a primary defect in many analyses of the efficiency of public project. The only effects that should be taken into account in enumerating the costs and benefits of a public project are the real or technological externalities, that is, those that affect total opportunities for production and consumption, as opposed to pecuniary externalities, which do not affect production or consumption.

Valuation of Costs and Benefits

In general, *benefits* should measure the value of the additional goods or services produced or the value of cost sayings in the production of goods or services, while *costs* should measure the value of real resources displaced from other uses.

Assuming a competitive economy, the benefits and costs are valued on the basis of the observable market prices of the outputs and inputs of the program. More precisely, the benefits are valued either on the market price of the output of the program or on the amounts the users are willing to pay if they were charged (that is, the consumers' surplus, which is the difference between the aggregate willingness to pay and the costs of the projects).

Where market prices do not accurately reflect the value of market transactions to society as a result of externalities, shadow prices, as adjusted or input prices, may be used. The general principle for estimating shadow prices for the output of public projects is to simulate what users would be willing to pay if they were charged as if the goods were sold in perfectly competitive markets.

Investment Criteria

Cost-benefit analysis is a method used to evaluate long-term projects. As such, the benefits and costs of each project have to be discounted to be comparable at time 0 when evaluation and decisions on the projects have to be made. There is a need to rely on some form of discounting in the choice of investment critetria. There are three possible investment or decision criteria. The first is the net-present-value method. Under this method the present value of a project is obtained by discounting the net excess of benefits (B_t) over costs (C_t) for each year during the life of the project back to the present time using a social discount rate. More explicitly,

$$V = \sum_{t=1}^{\alpha} \frac{B_t - C_t}{(1 + r)^t}$$

where V = Value of the project,
B_t = Benefit in year t,
C_t = Cost in year t,
r = Social discount rate, and
α = Life of the project.

Basically, a project is found acceptable if the present value V is positive. If there are binding constraints on a project (for example, budget appropriation, foreign exchange, private investment opportunity foregone), then the following model proposed by George A. Steiner[47] would be more appropriate:

$$V = \sum_{t=1}^{\alpha} \frac{B_t - C_t}{(1 + r)^t} - \sum_{j=1}^{n} p_j k_j$$

where p_j = Shadow price of binding constraint, and
k_j = Number of units of a constrained resource.

Second is the benefit-cost ratio. Under this method the decision criterion is expressed in terms of the ratio of the present value of benefits to the present value of costs (both discounted at the social discount). More explicitly, the benefit-cost ratio is:

$$\frac{\sum_{t=1}^{\alpha} \frac{b_t}{(1 + r)^t 1'}}{\sum_{t=1}^{\alpha} \frac{c_t}{(1 + r)^t}} = 0$$

Basically, all projects that are not mutually exclusive with a benefit-cost ratio in excess of 1 are acceptable.

Last is the internal rate of return. Under this method the decision criterion is expressed in terms of the internal rate of return; that is, the discount rate will equate the net benefits over the life of the project with the original cost. In other words, 2 is the rate of interest for which

$$\sum_{t=1}^{\alpha} \frac{b_t}{(1+r)^t} - \sum_{t=1}^{\alpha} \frac{c_t}{(1+r)^t} = 0$$

Basically, all projects with an internal rate of return which exceeds the closer social discount rate are deemed acceptable.

Choice of a Discount Rate

The choice of a discount rate is important for at least two reasons. A high rate will mitigate against the firm or the government undertaking the project while a low rate may make the project more acceptable from a return point of view. Furthermore, a low discount rate tends to favor projects yielding more current net benefits. Choosing the appropriate interest rate becomes therefore an important policy question. There are several possible alternative rates.

The first is the marginal productivity of capital in private investment. Given that the discount rate allows the allocation of resources between the public and private sectors, it should be chosen so that it indicates when resources should be transferred from one sector to another. This means that the discount rate should represent the opportunity cost of funds withdrawn from the private sector to be used in the public sector. As William J. Baumol states, "The correct discount rate for the evaluation of a government project is the percentage rate of return that the resources utilized would otherwise provide in the private sector."[48]

The following considerations enter into the choice of the marginal productivity of capital as a discount rate: an effort to minimize governmental activity, a concern for efficiency, and a belief that the source of funds for government investment in the private sector or that government investment will displace private investment that would otherwise be made.[49]

Second is the social rate of time preference, which expresses a concern for future generations in the sense that the welfare of the future generations will be increased if investments are made now. It follows that the discount rate should be the social rate of time preference, that is, the compensation required to induce consumers to refrain from consumption and to save. One study committee argued that the federal government should use the president in consultation with his advisers, such as the Council of Economic Advisers.[50] The strongest argument for the social rate of time preference was made by A. C. Pigou when he suggested that individuals were short-sighted about the future ("defective telescopic faculty") and the welfare of future generations would require governmental intervention.[51]

Advantages and Limitations of Cost-Benefit Analysis

There are thousands of cost-benefit analyses of government projects. The popularity of the method is a witness to some of its advantages; there are also some limitations well recognized in the literature. Among the advantages are the following. (1) It has been pointed out that cost-benefit analysis is most effective in dealing with cases of intermediate social goods.[52] (2) It establishes a framework for a reasonably consistent evaluation of alternative projects, especially where the choice set is narrow in the sense that the projects are not only similar but generate the same volume of externalities. (3) It allows decisions to be made which are most advantageous in terms of the objectives accepted. Among the limitations are the following. (1) There are limits within which social objectives can be measured in money terms. An example of nonefficiency objectives which are not measurable in dollar terms is an equitable distribution of income. (2) Cost-benefit analysis falls under what is known as partial equilibrium analysis. It is useful in evaluating only those projects which have negligible impact outside the immediately affected areas of the economy. (3) There are obvious problems of enumeration and evaluation of the costs and benefits of particular projects.[53] A committee of the U.S. House of Representatives, pointing to the difficulty inherent in estimating the direct effects of a policy and assigning dollar terms to them, argued that such estimates are seldom accurate.[54] Similarly, Michael S. Baram cites an inappropriate treatment of factors that transcend economies.[55]

STANDARDIZED ACCOUNTING AND ECONOMIC DEVELOPMENT

Given the important role of accounting in economic development in general and development planning and project appraisal in particular, there may be a need to ensure that the developing countries develop accounting systems capable of providing efficient and organized economic and financial data. One way of achieving this general objective is to simplify and unify all aspects of accounting information systems in order to improve reliability and consistency of information. That is exactly the role of standardized accounting. It has been adequately defined as follows: "It [standardization] involves establishing methodological standards of definition and terminology; criteria for the identification, collection, measurement, and processing of data, and for the layout of accounts and tables, procedures for integrating information into cohesive models; and standards for evaluating and communicating such information."[56]

Standardization may involve one of the following three methods:

(i) more uniform application of concepts, principles and rules, reporting procedures and legislation;

(ii) adherence to more unified charts of accounts and statements, which specify the classification categories by economic units, industries and sectors, and which preferably are applicable on an international scale; and

(iii) greater systematization of all accounting activities particularly standardized plans of accounts. (This would not only include the classification charts but also the quantitative and qualitative aspects of data.)[57]

Various schemes for standardizing accounting are already in practice, for example, the French *Plan Comptable Général*, the Belgian *Plan Comptable* (Plan Raymond Mayer), the German Framework of Accounts (*Kontenrahmen*), and the various EEC "directives" aimed at achieving harmonization of financial statements. These schemes are aimed at achieving better comparability among financial statements; better consolidation and integration of data at the corporate, sectoral, and national levels; better formulation of development and economic policies and plans; effective fiscal policy and administration; enhanced accounting theory; better-run small organizations; easier internal and external control and auditing of accounting by private accountants and governmental agencies; and a more specifically oriented training of personnel to administer the accounting system.[58]

A good description of these schemes follows:

1. The French *Plan Comptable Général*
This standardization plan for enterprises is geared to the whole economic sphere and consists of the following fundamentals: a uniform terminology, a uniform classification of accounts, a standardized method for registration, and general rules of valuation on a historical cost basis. The objectives of the French system are: improvement of fiscal control, systematic information for social accounts and standardization of presentation in company financial statements.

2. The German Framework of Accounts (*Kontenrahmen*)
This system includes a standard chart of accounts and flowcharts for industries. The flowcharts present all transactions occurring in an enterprise and are integrated with the chart of accounts. The whole system is micro-oriented for the comparison of industrial data.

3. Standardization in the USA
The standardization of accounting in the United States focuses largely on three aspects: generally accepted accounting principles, the presentation of the account layout, and the uniform pattern of reporting and costing for utilities and certain other industries, as required by federal agencies. The SEC provides a balance sheet model and a profit and loss statement for firms over which it has supervision, and requires strict adherence to this chart.

The U.S. Cost Accounting Standards Board, part of the U.S. General Accounting Office, has outlined cost accounting standards to achieve comparability, reliability and consistency of cost data for contract purposes, while maintaining equity and adherence to sound accounting principles.[59]

ACCOUNTING EDUCATION AND ECONOMIC DEVELOPMENT

Given the importance of the role of accounting in development planning in general and project appraisal in particular, accounting education in the Third World appears to have a major importance. There is obviously a need for systematic accounting education in connection with technical assistance programs to give a better chance for development planning to be effectively implemented.

The actual situation of accounting education in the developing countries is far from compatible with what should be required for an effective implementation of development planning. There are various accounting practice problems, and accounting education in the developing countries could be considered adequate in its role of facilitating economic development. A recent survey of experts gives a rough ordering of the relative importance of the major accounting practice and education problems and their causes in the developing countries and shows that many of the most important accounting problems are believed to result from important causes deeply rooted in accounting education.[60]

These problems include the following:

1. Shortage of qualified accountants at all levels and in all areas of accounting and practices.
2. Accounting information is either not available or is not available in the proper form, or is received by users too late to be useful.
3. The failure to utilize accounting information advantageously for internal management purposes.
4. Lack of legislation relating to accounting and auditing standards and procedures.
5. Inadequate teaching of accounting subjects at the college level.
6. Lack of qualified accounting instructors at the college level.
7. Locally authored textbooks are inadequate.
8. Lack of professional development opportunities for accounting educators and practitioners.
9. Inadequate accounting education for managers and prospective managers.
10. Lack of strong national associations of accountants.
11. Lack of adequate accounting in government agencies and government-owned businesses.

The problem of education is at the center of the need for improving the human resources of the developing countries. The general mechanism used is the formal education system, which takes place in schools, uses the traditional academic curriculum and prepares students to join the modern economic lifestyles. There are, however, other types of education most

beneficial to the developing countries, namely, *informal education,* or learning by doing, which involves various forms of training programs, and *education for self-reliance,* or problem-posing education, which teaches people to study together and realize the political and economic determinant of their poverty.

Given the inadequacy of formal education, various developing countries have experimented with informal education and education for self-reliance. The results are far from conclusive at this time. So the call for educational reform beyond the boundaries of formal education continues to stir interest and debate in the developing countries. Most calls for education reform stress the need for a curriculum most beneficial to and in accordance with the real needs of each developing country and more relevant to the development needs.

To improve accounting education in the developing countries and eliminate some of the problems identified, some foreign support is needed—not only as a matter of economic interest to the developed countries but also as a mortal obligation. In this regard, a report to the U.S. Congress by former comptroller general Elmer Staats, *Training and Related Efforts Needed to Improve Financial Management in the Third World,* states:

> The absence of effective financial management is a major obstacle to the optimum use of resources, both internal and external, that are available to improve the standard of living in Third World countries. Effective financial management is essential because anything less dissipates available resources and thwarts development. To improve financial management developing countries must:
>
> 1. Develop effective accounting and auditing practices.
> 2. Insure the presence of skilled personnel to effectively run their financial management systems.
> 3. Develop a comprehensive and up-to-date training program at both the national and regional level. . . .
> 4. Increase their commitment to the realization of an effective training development program.[61]

Various programs have been recommended for adoption by the developing countries. One noteworthy example is a distinct body of knowledge, called "economic development accountancy," which is recommended as the way to cater effectively to the needs of socioeconomic development. "Economic development accounting can be described as the application of existing and potential accounting systems, techniques, procedures and data to enhance economic development within a nation and among nations."[62]

It is a concept more compatible with the requirements of development planning and of accounting for economic analysis, planning, and policies. It

is intended to serve both micro and macro socioeconomic decisions.

To solve these problems and create a supportive accounting profession, the overall planning endeavor of the developing countries may have to adopt a multidimensional strategy focusing not only on accounting education issues but also on the national and international factors that achieve a better link between societal-practical demands and educational pursuits. To achieve this goal the following steps have been proposed:

1. An *accounting inventory and planning* framework should evaluate the types, levels and skills for accountants. Such a layout is not only important for internal appraisals in both developing and developed countries, but also for organizations supplying technical accounting (educational) assistance.
2. *Better links* may have to be established between: governmental agencies, the accounting profession, industry, and educational institutions to enhance accounting training, research and development activities.
3. An *accounting education and development report* is needed, outlining a program for international and regional development, to be submitted for implementation to countries and regional and international agencies. Such a report, with input from educators and practitioners around the world—possibly subdivided by region—might be along similar lines to the recently issued United Nations/World Bank Brandt Commission Report, dealing with international economic development. The report should also cover future accounting needs, the ways and means to satisfy them from a practical and educational point of view, and scope for better theoretical norms. Such a comprehensive educational survey should be supported by the United Nations, the World Bank or other agency.
4. An *international association for accounting development* should be established, especially to cater for the requirements of the Third World countries in the areas of accounting education, training, research and clearinghouse activities. International and regional certification and coordination of educational programs would also have to be considered, broken down by levels and areas of competency.
5. *Accounting development centers* should be considered for countries and regions to upgrade accounting instructors and pursue research and writing in various fields of accounting. Internationally and regionally, a better *theoretical framework,* and related concepts, will have to be jointly explored and researched.[63]

NOTES

1. The problems and policies needed to correct them are examined in Ahmed Belkaoui, *International Accounting: Issues and Solutions* (Westport, Conn.: Greenwood Press, 1985), Ch. 11.

2. George M. Scott, *Accounting and the Developing Nations* (Seattle: University of Washington, Graduate School of Business Administration, 1970).

3. Society for International Development, *The Role of Accounting in Economic*

Development, International Seminar (Washington, D.C.: Society for International Development 1976), pp. 13-15.

4. I. L. Fantl, "The Dilemma of International Accounting," *New Jersey CPA* (Spring 1968), pp. 3-8.

5. Mahmoud Qureshi, "Pragmatic and Academic Bases of International Accounting," *Management International Review* 2 (1979), pp. 61-68; Thomas R. Weirich, Clarence G. Avery, and Henry R. Anderson, "International Accounting: Varying Definitions," *International Journal of Accounting Education and Research* (Fall 1971), pp. 79-87.

6. Weirich, Avery, and Anderson, "International Accounting."

7. Ibid., p. 79.

8. Ibid.

9. Ibid.

10. F. E. Amenkhienan, *Accounting in the Developing Countries: A Framework for Standard Setting* (Ann Arbor, Mich.: UMI Research Press, 1986), p. 20.

11. Ibid.

12. Ibid., pp. 22-26.

13. Adolf J. H. Enthoven, "U.S. Accounting and the Third World," *Journal of Accountancy* (June 1983), p. 112.

14. Belverd E. Needles, Jr., "Implementing a Framework for the International Transfer of Accounting Technology," *International Journal of Accounting Education and Research* (Fall 1976), p. 51.

15. Ibid.

16. Amenkhienan, *Accounting in Developing Countries*, p. 24.

17. Scott, *Accounting and the Developing Nations*, p. 12.

18. Ibid., p. 25.

19. Belkaoui, *International Accounting*, p. 49.

20. Joseph P. Cummings and Michael N. Chetkovich, "World Accounting Enters a New Era," *Journal of Accountancy* (April 1978), p. 52.

21. International Accounting Standards Committee, *Objectives and Procedures* (London: IASC, January 1983), par. 8.

22. Ibid., par. 27.

23. Sir Henry Benson, "The Story of International Accounting Standards," *Accounting* (July 1976), p. 34.

24. T. R. Douglas, "International Accounting Standards," *CA Magazine* (October 1977), pp. 49-50.

25. "The Time is Now," *CA Magazine* (November 1980), p. 68.

26. Group of Experts on International Standards of Accounting and Reporting, *International Standards of Accounting and Reporting for Transnational Corporations* (New York: United Nations, 1977), p. 7.

27. Office of Economic Cooperation and Development, *International Investment and Multinational Enterprises* (Paris: OECD, 1976), pp. 14-16.

28. Office of Economic Cooperation and Development, "Declaration on International Investment and Multinational Enterprises," *OECD Observer* (July-August 1976), p. 14.

29. Commission of the European Communities, *Amended Proposal for a Fourth Council Directive for Co-Ordination of National Legislation Regarding the Annual Accounts of Limited Liability Companies* (Brussels, 1974).

30. *The Fourth Directive* (London: Deloitte, Haskins & Sells, 1978), p. 1.

31. T. L. Wilkinson, "United States Accounts as Viewed by Accountants of Other Countries," *International Journal of Accounting Education and Research* (Fall 1965), pp. 11-12.

32. Richard J. Briston, "The Evolution of Accounting in Developing Countries," *International Journal of Accounting Education and Research* (Fall 1978), p. 113.

33. J. M. Samuels and J. C. Oliga, "Accounting Standards in Developing Countries," *International Journal of Accounting Education and Research* (Fall 1982), p. 72.

34. Briston, "The Evolution of Accounting," pp. 117-18.

35. United Nations, *Planning the External Sector: Techniques, Problems, and Policies* (New York: United Nations, September 1965), p. 12.

36. Derek T. Healey, "Development Policy: New Thinking about an Interpretation," *Journal of Economic Literature* 10, no. 3 (1973), p. 794.

37. Todaro, Michael P., *Economic Development in the Third World,* 2d ed. (New York, Longman, 1977).

38. Adolf J. H. Enthoven, *Accountancy and Economic Development Policy* (Amsterdam: North Holland Publishing, 1973), p. 149.

39. Jan Tinbergen, *Development Planning* (New York: McGraw-Hill, 1967), p. 76.

40. This approach differs from the one taken by Enthoven in *Accounting and Economic Development Policy*. He foresees a role of accounting in the first two phases as follows:

(a) macro-phase-focal accounts and their components (e.g., national income, consumption, investments). Production functions data will be particularly relevant to this phase, although also extensively used in the subsequent phase.

(b) middle-phase-focal accounts broken down by sector and region on product and income, price indices, wage rates, and labor productivity. Input-output data by sector tend to be of special value in this phase. Shadow price estimates are also useful.

41. A. R. Prest and R. Turvey, "Cost-Benefit Analysis: A Survey," *Economic Journal* (December 1965), pp. 683-735.

42. The major components of a PPBS are presented in this chapter.

43. Another test for potential Pareto improvements is that everyone in society could be made better off by means of a costless redistribution of the net benefits.

44. Otto Eskstein, "A Survey of the Theory of Public Expenditure Criteria," in *Public Finances: Needs, Sources and Utilization*, ed. James M. Buchanan (Princeton, N.J.: Princeton University Press, 1961).

45. Jesse Burkhead and Jerry Miner, *Public Expenditure* (Chicago: Aldine-Atherton, 1971), p. 225.

46. R. N. McKean, *Efficiency in Government through Systems Analysis* (New York: Wiley, 1958), Chap. 8.

47. George A. Steiner, "Problems in Implementing Program Budgeting," in *Program Budgeting,* ed. David Novic (Cambridge, Mass.: Harvard University Press, 1965), pp. 87-88.

48. William J. Baumol, "On the Discount Rate for Public Projects," in *Public Expenditures and Policy Analysis,* ed. Robert Margolis and Julius Margolis (Chicago: Markham, 1970), p. 274.

49. Burkhead and Miner, *Public Expenditure*, p. 232.

50. Report of Panel of Consultants, Bureau of the Budget, *Standards and Criteria for Formulating and Evaluating Federal Water Resources Development* (Washington, D.C.: Bureau of the Budget, 1961), p. 67.

51. A. C. Pigou, *The Economics of Welfare*, 4th ed. (London: Macmillan, 1932).

52. R. A. Musgrave, *Fiscal Systems* (New Haven, Conn.: Yale University Press, 1969), pp. 797-806.

53. Prest and Turvey, "Cost-Benefit Analysis," pp. 729-31.

54. U.S. House of Representatives, 94th Cong., 2d Sess., Committee on Interstate and Foreign Commerce, Subcommittee on Oversight and Investigations, *Federal Regulation and Regulatory Reform* (1976), Chap. 15 (Subcommittee print).

55. Michael S. Baram, "Cost Benefit Analysis: An Inadequate Basis for Health, Safety, and Environmental Regulatory Decision-Making," *Ecology Law Quarterly* 8 (1980), pp. 473-531.

56. Adolf J. H. Enthoven, "Standardized Accountancy and Economic Development," *Management Accounting* (February 1976), p. 19.

57. C. W. Nobes and R. H. Parker, eds., *Comparative International Accounting*, 2d ed. (London: Philip Allan, 1985), p. 196.

58. Enthoven, *Accountancy and Economic Development Policy*.

59. Nobes and Parker, *Comparative International Accounting*, p. 197.

60. Committee on Accounting in Developing Countries, "Report of the Committee on Accounting in Developing Countries," *Accounting Review*, supplement (1975), pp. 198-212.

61. Elmer Staats, *Training and Related Efforts Needed to Improve Finance Management in the Third World*, ID 79-46 (Washington, D.C.: General Accounting Office, 1979), p. 1.

62. Enthoven, *Accountancy and Economic Development Policy*, p. 168.

63. Adolf Enthoven, "Accounting in Developing Countries," in *Comparative International Accounting*, ed. C. W. Nobes and R. H. Parker (London: Philip Allan, 1985), pp. 212-13.

SELECTED BIBLIOGRAPHY

Adelman, I., "A Reassessment of Development Economics: Development Economics—A Reassessment of Goals," *American Economic Review* 65, no. 2 (1975), pp. 302-5.

Amenkhienan, F. E., *Accounting in the Developing Countries: A Framework for Standard Setting* (Ann Arbor, Mich.: UMI Research Press, 1986).

Bailey, Derek K., "Towards a Marxian Theory of Accountants," *British Accounting Review* (Autumn 1984), pp. 21-41.

Belkaoui, Ahmed, *International Accounting: Issues and Solutions* (Westport, Conn.: Greenwood Press, 1985).

______, *Socio-Economic Accounting* (Westport, Conn.: Greenwood Press, 1984).

Briston, Richard J., "Accounting Standards and Host Country Control of Multinationals," *British Accounting Review* 16, no. 1 (1985), pp. 12-26.

______, "The Evolution of Accounting in Developing Countries," *International Journal of Accounting Education and Research* (Fall 1978), pp. 105-120.

Chenery, Hollis B., "The Structuralist Approach to Development Policy," *American Economic Review* 65, no. 2 (1975), pp. 310-15.

Committee on Accounting in Developing Countries, "Report of the Committee on Accounting in Developing Countries, *Accounting Review*, Supplement (1975), pp. 198-212.

Committee on International Accounting, *Accounting Education in the Third World* (Sarasota, Fla.: American Accounting Association, 1982).

Cummings, Joseph P., and Michael N. Chetkovich, "World Accounting Enters a New Era," *Journal of Accountancy* (April 1978), p. 52.

Elliot, Edward L., *The Nature and Stages of Accounting Development in Latin Amèrica* (Urbana, Ill.: Center for International Education and Research in Accounting, 1968).

Engelmann, Konrad, "Accounting Problems in Developing Countries, *Journal of Accountancy* (January 1962), pp. 53-62.

Enthoven, Adolf J. H., *Accountancy and Economic Development Policy* (Amsterdam: North Holland Publishing, 1973).

______, *Accountancy Systems in Third World Economies* (Amsterdam; North Holland Publishing, 1977).

______, "Standardized Accountancy and Economic Development," *Management Accounting* (February 1976), pp. 19-23.

______, "U.S. Accounting and the Third World," *Journal of Accountancy* (June 1983), pp. 110-18.

Group of Experts on International Standards of Accounting and Reporting, *International Standards of Accounting and Reporting for Transnational Corporations* (New York: United Nations, 1977).

Healey, Derek, T., "Development Policy: New Thinking about an Interpretation," *Journal of Economic Literature* 10, no. 3 (1973), pp. 757-97.

Lall, Sanyaya, "Is Dependence a Useful Concept in Analyzing Underdevelopment?" *World Development* 3, nos. 11 and 12 (1975), pp. 799-810.

______, "Less-Developed Countries and Private Foreign Direct Investment: A Review Article," *World Development* 2, nos. 4 and 5 (1974), pp. 43-48.

Lee, T. A., *Cash Flow Accounting* (London: Van Nostrand Reinhold, 1984).

Lewis, N. R., L. D. Parker, and P. Sutcliffe, "Financial Reporting to Employees: Towards a Research Framework," *Accounting and Business Research* (Summer 1984), pp. 229-39.

Needles, Belverd E., Jr., "Implementing a Framework for the International Transfer of Accounting Technology," *International Journal of Accounting Education and Research* (Fall 1976), p. 51.

Palma, Gabriel, "Dependency: A Formal Theory of Underdevelopment or a Methodology for the Analysis of Concrete Situations of Underdevelopment?" *World Development* 6, no. 10 (1978), pp. 881-924.

Pazos, Felipe, "Regional Integration of Trade among Less Developed Countries," *World Development* 1, no. 7 (1973), pp. 1-12.

Qureshi, Mahmoud, "Pragmatic and Academic Bases of International Accounting," *Management International Review* 2 (1979), pp. 61-68.

Samuels, J. M., and J. C. Oliga, "Accounting Standards in Developing Countries," *International Journal of Accounting Education and Research* (Fall 1982), pp. 69-88.

Scott, George M., *Accounting and the Developing Nations* (Seattle: University of

Washington, Graduate School of Business Administration, 1970).

Seidler, Lee J., *The Function of Accounting in Economic Development* (New York: Praeger, 1967).

Simmons, John, "Education for Development, Reconsidered," *World Development* 7 (1979), pp. 1005-16.

Singer, Hans W., "Dualism Revisited: A New Approach to the Problems of Dual Society in Developing Countries," *Journal of Development Studies* 7, no. 1 (1970), pp. 60-75.

Society for International Development, *The Role of Accounting in Economic Development,* International Seminar (Washington, D.C.: Society for International Development, 1976).

Streeten, P. P., "Trade Strategies for Development: Some Themes for the Seventies," *World Development* 1, no. 6 (June 1973), pp. 1-10.

Teitelbaum, Michael S., "Population and Development: Is a Consensus Possible?" *Foreign Affairs* (July 1974), pp. 742-60.

Tinbergen, Jan, *Development Planning* (New York: McGraw-Hill, 1967).

Tinker, Tony, *Paper Prophets: A Social Critique of Accounting* (New York: Holt, Rinehart and Winston, 1985).

Weirich, Thomas R., Clarence G. Avery, and Henry R. Anderson, "International Accounting: Varying Definitions," *International Journal of Accounting, Education and Research* (Fall 1971), pp. 79-87.

Wilkinson, T. L., "United States Accounts as Viewed by Accountants of Other Countries," *International Journal of Accounting Education and Research* (Fall 1965), pp. 11-12.

INDEX

About the Author

AHMED BELKAOUI, Professor of Accounting at the University of Illinois at Chicago, is a recognized authority on accounting and has served as a consultant to corporations, institutions, and governments throughout the world. Among his recent books are *Industrial Bonds and the Rating Process, International Accounting, Socio-Economic Accounting, Public Policy and the Problems and Practices of Accounting, The Learning Curve, Handbook of Management Control Systems, Quantitative Models in Accounting,* and *Inquiry and Accounting* (all published by Quorum Books). He is the author of more than 70 articles and reviews.